CW00523511

Saving sick Britain

MANCHESTER
1824

Manchester University Press

Saving sick Britain

Why we need the 'Health Society'

Martin Yuille and Bill Ollier

Manchester University Press

Copyright © Martin Yuille and Bill Ollier 2021

The right of Martin Yuille and Bill Ollier to be identified as the authors of this work has been asserted by them in accordance with the Copyright, Designs and Patents Act 1988.

Published by Manchester University Press
Altrincham Street, Manchester M1 7JA
www.manchesteruniversitypress.co.uk

British Library Cataloguing-in-Publication Data
A catalogue record for this book is available from the British Library

ISBN 978 1 5261 5228 2 hardback

First published 2021

The publisher has no responsibility for the persistence or accuracy of URLs for any external or third-party internet websites referred to in this book, and does not guarantee that any content on such websites is, or will remain, accurate or appropriate.

Typeset by
Servis Filmsetting Ltd, Stockport, Cheshire
Printed in Great Britain by
Bell & Bain Ltd, Glasgow

'Preventive medicine – which is merely another way of saying health by collective action – builds up a system of social habits that constitute an indispensable part of what we mean by civilization.' (Aneurin Bevan (1897–1960), Minister of Health. From *In Place of Fear*, 1952)

'Among the experiments that may be tried on man, those that can only harm are forbidden, those that are innocent are permissible and those that may do good are obligatory.' (Claude Bernard (1813–78), founding father of physiology. From *An Introduction to the Study of Experimental Medicine*, 1865)

We dedicate this book to the countless millions who continue to endure avoidable long-term conditions while society dithers.

We also dedicate this book to each of our families, friends and teachers. They know why.

Contents

Postscript – the COVID-19 pandemic
In a new chapter (Chapter 18), the authors spell out the lessons from the COVID-19 pandemic. Written as the book went to press, it links rapidly changing events to the book's arguments for the construction of the 'Health Society'.

Contents

Part IV

List of figures

List of figures

List of figures

List of figures

List of tables

Preface

We have worked together closely in the field of human genetics research for over two decades. But not so long ago we decided we had to think about a much broader topic – the health of the population. So, why are two specialists in a tightly defined area of science now writing about a matter that belongs, as it were, to health professionals and epidemiologists, to clinicians and policy wonks?

The answer is that we were driven to it by experience and by the logic of our specialism. For each of us there was a moment of truth.

In Bill's case, it was when he became Director of Research and Development at a Greater Manchester teaching hospital – the Salford Royal NHS Hospital Foundation Trust. This quickly exposed him to the reality of modern medicine struggling to treat a rising tide of people coming into the Accident & Emergency Department. He saw that the majority of the hospital's resources went into dealing with 'chronic' (i.e. 'long-term') conditions which were often fully preventable. Where was the activity that would stop people becoming unwell in the first place and so relieve the relentless and increasing pressure put on the Accident & Emergency Department? Since 2000, the hospital had been holding electronic health information on virtually everyone in Salford and this information could be used to guide work on prevention.

Salford's pioneering approach of combining data from both the hospital and doctors' surgeries had been supporting improved treatment – after patients had become ill. But, it had not been used in any meaningful way to improve prevention. A major opportunity was being missed. This was perpetuating unfairness because the records revealed that underlying health inequalities were linked to where people live: long-term conditions were much higher in the more deprived parts of the city. This inequality goes back a long way, at least to the early days of the Industrial Revolution.[1] But, the electronic record system data made action possible here and now.

In Martin's case, he had worked on the international Human Genome Project, which had defined the precise sequence of 3bn 'letters' that make up our chromosomes. At the time, in 2000, he did not question the promises that this knowledge would – within a decade – provide new cures across the board. But, ten years later, the promises were unfulfilled. So, how could science actually use all the data collected on human DNA sequences? The answer eventually came from Ken Muir, a new colleague of both Martin's and Bill's. Ken explained how information about the factors that confer risk of a condition can be used in mathematical models to calculate the risk of a future health condition. This information then creates opportunities to reduce that risk. The penny dropped: a given variation in a sequence of DNA may be statistically associated with an abnormally high (or low) risk of some health condition affecting a population. The variation can represent a risk factor in Ken's mathematical models. So, use of this knowledge of variation might just help the prevention of conditions. It was not just a question of finding new treatments. Martin concluded that a new frontier for studies on human DNA was the improvement of prevention. This turns out to be an over-simplification because prevention requires us to measure decreasing (or increasing) risk, but DNA sequence only tells us about fixed risk – called lifetime risk or non-modifiable risk.

At much the same time, the medical faculty at Manchester University was undergoing one of its alarmingly frequent reorganisations. We jointly directed a research department that aimed to develop collaborations, out of which would come innovations based on human DNA sequence and its variations. We faced the question: where did our department belong in the reorganised faculty? We agreed that the question really should be: with whom did we find it easiest and most constructive to work? And we agreed that the answer was with epidemiologists (who conventionally study risks to health in human populations) and public health researchers (who additionally propose policy solutions to promote the health of populations).

The two of us also share a common outlook. Like most researchers, we started off many years ago by being in awe of the scientific method. Its aim is to improve our human condition by uncovering successive layers of truth about how the world works. The scientific method is based on observation, experimentation and reasoning (logic) applied first to a facet of the natural world and, after that, to devising means of improving the human condition. These two steps in the scientific method are both very demanding. Often people focus on just one or the other. Occasionally circumstances arise where the researcher attempts both steps. Those are the circumstances in which we found ourselves. We were prepared to step outside our own comfort zones because we were driven by our emotions of respect and frustration. There was the respect we feel for our fellow human beings who must endure long-term ill health and suffering. And, there was frustration that the scientific method was not in practice being applied extensively and rigorously to end that suffering.

So, rather than being influenced by medical research (where the over-riding concern is to identify, treat and cure disease), we were influenced by epidemiological research (where the focus is on measurement and reduction of risk of conditions and diseases).

Preface

With our general knowledge of medicine (neither of us is clinically qualified but we have researched different kinds of common and rare diseases over the years), this was perfect: working on risk of a condition does not necessarily require detailed knowledge of its treatment. Not to pull any punches, it might just be an advantage to have a perspective and experience that differs from that of most medics. We certainly needed to understand risk and biology. But, as we soon discovered, we also needed to understand some basic elements of public policy. You cannot divorce science from public policy for long.

We started a long journey and this book is the result. It is a 'public policy book' as much as it is a 'science book' aimed at non-specialists. It is a manifesto as much as it is a treatise. Our aim, we decided, is not to educate anyone on biomedical science. Yes, some technical issues have to be described. But, the main aim is to reveal human health as part of an interactive system; to identify how improving health requires modification of the system as a whole; and to specify practical modifications needed right away. One cannot reduce it to improving the health of individuals and, at the same time, one cannot ignore the health of individuals. We follow a 'systems biology' approach to the problem. This is the approach favoured by today's leading biologists[2] and it stands in stark contrast to the one dimensional genetic determinism to which some popular science writers adhere.[3]

If we were to adopt this systems approach, we realised we had to cover a lot of ground, from molecular biology to human biology to medicine to public health to public policy. This could either be a heavy read that few people could wade through, or it could at least try to be popular. That was an easy decision for us. The hard part followed and you, dear reader, are the judge of whether what we have written is the basis for the health and societal innovation that our advanced post-industrial society – and other similar high-income societies – need.

Acknowledgements

We are grateful to our colleagues at the Centre for Epidemiology at the University of Manchester. We have already mentioned Ken Muir. But, equally, there is also Artitya Lophatananon, Raymond Agius, Arpana Verma, Mike Donmall, Andy Povey and Adrian Heald. Together, we had long debates and examined early discussion papers.

The Fondation Brocher generously supported our residency at their institute outside Geneva where we had tranquil surroundings to write and to mull over the problems of prevention. We are grateful to Manchester University Press for their confidence in our endeavours and we especially value the support of our editors, Tom Dark and Lucy Burns. We also appreciate the input of Ralph Young and of anonymous reviewers who helped our project mature.

Introduction:
the heart of the matter

This book is not about healthcare policy. Glancing at the title, the reader might think differently. Actually we are concerned with public policy – the whole of it and not just healthcare policy. This is because we have undertaken a redefinition of 'health'. Our new definition forces us to widen our scope. Imagine this was a book on the case for overhauling the nation's infrastructure. Would it discuss only drains and trains? Or would it also examine issues in urban and rural planning, in transport, housing, education, health and so on? It is the same for us: we think health policy has been pigeon-holed for too long and we say it has to stop.

Nor is this book about healthcare – the current euphemism for treating the sick. We are concerned about what happens before you get sick, before you show symptoms, before you get medicines and therapy. This book is about what we need to do to prevent disease in the first place. Too often, we see a news story about prevention and it turns out to be a story about some new life-saving treatment. In other words, people muddle the prevention of death with the prevention of disease. This muddle has to stop too.

It is widely recognised that prevention of disease is better than cure. Hippocrates first hit on this idea over 2,300 years ago. But, what does that mean for developed post-industrial societies today where it is not so much infectious diseases as common long-term conditions that are a risk, first to our health and then to our lives? In days gone by, societies were afflicted with infectious diseases that, in some cases, rapidly wiped out a large fraction of the population. Without vaccination and drugs like antibiotics, humanity could not avoid such devastating plagues. However, today, we have a group of long-term conditions that afflict a similarly large fraction of the population: we have the modern plagues of diabetes, depression, heart disease and cancer.

Yes, medicines or other treatments can help patients once they have been diagnosed with these conditions. This can extend life, even if treatment cannot overcome all the disability that follows on from diagnosis. But there is no drug or vaccination that can unfailingly prevent the development of these conditions. Other methods are needed for the prevention of the plagues of our times.

Surely, you might say, preventing the inevitable is impossible. Yes, of course, it would be impossible to eliminate every case of diabetes, heart disease, depression, cancer and other long-term conditions. However, it is the risk of getting those conditions that we can reduce. In so doing, we can reduce incidence and prevalence – that is the number of people who get these conditions and the numbers who must endure them for years or decades. This idea is at the heart of this book.

We need, first, to recognise the scale of the problem: how many people are affected in what ways? Then we need to understand what creates the risk of getting one of these long-term conditions? There are two types of risk: modifiable and non-modifiable. Modifiable risks are amenable to being reduced, comprising factors such as social isolation, physical inactivity, obesity and pollution. Non-modifiable risk is genetic risk. This is due to small variations in people's genes, which act to promote – or to inhibit – processes that can result in one or more long-term conditions. These many variations are not amenable to modification. Therefore, prevention means focussing on reducing modifiable risks.

Introduction

But reducing these risks turns out to require challenging, across-the-board changes in our way of life, in the way we organise our societies and cultures. That is a big ask for some politicians: quick fixes that only appear to be tackling the problem are easier. The plan of action that we outline here involves profound individual and societal change. It will shake society to its core. Such a shake-up is justified only if there is clear evidence that it is needed along with a simple and practical plan of action.

We will present the evidence that today's common long-term conditions comprise the modern plagues that kill millions and burden us with years of lingering disability. Lives were lost to past plagues because society did not know what to do. When the bubonic plague struck – most famously in the Black Death that swept round the world in the fourteenth century – people could pray to their gods, run away or do both. To prevent today's common long-term conditions, we know what we must do: we have to reduce our modifiable risk factors.

However, we are not doing that: our societies dither and tinker as the modern plagues spread further and further. This cannot be an option when these plagues pose systemic risks to society. Such risks include social fragmentation, losses of productivity and, ultimately, an undermining of democracy.

Our way of life is the product of public policy as a whole. So, to change our way of life, public policy has to change. Social habits, personal habits, customs, culture, economics and politics can all stand in the way. So, those are the problems on which to focus. There are also some scientific and technical issues to act on, but there can be no purely technological fix. There is not, for example, any magic potion, pill or elixir coming along any time soon to lengthen our healthy lives. Such magic goes back to Bronze Age China and Ancient Greece. Pills may change our biology but they cannot alter the modifiable factors that have promoted the modern plagues in the first place.

Introduction

The heart of the matter

Introductions often give readers a preview of the main idea at the heart of a book. Here, the main idea will appear to be different depending on whether the reader is a well-informed person, a natural scientist or a social scientist.

For a natural scientist (one that researches the natural world), the main idea we propose is 'Systems Prevention'. This is the term we give to a consequence of the particular capability of our species for advanced communication – for speech and its related property of abstract thought. This capability allows us to act consciously to achieve things that other species leave to natural selection. Just as the origin of species is down to natural selection, so is the preservation of characteristics that allow members of a species to avoid a predator or disease. That is why Charles Darwin refers to 'preservation' in the title of his famous book.[1] Humanity, however, can preserve itself in a unique way. It can prevent conditions and diseases by working out how to do so and then following through with action. 'Systems Prevention', then, refers to the way that common long-term conditions require humans consciously to work for their prevention, based on our recognition of a web of connections (a system) that exists between the different levels of organisation of our species. This web links the smallest molecule to the biggest influences of our societies and the natural world around us. We have borrowed this idea of connectivity from a contemporary biologist, Denis Noble, who proposed a principle of biological relativity. Noble's idea focusses on how biological systems work normally. We have extended the idea to when systems become abnormal. We discuss Systems Prevention in Part III and we shall use the idea – expressed less technically as the 'Health Society' – in Part IV.

For people with a background in the social sciences or humanities, our main idea is that society needs a new framework for the whole of public policy. This framework is rooted in what a

4

Introduction

Roman lawmaker – Cicero – wrote 2,000 years ago: 'the health of the people is the supreme law'. There is debate as to whether Cicero took 'salus' in Latin to mean health or something else (like well-being, welfare, security or simply goodness). We are happy to use 'salus' to mean health and we are happy to use the phrase 'supreme law' to mean a fundamental guiding idea. We then borrow from political philosophy[2] the notion that 'health' comprises the optimal satisfaction of human needs where these needs fall into three categories: vital, social and agency needs. We assert that this provides a positive definition of health in place of the conventional negative definition (as an absence – an absence of disease). This positive definition directly guides action to improve population health. So, we conclude that public policy as a whole should have as its guiding idea the optimal satisfaction of human needs. Those needs change over time and priorities change too. That is all a matter for new evidence and free debate.

For the well-informed reader with a range of interests, the main idea we propose is for the Health Society. We in the UK are proud of our National Health Service (NHS) but we also complain that it is, in effect, only a national disease service. It seems to act only when we are already unwell. While it does a great job preventing us getting infectious disease, prevention of non-infectious long-term conditions has not worked. We do not blame the NHS for this – it is a problem for all our institutions and organisations. So, we propose a number of policy innovations that can begin to change things. For example, we endorse the proposal of a recent Chief Medical Officer that obesity be treated as a national risk. What that means is placing obesity onto the National Risk Register and all the local Community Risk Registers. The other key modifiable risk factors (high blood pressure and social isolation) also may need to go on the risk registers. The practical effect of adding these risk factors is that all departments of national and local government would be required by law to put in place cross-departmental plans to reduce risks. Infectious diseases like flu are already on the registers. So, why not the modifiable risk factors for common long-term conditions as well? We also propose that policy on the prevention of conditions and diseases should be the central organising principle of government. One way of ensuring this is by giving that responsibility directly, explicitly and wholly to the Deputy Prime Minister. This then gives a flavour of our plan for a National Health Society.

So, that is the heart of the matter. First, science points to the web of connections between the organism, the environment and health. Second, public policy can deliver the public good expressed as 'health' if it optimally satisfies (or, more precisely, if it establishes and maintains the conditions required for optimal satisfaction of) our individual and social needs. Third, science and public policy together give rise to a plan for the construction and maintenance of the Health Society.

To build these arguments, the book is divided into four parts. Part I describes what is driving the need for change – the high prevalence of a set of common long-term conditions. We examine these conditions, their scale and their social, economic and political impacts. Public policy has failed to prevent or end these plagues. Part II looks at key problems in prevention of common long-term conditions – problems in epidemiology and biology, the nature of risk and barriers in society. Part III notes the failure of public policy and starts the process of re-thinking the basic issues. It develops a new definition of 'health' based on modern biology and philosophy: health is the condition where human needs are optimally satisfied: satisfaction of needs prevents the modern plagues. Part IV then uses this definition to propose actions that can minimise the prevalence of the common long-term conditions and thereby end the modern plagues. These actions comprise the construction of the Health Society where our institutions are reformed, modern technology is deployed, and businesses and communities are engaged, involved and empowered. Actions are proposed that are bottom-up as well as top-down because a profound change in our way of life is needed – not just some minor modifications to individual behaviour with which 'nudge' theorists choose to concern themselves.

While you read this book, please hold very tight. We shall be saying things that are unsettling to numerous interest groups. We shall range very widely over the humanities and the natural sciences. Sometimes you may feel that you don't understand on first reading what we're saying. But don't give up. Because the change we want is worth it.

Part I

The health of millions of people is affected by one or more common long-term conditions. These are the 'modern plagues'. But are they really plagues? How are these long-term conditions related to each other? How are other people and society affected by the consequences of these plagues? And how have society and successive governments responded to all this?

1

Words about words

Words are slippery things: they can have different meanings in different contexts at different times. So, before we get going, we need to do a little housekeeping to make sure that the meanings that we ourselves have in mind for some common words are clear to all. The words we want to look at are: disease, risk, obesity, prevention, lifestyle and health. There may be some readers who would rather refer back to this chapter if, later on, they become unsettled by our arguments.

Disease

When it comes to diseases, the truth is people just don't like calling a spade a spade. Yes, health professionals try to use precise language. But, most of us want to fudge the issue much of the time or even make light of it all.

So we tend to describe the situation with words or phrases such as: I feel a bit upset, below par, crappy, crocked, crook, crappy, crummy, funny, green around the gills, grotty, in a bad way, liverish, lousy, not myself, not up to snuff, off colour, out of kilter, out of sorts, peaky, peculiar, poorly, queasy, ropey, rough, run down, seedy, taken badly, under par, under the weather.

Many of these words try to downplay the problem that we have. This can be the case for the layperson as much as the expert. Experts may question whether a set of symptoms should be described as a disease, or a condition, or a disorder or a syndrome. Even this begs the question: what does 'symptom' mean? Ultimately, perhaps it does not matter too much which word is used, as long as no-one with a particular condition feels they are pre-judged in some way. However, from a biologist's perspective, a word is needed which indicates that things are not in order or, in other words, that indicates some kind of imbalance in an individual's biological systems. For now, we use the word 'condition' to refer to the common ways that an individual's biology may become unbalanced, but in Chapter 7 we want to discuss the word 'homeostasis', since this refers to balance or equilibrium in biological systems. This is not to say that clinicians and others should stop using the words they want to use. However, a range of conditions will be under discussion, which seem clinically unrelated but that, from the point of view of preventing them, share important features. That is why we want to use just one word for the diseases, disorders or conditions that comprise today's common long-term conditions.

Risk

My risk of getting cancer is about one in three. The odds of my favourite horse winning are about twenty to one. My chance of winning the lottery is about one in ten million. Which of those outcomes are we least likely to do anything about?

When the probability of an event that we want to happen is small or vanishingly small, we may bet our shirt on it. And, once we've lost our shirt, we bet the house. We act and we act fast. But, when the probability of an event that we don't want to happen is high, all too often, we do nothing.

In English, there are many words for 'risk' and the word we choose to use often depends on whether we welcome or fear the event to which we are referring. The two main synonyms of 'risk' are words about danger (jeopardy, peril, hazard, menace, threat) and words about probability (possibility, chance, gamble and stake). In addition, any sentence that we use which contains the words 'if' or 'may' is, actually, a sentence about risk. 'If it rains tomorrow, I won't go out.' 'It may rain tomorrow, so I'll stay in.'

As they say, prediction is hazardous, especially about the future. You might think that all we can really do is put a number on it and let people decide. But that is missing the point: we can also change perceptions of risk. There is no doubt that society has had partial success in changing perceptions, for example, of the risks associated with tobacco-based nicotine addiction.

Smoking rates have dropped steeply – although there are still millions of smokers in the UK and the tobacco companies continue to make new addicts of millions more around the world. Nicotine is so highly addictive and ingestion by inhalation such an effective way of delivering the drug, that the Isle of Man's prison banned tobacco and offered nicotine patches instead. Some prisoners got round the ban by extracting nicotine from their patches, soaking hair and shredded banana skins with the extract and then making roll-ups.[1] However, the prison persisted in its efforts to cut smoking and eventually offered e-cigarettes to the inmates. This worked. The governor was surprised that so many prisoners went on to ask for help in quitting smoking altogether.[2] It seems that changing people's perceptions of risk can happen even when prison walls intervene: perceptions have changed throughout the UK and many other countries.

This change in perceptions is due to knowledge and education on the risks themselves and due to the availability of support. But it is also due to people feeling they actually have the power to reduce the risk they take on from tobacco use. This feeling of power comes from the fact that risk reduction involves just one straightforward action by them, namely quitting.

The problem with the word 'risk' is not only that it has lots of tricky mathematics behind it, but also that in everyday life we use the word without any mathematics. We continuously weigh up risks on some matter and then decide that a given risk is worth it or not worth it. Our decision-making processes are, in effect, risk assessments that may have some experience behind them but are largely just a guess. Furthermore, when we make decisions we don't necessarily want to do the rational thing. We want to be spontaneous (i.e. we want to avoid making risk assessments). We want to be daring (i.e. we want to ignore any risk assessments that may be out there). In other words we only want to do the rational thing when we have to (say, at work) or when we see it as a serious matter (i.e. we already have enough knowledge) or when our friends want us to be rational.

Synonyms for risk seem to fall into two groups: risks where we have already made up our minds (perils are bad, while gambles are good) or where we are trying to be open-minded and rational (probability when risk is high; possibility when risk is low). In this book, we, of course, want to be as open-minded and rational as possible. So for now let us simply note that an understanding of risk is rooted in a branch of mathematics called probability theory, but the perception of risk is a matter for the humanities and social sciences.

A keen appreciation of risk exists in the insurance world. The pensions that people save up for have behind them an annuity: a pot of money that needs to be fully used up, along with its interest, by the saver's date of death. Calculating the most probable date of death is important to enable regular pension payments. This calculation is undertaken by actuaries and involves consideration of the changing size of risk factors for one person. If the actuary gets it wrong and sets a pension that is too high or too low, the insurance company either loses profits or breaks the law. The giant insurance industry that uses risk to set pensions stands in contrast to society's feeble efforts at using risk to promote risk-reduction activities that would improve the health of the nation.

Obesity

We have seen that the common words we use to refer to a health condition often play things down. The same is true for obesity. At the other extreme, the words we use for obesity may be intentionally hurtful.

It is not hard to tell whether a word is playing things down or is hurtful: ample; beached whale; big; big-boned; broad; bulky; chubby; chunky; curvaceous; extra-large; fat; flabby; hulk; fleshy; fuller figure; gargantuan; heavy; hefty; jumbo; king-size; lardy; large; love-handles; mammoth; man-boobs; plump; podgy; portly; putting on size; rotund; slabba; solid; stout; sturdy; substantial; thick-set; tubby; well-covered.

What people need are terms that are not judgemental. Terms used by health professionals are all intended to be non-judgemental: Grade I, Grade II and Grade III obesity, morbid obesity, overweight and excess adiposity. Behind most of these terms there is usually a reference to an individual's position on a numerical scale. This is comparable to the way that weather forecasters talk about a day being mild or warm so as to indicate a specific temperature range. When one expresses an individual's weight in a way that takes account of their height, this measurement is called the Body Mass Index (BMI). By measuring BMI in a large number of people, one can calculate the average for the whole group or for a sub-group of people defined by age, gender and so on. Using these calculations, one can then describe an individual as being underweight, normal, overweight or obese. If someone is morbidly obese then they have a symptom such as reduced mobility that is recognised to be statistically associated with obesity.

One of the problems with BMI measurements is that sports enthusiasts may have an elevated BMI because of their bigger muscles. They protest vigorously that they are not overweight. They often prefer a measure called adiposity that takes account of the ratio of muscle to fat in the body.

However, the biggest issue with BMI is what lurks behind it. The assignment of an individual to any of the four groups (underweight, normal, overweight, obese) is closely connected to their estimated risk of a specific event like a diabetes diagnosis within a given time period. A person's low BMI is associated with elevated risks of poor health and reduced life expectancy. A person's high BMI is associated with elevated risks of death from common long-term conditions. So, in truth, we could replace BMI with a series of estimates of risk for different outcomes. BMI is a rough surrogate measure of those risks.

Our sensitivity about our weight helps to make it invisible. We don't want to acknowledge that our shape is 'imperfect'. We don't want to be mocked for our imperfection. So we go into denial and, if denial doesn't work, then we resort to defiance and hostility. We stick out our chins and say: 'I can be overweight if I want to be. It's my business. Back off. I'm happy this way. You're no size-zero fashion model.' Shame, mockery, denial, defiance and hostility: these are aspects of behaviour that tend to impair health.

However, it gets more complicated. Industries have come into being that play on our anxieties about body shape. They make promises to us that perfection is only a financial transaction away. You dislike the 'before' image and we promise you the 'after' image. Have these industries done more harm than good? To what extent is playing on anxieties about body shape increasing the risk of anorexia, bulimia, anabolic steroid abuse and mental health problems? It is time for some answers.

Prevention

If I see a child step off a kerb into heavy traffic, I hope I would have the presence of mind to prevent an accident by grasping that child by the arm and pulling them back to safety. I would have prevented a tragedy. At that moment, I would have reduced a risk of injury or death to zero. Prevention is, in this context, an all-or-nothing action.

But the same word can be used to mean something less certain. Perhaps the local council will have decided – after pressure from parents – to create a zebra crossing outside a school. So here, we are talking about prevention as an action that reduces risk – not an all-or-nothing action. Some accidents may still happen.

The prevention of common long-term conditions has this second meaning. It refers to reducing the risk of diagnosis or onset of those conditions. It is unrealistic to hope to stop every diagnosis of diabetes, depression, heart disease or cancer in a population. But, one can stop onset in some and one can delay onset in others. While just achieving a delay may sound feeble, in fact it is what we really all want – a delay to our own death.

When it comes to the prevention of infectious diseases, this is generally seen as straightforward (except when a brand new infection comes along). Population-wide vaccination has wiped out polio worldwide, although it persists in some isolated conflict zones where superstitions prevail. Annual vaccinations against 'seasonal flu', when provided widely, appear for now to be effective in preventing worldwide epidemics – called pandemics. The success of vaccination programmes in preventing infectious disease has perhaps made us think that prevention of all diseases and conditions could be that effective. Not so: prevention of common long-term conditions is far more difficult.

The US Commission on Chronic Illness in 1957 saw two aspects to the prevention of disease, which it called primary and secondary prevention.[3] Primary prevention, said the commission, seeks to avoid development of disease, while secondary prevention seeks to prevent progression of disease. The term 'tertiary prevention' was also introduced and sought to refer to reducing the impact of established disease. These ideas have persisted.[4] However, we think they muddy the waters for common long-term conditions because the way in which secondary and tertiary prevention work differs so much from the way primary prevention works. Acting to reduce the risks of a future long-term condition involves no clinical intervention because there are no clinical symptoms. So primary prevention is a non-clinical set of activities. On the other hand, both secondary and tertiary prevention involve clinical interventions such as medicines and other therapies and their attendant risks. These distinctions are so important that we only use the word 'prevention' to refer to non-clinical activities undertaken before a condition has been diagnosed. Actions taken to reduce or delay the impact of an existing condition are forms of treatment – not forms of prevention.

Moreover, we coin our own term: 'Systems Prevention' (see Chapter 13). This refers to prevention policies and practices that are guided by systems biology – the efforts that biologists are making to understand living organisms and their environment as a whole. For many decades, biological research has drilled down through the levels of organisation of living systems often ending up focussing on just one molecule. Researchers have worked away in separate specialisms such as molecular biology, genetics, physiology, clinical science, epidemiology, ecology, social science and so on. But, today, systems biologists are trying to put all those pieces back together. They are seeking a unified understanding of systems made up of atoms, molecules, cells, tissues, organs, then of the entire organism and its interaction with other organisms of the same species (social organisation) and of all different species, each living in a niche that can support particular species. Briefly put, systems biologists are being systematic – exactly what our society needs to be to reverse the rise in common long-term conditions. So Systems Prevention sits within systems biology.

Lifestyle

The word 'lifestyle' will hardly appear in this book. Instead we shall be referring to 'way of life' or 'social habits' (more strictly, the 'system of social habits'). So why are we banning 'lifestyle'?

Words about words

Psychologist Alfred Adler was the first to put the words 'life' and 'style' together in one German word – 'Lebensstil'. For Adler, the compound noun referred to someone's basic character. He claimed there were four categories or 'styles' that people adopt from childhood so as to undertake the 'tasks' of friendship, love and work. Three of these styles (ruling, getting, avoiding) are 'mistaken' and the fourth (socially useful) is not mistaken. To adopt that socially useful style one needs, it seems, the benefits of Adler's 'depth psychotherapy'.

This meaning may persist in psychotherapeutic circles, but by the 1960s, with the rise of consumerism, its common meaning became, according to the Oxford English Dictionary, 'the way in which a person lives'. There is no suggestion that lifestyle arises from the way our character develops as children, as Adler would want. Rather, the implicit or explicit suggestion is that lifestyle is a set of 'free choices' that individuals can make as they see fit. As a result, the word is often used in conjunction with 'choice': a lifestyle choice. Life is reduced to a set of choices of what to buy or do, and advertisers inform us of what is the best choice to make.

To emphasise this point, search for 'Lebensstil' in your browser. The first hit we got was on the 'Lebensstil Kollektion' website where you will find a collection of bespoke kitchenware that you may choose to buy if it suits your lifestyle – and pocket. Or take a look at examples in dictionaries of how the word 'lifestyle' is used:

- 'The benefits of a healthy lifestyle.'
- 'And, why would executives that are enjoying a lavish lifestyle be sending alarm signals?'
- 'Finally, he says, people's inactive lifestyles have also contributed to the problem.'
- 'The balance of the articles can be used by either gender to promote a healthy bodybuilding lifestyle.'
- 'But, how could a hunter-gatherer lifestyle feed the 20m-strong population of Australia?'

- 'And, he was almost as famous for his playboy lifestyle as his driving skills.'
- 'In today's busy lifestyle, why not reward yourself?'
- 'Adopting healthy lifestyle changes and taking medications can help you manage your disease.'
- 'Simplifying health empowers people to feel confident in making energizing lifestyle choices.'
- 'If your busy bodybuilding lifestyle makes it impossible to buy fresh veggies often, the next best bet is frozen.'
- 'A mother who stole £715,000 from her bosses to fund a jet-set lifestyle has been jailed for five years.'
- 'He was already obese and he was already living a sedentary lifestyle.'

So many of these common usages relate to health. Health is treated as a matter of style, and style, of course, is a matter of choice. In truth, this is, at best, a gross exaggeration because it is palpably untrue, for example, that the sedentary jobs that predominate in the world of work are a matter of choice or style. Most jobs are in towns and cities and if we live in one, we are constrained to work there. That usually means work in a not-so-stylish office. In the country, a farmer is obliged to maximise productivity and that means sitting on a tractor or some other machine. In theory, the farmer could perhaps scrap the tractor and plough the field behind a stylish horse. In practice, this only happens on TV 'reality' shows. In truth, jobs are only a matter of choice for a minority.

Then, after work, a long commute ensures that many arrive home ready to slump on the sofa, order a takeaway and stare at a TV screen until it's time to collapse in bed.

This may not be how people want to live. But it is how billions of us do, with few variations. To call it stylish or even to call it a choice is stretching the meanings of words. It is surely more accurate to say these are 'social habits' or part of today's 'way of life'. The ways of working and living are habitual in our society. They arise not from individual choices but from the way things are run in our society. They could be run differently. But now we are racing ahead of ourselves.

We want to think as clearly as possible about how our societies can get out of this unhealthy mess. Thinking clearly means, in part, finding the right words. Lifestyle and choice are not the right words. We have already referred, at the start of the book, to Aneurin Bevan's insightful recognition that prevention of disease requires us to change our 'system of social habits'. This phrase goes far beyond the jobs we do, the commuting, the takeaways and the TV and it goes beyond simply changing individual habits. Unfortunately, Bevan does not explore the implications of this pointed phrase. So, instead, we shall be trying to do it.

'Habit' has a far less contentious history as a word. It comes straight from the Latin 'to have' (habere), which also meant 'to wear' and this meaning comes directly to our times when we refer to a nun's habit. It is what we wear without any show or fuss because it is just part of our everyday routine. That sense then widens out into 'habit' as a tendency to act in a certain way – the habits of daily life.

If 'lifestyle' is inappropriate because it hides the major determinants of our health, the word also has another serious problem: it sits in a narrative that blames the victim for bad public policy. It is your own fault if you eat too much, don't socialise or exercise enough, drink, smoke or take drugs. They are, we are continually told, your own lifestyle choices and you should know the consequences. You should take the blame. Some people don't eat too much, they do exercise and so on. So, why not you? You are feckless or reckless. You should be grateful for the efforts that the government makes to improve health. But don't expect it to nanny you.

This points to a dispute that has a very long history. Should one blame society or the individual? We think the dispute is a waste of valuable time. While we and our governments continue to blame 'lifestyles' for the epidemics in obesity, diabetes, depression, heart disease and so on, we let government and other key stakeholders off the hook and fail to stem, let alone reverse, those epidemics. When a government plays this blame game, its aim is primarily to distract people from its own inadequacies.

Where does the phrase 'way of life' come from? Politicians sometimes use the phrase to refer to practices such as democracy. By contrast, anthropologists refer to 'lifeways' to distinguish between the ways of life of, for example, the hunter-gatherer and the farmer. Historians of human biology do the same, suggesting that common long-term conditions reflect maladaptation to today's lifeway.[5] 'Way of life' is synonymous with 'lifeway' but we prefer the former. Now, that is truly just a matter of style.

Health

We all go round and round in circles defining 'healthy' as the opposite of 'ill' and 'ill' as the opposite of 'healthy'. We seem never to get further than defining health by its absence. After World War Two, the United Nations set up the World Health Organization (WHO). It defined health as 'a state of complete physical, mental and social well-being and not merely the absence of disease or infirmity'.[6] This appears to solve the problem of defining health by its absence but is 'well-being' really such a helpful idea? It so easily slips into the same problem: well-being means not being unwell. The saving grace of the definition is that 'well-being' implies a prolonged state of one's health: it implies an absence of long-term conditions.

The problem with only having a negative definition of health is that it leaves us no wiser on what needs to be done. If we defined 'road safety' as an absence of accidents, it would not tell us that we need driving tests, education for cyclists and pedestrians, zebra crossings or traffic lights. Those are some of the preconditions for road safety. A complete list of those preconditions is what road safety is. We can discuss the importance of any one of them. We can test the effects of removing one of the preconditions or of adding another as times change. We can be practical in a way that escapes us if we have abstract definitions.

So, there really has been a problem in defining 'health' satisfactorily. In 1986, forty years after its formation, the WHO returned to the problem and adopted the Ottawa Charter. This specifies 'peace, shelter, education, food, income, a stable eco-system, sustainable resources, social justice, and equity' as the 'prerequisites for health' and as the 'fundamental conditions and resources for health'.[7] The underlying idea is that you need to define health by defining the conditions that must be met for individuals and populations to minimise the risk of disease. If society can satisfy those conditions fully, then it will have done everything it can to ensure and to prolong health. We agree with that general approach, though we have some different ideas about the conditions that must be met. And then we go one step further by defining health simply as the state that exists when those conditions are fulfilled (see Chapter 12). That state does, of course, not mean that no-one ever gets ill or dies.

2

The modern plagues

We shall be proposing big changes to our way of life and this will entail proposing big changes to public policy as a whole. But, there is no point in making such proposals unless people have a crying need for them. The modern plagues are the reality that makes change imperative. So let us start by looking at them, at the common long-term conditions of diabetes, depression, heart disease and cancer. What are these conditions? How common are they? Why just these conditions, when there are many more that cause disability and death? Why do we draw a parallel between these conditions and the epidemics or plagues that decimated populations in the past?

Why 'plague' is the right word

Our way of life today is inflicting enormous harm on our species. The extent of this harm is so great that it is reminiscent of past times of the 'Black Death' of the fourteenth century and the 'Great Plague' of the seventeenth century. Back then, humanity could plead ignorance in its failure to prevent bubonic plagues or other infections. Even as late as the last century, when the influenza pandemic killed millions after World War One, a plea of ignorance was increasingly tenuous but just possible. But today, there is no such excuse for society's self-inflicted harm due to infectious or non-infectious epidemics. The evidence is all around us of people whose once healthy lives are brought to an end by the onset of diabetes, depression, heart disease or cancer. This then affects the rest of society, constraining prosperity and damaging the social fabric, as we shall show shortly.

The numbers of people diagnosed with these common long-term conditions have been rising continuously over recent decades. But, the increases have led neither to the rapid reactions nor even the panics that infectious epidemics have caused. It is worth taking a look at flu epidemics. This is something that society takes really seriously, yet the numbers of people diagnosed with flu are far lower than the numbers diagnosed with the common long-term conditions. We say there is an epidemic when the frequency of occurrence of a disease in a specified time (its incidence) in a population is above a certain threshold. Emergency planning is continually reviewed and, when the threshold is breached, planning is transformed into action. The threshold is set not only by the incidence, but also by the severity of the symptoms due to that year's strain of flu.

Figure 2.1 shows a graph with the number of flu cases each year between 1966 and 2015. Every winter there is a spike in the number of cases. But the biggest spike in numbers of flu-like diagnoses was in the winter of 1969 when the rate was 1,300 diagnoses per 100,000 people at the peak of the epidemic. That corresponds to about 1.3% of the population. In winter 1975, it was 0.8%. Of course the total number of cases for a whole epidemic is higher than this.[1] Note how this illness may be less frequent nowadays in England and Wales with the advent of NHS vaccinations.

As we shall see, the impact of the common long-term conditions is greater. The numbers have risen more slowly than seen during flu epidemics, but the proportion of people affected is far larger. Their prevalence (the affected proportion of a population) is at a level comparable to the pestilential plagues of ancient times and

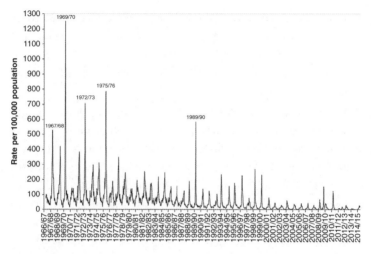

Figure 2.1 Year on year variation in influenza-like illness between 1966 and 2015 in England and Wales. The graph shows that most years there is a surge in the number of cases per 100,000 people. Note how some years show a bigger surge to more than 1% of the population. Also note how this illness may be less frequent nowadays in England and Wales (with the advent of NHS vaccinations).

the Middle Ages. This is, then, good enough reason to use the phrase 'modern plagues'.

Diabetes, heart disease, cancer and depression

Deciding which long-term conditions are the plagues of our times is not easy. The four we have selected could be replaced by other long-term conditions, say dementia or lower back pain. In some cases we do not have all the data we need to prove exactly how common a condition is. With diabetes, the picture is very clear. With the common conditions of anxiety and depression, we know prevalence is high but we also know it is repeatedly overlooked. With heart disease, we have conditions that are a major focus of service-based prevention activity in the UK. With cancer, there is massive public concern. So you can see we are using a number of different standards to identify the plagues of our times. You may find this unsatisfactory, but we shall see that when it comes to prevention of each of them, it turns out they all share critical factors that alter risk and that society can modify. So, if we eliminate a source of risk for one condition, this will eliminate a source of risk for another condition too.

Diabetes is a condition where the concentration of glucose in the blood (called blood glucose or blood sugar) is too high. Normally, a protein called insulin, which is made in the pancreas, prevents this by enabling sugar to be moved out of the blood into the tissues of the body. But, in Type 1 diabetes, the pancreas is damaged, while in Type 2 diabetes, the pancreas fails to release insulin appropriately and the cells in tissues do not respond appropriately. This then raises blood sugar. In the longer term this can result in serious disabilities affecting eyes, heart, blood circulation, nerves and so on. Clinicians also recognise 'pre-diabetes', when blood sugar is toward the top of the normal range, indicating an increased risk of diabetes and its consequences.

Cardiovascular conditions (commonly called 'heart disease') are a range of conditions affecting the tubes that carry blood around the body (blood vessels). Among these, heart attacks (myocardial infarction or ischemic heart disease) and strokes (where a vessel in the brain becomes blocked or ruptured) are prominent and can be rapidly fatal, as can the rarer aortic aneurysms. Other cardiovascular conditions include angina (chest pain), congestive cardiac failure (heart failure), atrial fibrillation (palpitations) and peripheral arterial disease (reduced flow of blood to the limbs). Hypertension (high blood pressure) is common, with its symptoms of severe headache; confusion; vision problems; chest pain; difficulty breathing; irregular heartbeat; blood in urine; and pounding in chest, neck or ears. Clinicians also recognise 'pre-hypertension', when blood pressure is toward the top of the normal range but the symptoms of hypertension are absent.

Cancer comprises over 200 conditions where the body's usual control over the growth of a cell is disrupted. This disruption means that the cell may grow and divide many times more than usual. This can then lead to a clump of cells. When some of these cells break off the clump, they may form a new clump elsewhere in the body. The cancer cells can cause a blockage in a blood vessel, for example, or they can disrupt the normal functioning of organs and tissues. Loosening of control over a cell's growth arises usually from the influence on a cell of an 'agent' (say, radiation, or a virus, or too much or too little of a chemical), but other influences increase the risk of cancer as well. One of these influences is being overweight or obese: twelve of the most common types of cancer are associated with obesity.[2] Cancer is sometimes said to be a 'genetic' condition, but this refers only to some of the links in the chain of events that result in the condition. So, at the start of the millenium, hope was misplaced that knowledge of the human genome sequence would rapidly usher in cures for common cancers.

Depression and anxiety are termed 'common mental disorders' (or sometimes 'neurotic disorders'). Key symptoms are marked emotional distress and an interference with the ability of people to perform everyday functions. Symptoms of depressive episodes include low mood and a loss of interest and enjoyment in ordinary things and experiences. They impair emotional and physical behaviour. Anxiety conditions include generalised anxiety disorder, panic disorder, phobias and obsessive compulsive disorder. Symptoms of depression and anxiety frequently exist together. The causes of depression have been described by the National Health Service: 'There's no single cause of depression. It can occur for a variety of reasons and it has many different triggers. For some people, an upsetting or stressful life event, such as bereavement, divorce, illness, redundancy and job or money worries, can be the cause. Different causes can often combine to trigger depression. For example, you may feel low after being ill and then experience a traumatic event, such as a bereavement, which brings on depression.'[3]

Living in a time of plague

With the bubonic plague, people were disabled by illness within hours and dead within days. By contrast, with the modern plagues, we get a diagnosis and slowly become less able to lead a full life. However, life can continue for many years and we may ultimately die of something completely different. So, while an old-fashioned plague is serious because of the proportion of the population that catch it and die, a modern plague is serious because of the proportion of the population that catch it and then lead increasingly more disabled lives. To understand the scale of today's common long-term conditions, the key quantity we need to know is their prevalence.

How that prevalence changes with time, age, gender, ethnicity, deprivation, location and so on is useful to know so as to guide action on prevention. Prevalence is different from incidence – how many people are diagnosed with a condition in a given time. If the incident rate goes up, then so does the prevalence but if, over time, the death rate goes down (due to improved medicines) then prevalence will rise. Improved prevention will reduce incidence and that eventually leads to reduced prevalence. A miracle cure, on the other hand, would not necessarily affect incidence but would reduce prevalence. Think of a bath tub with water flowing in and draining out: the water level inevitably rises if more water comes in or less drains out. To end the risk of the bath overflowing, you have to turn off the tap. So, which taps – what factors – are filling up the bath?

Diabetes

In 1980, the number of people worldwide with diabetes was 108m but in 2014 it was 422m. This four-fold increase in diabetes over 34 years is not explained by population growth since prevalence rose from 4.7% to 8.5%.[4] Diabetes is a global pandemic.

A research study showed that, in the UK between 2004 and 2014, diabetes prevalence rose year-on-year from 3.2% to 5.3%.[5] This rise was seen in all four nations comprising the UK. It was seen among both men and women. And it was seen for people regardless of their level of deprivation – although the least deprived 20% of the population benefitted in 2014, after years of increases, from a small decrease in prevalence. However it is important to bear in mind that this least deprived fifth of the population does not have uniformly better health: their health is worse in those areas of England where health is worse for everyone else.

A National Diabetes Audit in 2016 found that in one of the four nations, England, there were 2.8m diabetics (5.1% of the population) with around 200,000 new diagnoses every year.[6] From 2018, the NHS and Public Health England have been collecting the numbers systematically (not just through surveys) – a vital first step in tackling the problem.

Heart disease

One way of measuring the prevalence of conditions like heart disease is to examine the electronic health records kept by family doctors. It is not perfect because some people do not have a doctor and there is currently no single, national, managed set of data standards. However, records of over 1.2m people in England have been examined and results analysed in 2017 show that over one in five adults had a diagnosis of heart disease.

Hypertension was by far the most common at 18.6% prevalence.[7] In 2016, Public Health England estimated the prevalence of raised blood pressure (hypertension) across the population at approximately 24%[8] or some 13.4m people. This higher number includes undiagnosed cases as well – of which there were 5.6m. That this large number of people should have been missed suggests that primary care may not be the only setting required for prevention of major cardiovascular events.

The same study found that coronary artery disease was present in 3.5% of people. A separate study had found a prevalence of 3% in England, and 4% in Scotland, Northern Ireland and Wales.[9]

Heart disease remains the leading cause of death and, in particular, ischemic heart disease (where flow of blood to the heart is restricted). This, by itself, was the leading cause of death in the UK in 2007 and, despite a dip, remained so a decade later. This makes especially important the acquisition of continuous, systematic, full and accurate data. There is much to do.

Cancer

All cases of cancer in England are now recorded by the National Cancer Registration and Analysis Service. There is information on new cases and on five-year survival after treatment. This continuous and systematic approach is essential if action on prevention is to become effective. We also need to know about the health of people who have had a cancer diagnosis – in particular the disabilities they may have acquired and the risk factors for those disabilities. There is enormous public concern about cancer and that itself is one reason to consider it as a modern plague. Yet the incidence rate is not that high at about 0.06% per annum. However, improved treatments save lives and this then pushes up the prevalence of the disabilities associated with cancer. Between 2006 and 2016 the incidence rate rose for women by 4.8% (from 516 to 541 per 100,000 people) and for men it fell by 1.2% (from 671 to 663). This fall was due, in part, to a reduced incidence of prostate cancer.[10]

What we need to bear in mind is the fact that people have to lead their lives with the consequences of cancer treatments that are often invasive, disfiguring and unpleasant. For example, the most common type of cancer in women is breast cancer. If this requires radical mastectomy, the individual must live with that all their lives. Among men, prostate cancer is the most common type and, here, treatment can cause erectile dysfunction. Nearly all cancer treatments have effects that are not only psychological but also social. Surviving cancer is not a walk in the park. Prevention is preferable to cure.

Depression and anxiety

A survey is undertaken just once every seven years to measure the prevalence of different forms of mental illness in the UK. Four surveys have been conducted and the most recent Adult Psychiatric Morbidity Survey was in 2014.[11] The results were not made available until two years later. They give a national and regional picture, but there is no information for smaller areas. In addition, each survey done has looked at a different population, so it is tricky to identify trends in prevalence. For example, in 1993 and 2000 the populations were, first, those aged 16–64 and, then, those aged 16–74 in England, Scotland and Wales, while in 2007 the survey covered those aged 16–74 but only if they lived in England. Some idea of the local prevalence of depression and anxiety can be gleaned from the General Practice Patient Survey of individual doctors. The survey estimated prevalence of depression and anxiety in 2014 in England among those aged 16–74 at one person in six (15.7%). One in twelve (8.1%) had severe symptoms[12] These large figures have a still more troubling aspect. While one in six people would probably benefit from support and treatment, three out of five of them (61%) do not get either. Expressing this in numbers, we can say that about 8.5m people in England need support and treatment but nearly 5m miss out. Could it be that to get help with depression or anxiety one must first be severely ill? Have the numbers of people affected by anxiety and depression been increasing? The analysis of the 2014 survey answers this question with a 'Yes'. This conclusion is based on using the data from all four surveys between 1993 and 2014 and is illustrated in Figure 2.2. Within two decades, about a third more of the English

The modern plagues

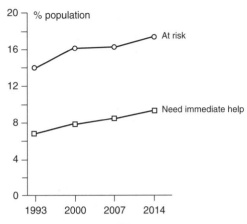

Figure 2.2 The increase of mental ill health in England between 1993 and 2014. The graph – based on the Adult Psychiatric Morbidity Survey – shows the increase in the population of England at risk or needing immediate help with depression or anxiety. Numbers increased by about a third in just two decades.

population became at risk of depression and anxiety or in need of immediate help.

The big picture

Just as the word lifespan identifies the age at which people die, so 'healthspan' identifies the age at which people come to the end of their fully healthy lives. Healthspan is the period of a person's life that is free of disability – where a disability is 'an umbrella term for impairments, activity limitations and participation restrictions' according to the World Health Organization (WHO).[13] So, we should not think of disability as simply referring to being confined to a wheelchair. If we find that we are no longer able to do some of the things we used to do, then we have acquired a disability. It is likely to start in a small way but it does not go away like, for example, a bruise eventually disappears. It goes on for a long time. We may ignore the disability or work our way around it. Then, sooner or later, another minor disability comes along and the list starts to grow. On top of that, one disability may accelerate the progression of others. For example, if we can't move freely because of an aching joint, we are likely to undertake less physical activity and then this in turn raises the risk of obesity, which then slows us down even more.

'Participation restriction' is an important disability: when people can't participate in, say, social activities then both they themselves and their community lose out. The individual becomes isolated, while the community loses the contribution of someone who may have been full of ideas, energy and fun. Note also that isolation increases the risk of poorer mental health, of greater physical inactivity and of compensatory over-eating.

The common sources of disability are the common long-term conditions. We can live a long time – sometimes decades – after healthspan has ended and before we die. This gap between healthspan and lifespan has been measured in each neighbourhood of England, from the most to the least deprived.[14] What has been found is that the most deprived can expect to live twenty years with disability while the least deprived live twelve years. To put it another way, the most deprived spend over a quarter of their lives with disabilities while the least deprived spend one seventh of their lives with disabilities. The gap between healthspan and life span is shown in Figure 2.3, adapted from the Marmot Review – a major study by leading epidemiologist Sir Michael Marmot. Notice how the gap gets smaller as deprivation declines. The most deprived fraction of the population has the shortest healthspan and endures disability for the longest time. The area in grey indicates the burden of disability on the population. Improving the health of the population means reducing the area in grey as much as possible.

We can imagine this figure as though there were a population of one-hundred people, each with a higher income than the previous person. The grey gap between healthspan and lifespan draws

The modern plagues

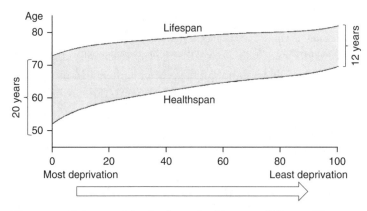

Figure 2.3 Influence of deprivation on healthspan and lifespan. The most deprived fraction of the population has the shortest healthspan and endures disability for the longest time. The area in grey indicates the burden of disability on the population. Improving the health of the population means reducing the area in grey as much as possible. The diagram is based on information from the Marmot Review (see text).

attention to the fraction of our lives when disability means our income is under threat (because disability reduces productivity at work), when we spend more time getting medical attention and less time with friends and in our community and when there are ever-increasing health costs. The data for the Marmot Review was collected between 1999 and 2003. If inequality were to increase, then, the grey area of the figure will change shape so that the most deprived spend more time disabled and the least deprived may also show more time disabled. Today, inequality is indeed growing. According to the House of Commons Library, the top 10% of the population will have 4.5 times more disposable income in 2021 than in 2018 when they had 4.0 times more.[15]

What about all the other conditions?

Comparative data on different conditions can be hard to come by but this problem has started to be tackled by the Bill and Melinda

Table 2.1   Global changes in the causes of death and disability between 2004 and 2017

What caused the most deaths in 2017?	% change	What health problems caused the most disability in 2017?	% change
Ischaemic heart disease	−13.4	Lower back pain	+10.2
Alzheimer's disease	+31.3	Headache disorders	+5.7
Stroke	−7.6	Depressive disorders	+7.6
Lung disease (chronic obstructive pulmonary disease)	+9.3	Neck pain	+8.3%
Lung cancer	+5.4	Diabetes	+42.8
Lower respiratory infection	+14.9	Falls	+16.5
Colorectal cancer	+9.1	Age-related hearing loss	+14.9
Breast cancer	+1.0	Lung disease (chronic obstructive pulmonary disease)	+10.0
Prostate cancer	+17.7	Anxiety disorders	+5.6
Pancreatic cancer	+19.5	Other musculoskeletal	+5.4

Source: based on data from the Global Burden of Disease project.
Note: conditions ranked for frequency as the most common causes of death and disability in 2017.

Gates Foundation of the Global Burden of Disease project. Its open access database covers 195 countries, 359 conditions and 63 risk factors.[16] We constructed Table 2.1 using data taken from the project.

The table shows the top ten causes for deaths in the UK alongside the top ten causes of disability for 2017. So as to get an idea of how things alter over time, the percentage change is also shown for each condition since 2004. When it comes to causes of death the top three are ischaemic heart disease, Alzheimer's disease and stroke, while the top three causes of disability are lower back pain, headache disorders and depressive disorders. Since 2004, the biggest rise in deaths has been due to Alzheimer's disease (up 31.3%) and the biggest rise in disability has been due to diabetes (up 42.8%). This analysis shows that prevalence of a condition does not correlate with cause of death or disability. And that, in turn, indicates that there needs to be continuous research and action on prevalence, death and disability so that society can prioritise prevention where it decides it is needed most.

3

Sorrows in battalions

Having any one of the common long-term conditions described in the last chapter is, without doubt, a serious problem. But, so often in life, one problem begets another. 'When sorrows come, they come not single spies but in battalions', says Hamlet's uncle reflecting on Ophelia's grief. To appreciate the cumulative impact of diagnosis with multiple long-term conditions, consider this brief anonymised case history based on a real person.

Dorothea Deauville lived a year or two longer than most women of average means. She died recently aged 84, but for six of her nine decades she was not only obese but also endured deteriorating health.

In her early forties she went on to medicines for hypertension (high blood pressure). After child-bearing, she had a prolapse of the uterus. Her muscles became stiff due to a condition called polymyalgia and, for this, she was treated long-term with steroids. She had to have a foam collar for the arthritis in her neck. She also had an operation for that, but the pain persisted and so she went onto painkillers for the rest of her life.

In her fifties she got gallstones. In her sixties she developed angina, survived a heart attack and went onto more pills. In her seventies she became diabetic. Kidney problems followed, including recurrent urinary tract infections. There was nerve damage in her foot causing it to drop. She had a mobility scooter. The wide range of pills she was on probably caused her dramatic skin rashes. These rashes gave rise to ulcers.

Dorothea was in and out of hospital for many years and received social care until she eventually developed pneumonia, went into renal failure and suffered major organ shut down.

Dorothea Deauville endured one long-term condition on top of another. How frequent is this? Was she simply unlucky or was there some complex and tangled web of cause and effect between all the conditions that affected her? Or are both ideas close to the truth: is it a combination of chance and of causality?

Let us ask first how frequently people get two or more long-term conditions. One would hope that such information was being collected and stored continuously. But it isn't. We have to rely on, and then interpret, various cross-sectional studies (in effect, snapshots) undertaken in different places. The studies described below used different definitions and, as a consequence, it is much harder to say if a trend exists toward more or fewer people having multiple conditions.

One study looked at 100,000 people over 18 who were on the records of 182 family doctors across England between 2005 and 2008.[1] Less than one in twenty of those aged 18–24 had two or more conditions. This is a small, but still troubling, proportion. In stark contrast, nearly half of all those aged 75–84 had two or more concurrent long-term conditions. Three-quarters had at least one long-term condition.

A second study looked at data for 2012 in a larger group of over 400,000 patients.[2] It reported a higher proportion of people with two or more conditions. For example, three quarters of those aged 75–84 had two or more conditions. This study sheds some light on what long-term conditions tend to go together. The top three most prevalent conditions are high blood pressure, depression/anxiety and chronic pain. What is associated with each of these conditions? If you have high blood pressure, then this is often associated with pain, diabetes and hearing loss. Depression and anxiety go along with pain, high blood pressure and irritable bowel syndrome. Chronic pain goes along with high blood pressure, depression or anxiety and hearing loss. In fact high blood pressure, depression and anxiety are frequent in all the top ten most common conditions.

To put some numbers on this, nearly one in five people had high blood pressure and of these, a quarter had chronic pain, one in five had diabetes and one in six had hearing loss. The multiple conditions that Dorothea Deauville had fit best with the coronary heart disease group: her disease went along with hypertension, a painful condition and diabetes. The fact that two things go together does not tell you how this comes about: only when you know the sequence of events can you start to see whether preventing the earliest event also prevents, modifies or delays subsequent events.

Other important observations from this study include the impact of deprivation and depression / anxiety. People living in the most socially and economically deprived neighbourhoods are about 5% more likely to have multiple conditions. But when one of those conditions is depression / anxiety, people in the most deprived areas are 12% more likely to have multiple conditions.

Analysis by the Department of Health backs up these findings. In its most recent compendium of information on long-term conditions – harking back to 2008 – it predicted a million more people with multiple long-term conditions over a ten-year period (2008 to 2018).[3] The numbers were set to rise from 1.9m to 2.9m. It also reports that the more long-term conditions you have, the more problems you have with walking, washing, dressing and performing everyday activities. For example, about one in twenty people have some difficulty walking. But for people with one long-term condition, this difficulty rises to one in four people. Furthermore, nearly two-thirds of people with three or more such conditions have difficulty walking. Over four fifths of people with a long-term condition say that their health is a barrier to the type or amount of work they can do.

Complications

If you have more than one long-term condition, is one the consequence of the other or is it chance? We just don't know. But we do have technical words with which to think about the problem.

Where there is a strong suspicion or evidence that the initial condition (one set of symptoms) frequently gives rise to another set of symptoms, we say that the initial condition has 'complications'. Clinicians sometimes use the word 'sequelae' to refer to the same thing. A medical complication is then considered to be an unfavourable result of a condition (or of some treatment given for the condition). Complications generally make the condition more severe or involve new signs or symptoms or harmful abnormalities. These may become widespread in the body and affect other organs. If those signs, symptoms and abnormalities correspond to some other known condition, then we can say that the complication has led to the development of a second condition in the patient.

If we are not confident that the second condition is a consequence of the condition that was detected first, then we use the word 'co-morbidity'. 'Morbidity' just refers to the state of having a condition or disease. 'Co-morbidity' refers to having two conditions and 'multi-morbidity' refers to more than two.

Here are some of the complications that are associated with diabetes.

Heart conditions. Over 68% of diabetics over 64 years die from a heart condition, while under half that proportion die in this way in the population as a whole.[4] Note that this does not prove that diabetes causes the heart condition. Proof would require us to uncover the precise mechanism. However, there are a number of factors that raise the risk of both diabetes and cardiovascular disease (e.g. obesity, insulin resistance, high blood cholesterol and triglyceride content, hypertension). Having risk factors in common is, again, not proof that one thing causes another.

Nerve damage. Long-term elevated blood glucose concentrations can eventually cause damage to many of the nerves in the body. Hands, feet, thighs, hips, the face and the internal organs are commonly involved.

Kidney damage. Symptoms include less urine, swelling of the legs and unexplained shortness of breath. A protein called albumin escapes through the kidneys and this is found in nearly half of diabetics.[5]

Eye damage. Long-term elevated blood glucose concentrations can lead to damage in the blood vessels of the retina of the eye. Vessels can burst or get torn or leak so that fluid enters the back of the eye. Blurred vision can lead on, for example, to blindness or retinal detachment.

Foot damage. Diabetes can reduce blood flow to the foot and this then can lead on to ulcers that become infected. If there is nerve damage present already, then the diabetic may not notice the damage and so may develop gangrene that then requires amputation.

Note that all this damage to different tissues can also be seen in conditions other than diabetes.

So, we can talk of 'complications' and of 'co-morbidity', depending on how confident we are that one thing has led to another. If we want to keep an open mind (or don't have a clue), we should talk about 'risk factors'. One can make the case that this is a better term to use: risks can be measured and then ranked (low, medium, high risk). Really, we ought not to say that A causes B until we understand why. When it comes to the long-term conditions, on the whole, we do not understand a great deal about their basic biology.

Leading Cambridge brain scientist, Ed Bullmore, suspects that inflammation is part of the problem in many long-term conditions.[6] This idea is based on the partial success of attempts to treat them using drugs known to target the immune system and the processes of inflammation. New treatments for rheumatoid arthritis and other auto-immune diseases that target inflammation were introduced in the 1990s, while today immunotherapy is used for some cancers. Low-grade inflammation, detectable by blood tests, is increasingly considered to be a reason why factors such as poverty, stress, obesity and ageing increase risk of the common long-term conditions.

Scientists are now even opening up to the idea that inflammation could be deeply implicated in mental illness including depression. But does inflammation cause depression? This hypothesis has been tested by performing two brain scans on volunteers, one before and one after an inflammatory response has been deliberately provoked by the injection of typhoid vaccine. If there is a difference in the two scans, that shows that bodily inflammation can cause changes in the way the brain works; if not, that would be a problem for the theory that inflammation can cause depression. Over a dozen versions of this experiment have been performed.[7] Overall they support the idea that inflammation alters brain activity. Clinical trials are now underway to see if anti-inflammatory drugs can be used to treat schizophrenia and Alzheimer's disease.[8]

Risk factors

Just because a factor that changes the risk of an event is not called a complication or co-morbidity does not mean that it is not useful. When it comes to prevention of a long-term condition, we shall see later that identifying a risk factor, measuring it and acting to reduce the risk are all essential. The key thing about a risk factor is that it is a statistical idea. It is the idea that one event is associated with another event so frequently that the association only has a measurably small chance of being a statistical fluke.

The risk factors that turn up in the context of the common long-term conditions include the following: obesity; overweight; physical inactivity; social isolation; age; socio-economic status; genetic variation; gender; smoking; diet (sugar), substance abuse (alcohol, drugs); pollution. This mish-mash of factors can be divided into two groups: those factors we can do something about and those that we can't. This is an important distinction: we can do little or nothing about our age, our gender or our genetic make-up. But we can do plenty about reducing the other risk factors, either as individuals or as a society. That is ultimately what this book is about.

Later on we shall be discussing factors about which we can do nothing – like our genetic make-up. The factors where society and individuals can do something break down into two groups: those where a little change can go a long way and those where much change is needed to get anywhere. Smoking, substance abuse and pollution are risk factors where a little change can go a long way.

Risks due to smoking, alcohol, pollution

Table 3.1 lists some of the risks associated with smoking tobacco and consuming too much alcohol.[9] The first column lists broad categories of different conditions and diseases. The second and third columns list specific risks to health.

Each year a research centre called the Health Effects Institute reports on 'The state of global air'.[10] The 2019 report highlights pollution due to ozone and due to particles inside and outside the home (from diesel engines, wood fires etc.). Of course there are other forms of pollution in the atmosphere, especially in the workplace. Particulate matter (PM) that is released into the air from diesel cars, buses and lorries is particularly risky if the particles are very small – this means about 2.5 microns in width (a micron is a millionth of a metre). Studies show that increased levels of this PM 2.5 in the air raises the risks of narrowing of the arteries (leading to heart attacks), blockages in the arteries (strokes), lung cancer, lung disease (especially chronic obstructive pulmonary disease), lung infections (pneumonia) and diabetes. Globally in 2017, about three million deaths are considered to have arisen from this form of pollution. For the UK, the number of deaths from PM2.5

Sorrows in battalions

Table 3.1   Diseases and conditions linked to smoking and excess drinking

	Risks due to smoking	Risks due to excess alcohol
Cancers	Lung, bladder, blood, cervix, colon, rectum, esophagus, kidney, larynx, liver, throat, mouth, pancreas, stomach, trachea	Mouth, nasal cavity, throat, windpipe, colon, stomach, breast
Heart disease	Stroke, heart attacks	Hypertension, heart attacks, heart failure, stroke
Diabetes	Diabetes	Diabetes
Liver	Cancer	Organ failure, cancer
Lungs	Lung disease (chronic obstructive pulmonary disease), breathlessness (emphysema)	Lung infections, pneumonia
Mental	Dementia, schizophrenia	Depression/anxiety.
Stomach	Cancer	Ulcers, anaemia, malnutrition
Bones	Osteoporosis, tooth loss	Osteoporosis
Sex	Infertility, erectile dysfunction	Infertility, erectile dysfunction, miscarriage
Pregnancy	Under-weight newborn	Foetal alcohol syndrome

Source: based on data from the World Health Organization.

was 22,300. These numbers have been rising in recent decades. Current levels of air pollution have reduced life expectancy by twenty months worldwide.

In brief, smoking, alcohol and air pollution are among the factors that increase the risk of the modern plagues. What is special about smoking, alcohol and air pollution is that there is a groundswell of opinion that society should legislate against them. However, their link to the modern plagues is not always recognised. Moreover, there are also commercial interests and cultural attitudes that resist action, including legislation, which would reduce these risks.

UK governments have, over the decades, restricted smoking ever more strictly. The very first legislation was in 1693 when MPs banned smoking in Parliament. Other workplaces did not benefit from such a ban until 2006 – over 300 years later. A requirement for smoke-free train carriages was introduced in 1868 but car passengers were not protected until 2014. Restrictions on tobacco sales and advertising, and raising prices, have been slow in coming. To be fair, the pace of progress has accelerated. An important new strategy was introduced in 1992: government committed itself to reducing smoking to 20% of the population. A new target was set in 2016 of 12% by 2022. The method has involved tighter restrictions plus public educational measures.

Smoking prevalence has indeed declined. In the 1950s over 80% of men and 38% of women smoked. By 2000 the numbers had halved for men while 10% fewer women smoked.[11] Then, between 2011 and 2017, the total adult population of smokers fell from 7.7m to 6.1m.[12] However, unemployed people (39%) were around twice as likely to smoke as people in work (21%)[13] and there are important regional differences. For example, more adults in Greater Manchester are smokers than the England average (19.5% of adults in England smoked in 2012, but this was 23.1% in Greater Manchester).[14] In 2014, among children, 2% of 13-year-olds, 4% of 14-year-olds and 8% of 15-year-olds smoke at least one cigarette a week.[15]

This leads us to be optimistic that regulation and public education can go some way to cracking the problem. However, there are still some 6m smokers in England alone. Moreover, there is evidence that the tendency to smoke is transmitted between generations within the home. For example, teenagers living with smokers are more likely to smoke. Some 17% of younger teens smoke if they live with three or more smokers but if they live with non-smokers then just 4% take up smoking.[16]

It seems unlikely that Parliament would legislate to ban smoking in a private house or flat so as to protect children. So we may have reached the limits of what the law and perhaps of what public education can achieve. A little change (a few laws and a low-intensity public education programme) has gone a long way in combatting smoking. But to deal with the rest of the problem – the 6m remaining smokers – much bigger changes, as described in Part IV, may be essential.

Similar considerations apply in the case of alcohol. Excessive use can be reduced by legislation and public education. But ensuring moderate use by us all will probably require bigger changes in our society. As for PM2.5 pollution, legislation alone may be sufficient, assuming there is sufficient public and private investment in the infrastructure required to run a green economy.

4

Your loss is my loss: we all lose

Biology and medicine are both challenged by the wish to understand and prevent the common long-term conditions. But, the challenge is not just to biologists and doctors, it is also to social scientists.

History suggests why. The Black Death of the 1350s was the most terrifying of the plagues in the Middle Ages. It killed about a quarter of our species – over 100m out of a global population of some 450m. Not dissimilar proportions of the population are at risk of today's common long-term conditions. But the Black Death did not simply reduce population size: it disrupted society. Feudal labour relations (serfdom) crumbled in the face of a shortage of labour, although some landowners tried to double down on their serfs. Serfs and peasants rose up in rebellion. The plague was blamed on Jews, causing their persecution. The power of landowners was challenged by merchants.

The plague changed European societies forever. Other times of plague also saw profound change. Here is how the ancient Greek historian, Thucydides, describes people's behaviour during the plague in Athens of 431 BCE:

> And, the great licentiousness, which also in other kinds was used in the city, began at first from this disease. For that which a man before would dissemble and not acknowledge to be done for voluptuousness, he durst now do freely, seeing before his eyes such quick

Figure 4.1 'The Dance of Death': a wood engraving from the *Nuremberg Chronicle*, 1493. An image from the time when people had no idea how to deal with plagues like the Black Death.

revolution, of the rich dying and men worth nothing inheriting their estates …

As for pains, no man was forward in any action of honour to take any because they thought it uncertain whether they should die or not before they achieved it. But, what any man knew to be delightful and to be profitable to pleasure, that was made both profitable and honourable.[1]

So it seems reasonable to suggest that the increasing prevalence of the common long-term conditions – our modern plagues – will also have profound consequences for society and human behaviours. There is evidence already that this suggestion is true. In 2018, a panel of over 200 academics warned: 'Insufficient vigilance about the changing global health challenges may well lead to further breakdown of trust and social order, and perpetuate health inequalities within and across countries.'[2]

Financial costs

Since 5 July 1948 Britain has maintained the following principles: that no-one should be denied medical treatment for lack of money; that no-one should pay for treatment when they are ill; and that the financial costs of illness should be paid through progressive taxation. British people are rightfully proud of their general adherence to these civilised principles. They want to use some of the nation's resources on this because they see a need for them to help to stop anyone from dying before their time.

But costs do not just arise from using resources for an individual's clinical diagnosis, treatment and follow-up. That individual takes a hit in other ways through loss of income or reduced prospects for promotion. Society as a whole loses out on the resources already expended on that individual, in education and skills, for example. Extending lifespan of the population is a major resource commitment by a civilised society, and here we look at this commitment, not because we want it to be reduced, but because we want the population's need for this commitment to be reduced.

First, let us see how many people today need these resources. Figure 4.2 shows the percentage of people in England with one, two or three long-term conditions.

One in seven people aged under forty reported having a long-term condition in 2009. This rose to well over half for people aged over sixty. Moreover, a quarter of the latter group had two or more long-term conditions. Most of the people living with a long-term condition are living in the gap identified in the Marmot Review described in Chapter 2: they endure life after healthspan has ended for a period that varies depending on factors linked to their degree of deprivation. It is in this gap that much of the money is spent to help each of us live longer with long-term conditions. The bigger

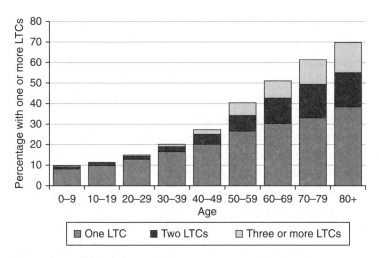

Source: General Lifestyle Survey 2009

Figure 4.2 Over time, people acquire one, then two, three and more long-term conditions. Each column represents a different age group in England and, within each column, the size of the rectangle represents the proportion of that group affected in 2009 by one, two, or three or more long-term health conditions. Older age groups tend to have more people with more long-term conditions (LTCs).

the gap between healthspan and lifespan, the greater the number of years the individual spends alive, albeit with disability. While we remain healthy, there are, of course, costs associated with preventing or treating infections (immunisations and antibiotics) or minor ailments. But the big costs arise once healthspan has ended.[3] The average annual cost for someone with no long-term conditions is £1,000. However, this then rises to £3,000, £6,000 and £7,700 as the number of conditions rises to two, three and more than three.

Toward the end of healthspan, continual treatment is needed, often with daily medication, to help us lead a life that is as close as possible to the life we led previously. The treatment goes on for as long as possible and tends to become more intense as time goes by. For every society, whether treatment is socialised or privatised, these costs affect the whole of society. If we just consider direct treatment costs in seven of the richer countries (the 'G7'), these costs worked out in 2014 at 9% of the total wealth that those countries produced in that year.[4] That corresponds to $3.1 trillion ($4,000 for every one of the 770m people who live in the seven countries). So, over $3 trillion that could have gone on preventing climate change, or on education, housing, transport and so on went, instead, on keeping our bodies ticking over. In other words, the common long-term conditions impede progress one way or the other.

If the G7 countries (or any other set of countries) all had effective prevention policies, average healthspan would increase and healthcare costs would fall. On the other hand, when the G7 countries have ineffective prevention policies and practices, then healthspan remains much the same, while advances in treatment continue to lengthen lifespan. But that then has the effect of increasing the gap between healthspan and lifespan, of increasing the years spent enduring long-term conditions. In other words the 770m people of the G7 risk living for an even longer time with disability, thus impeding progress. In other countries, where usually less resources go toward treatments, the temptation is to copy the G7 model and increase treatment spending. But it would be wise to use scarce resources for prevention as well.

We have looked at the financial implications of the burden of long-term conditions as a whole, so now let us turn to some of the individual conditions. There is some information for diabetes, cancer and heart disease as well as for obesity. We include obesity because it is the most widely recognised of the common modifiable risk factors for the common long-term conditions. Obesity may not itself be a disease, but it does consume national resources.

British MPs concluded that the total cost of obesity and overweight in England was £7bn a year in 2002.[5] Half this total was attributable to the costs of having a Body Mass Index (BMI) of above 30. The direct healthcare costs of treating obesity and its consequences (consultations by family doctors, inpatient and day case admissions, out-patient attendances and drug costs) was about £1bn. Premature deaths and absences from work carried a price tag of £2.5bn. Economists have argued that the costs are probably much higher.[6] The Marmot Review in 2009 reported estimates for the annual UK cost of obesity-related illness at £31–33bn for productivity losses and £20–32bn for lost taxes and higher welfare payments.[7] That means that over £50bn of the UK's national wealth goes to the consequences of just one of our common risk factors. The annual costs of sickness absence and unemployment associated with working-age ill-health are estimated to be over £100bn.[8]

Obesity also reduces wage levels of those in employment and may affect educational attainment.[9] In the US, workers have been measured for the time they need to complete tasks and for their ability to meet physical job demands. Workers with a BMI above 35 show a loss in productivity of 4.2%.[10] Production worth $42.8bn in 2006 was lost as a consequence of obesity among US full-time employees, Finkelstein et al. calculate.[11]

What is more, the costs of obesity are set to rise. The 2007 Foresight study commissioned by the UK government says that, by 2050, National Health Service costs attributable to overweight and obesity will rise to £10bn a year while the wider costs to society and business will be £50bn a year.[12] Cancer Research UK and the UK Health Forum have also made calculations indicating that obesity will add £2.5bn to health and social care costs by 2035.[13]

Employers have an obvious interest in having a healthy workforce. In the US it has been possible to calculate how much productivity has been lost as a consequence of obesity in the workforce. A National Health and Wellness Survey was undertaken using self-administered, web-based questionnaires to a panel of 63,000 people aged over 18 representative of the adult population. Levels of obesity were set so that Grade I obesity has BMI values 30–35; Grade II 35–40; and Grade III above 40.

Using this data one can look at the effects of increasing obesity on worker productivity. Two components of productivity that have been explored are absenteeism and presenteeism. Absenteeism due to obesity is the extra number of days off work taken when BMI is above normal. Presenteeism due to obesity is time lost at work due to six factors: the time between arriving at work and starting work when an employee feels unwell; the frequency at which employees: lose concentration; repeat a job; work more slowly than usual; feel fatigued at work; or do nothing at work.

It turns out that the annual costs of absenteeism in the US rise from $277 to $1,026 among men and from $407 to $1,262 among women as obesity goes from Grade I to Grade III. The costs of presenteeism rise from $391 to $3,792 among men and from $843 to $3,037 among women as obesity goes from Grade I to Grade III. The disproportionately high per capita and total cost of grade II and grade III obesity is particularly concerning given that this BMI range is the fastest growing subset of the obese population. Individuals with Grade II BMI represent 37% of the overweight population, yet they are responsible for 61% of the costs resulting from excess weight. Note that employers in the US generally pay for some treatment costs directly, while in the UK they pay indirectly.

When it comes to diabetes in the UK, its prevalence is predicted to rise by over 2m to 5.6m by 2035.[14] In 2010, diabetes took up approximately 10% of the total UK health resource expenditure. This is set to rise to 17% by 2035. That means a rise from £23.7bn in 2010–11 to £39.8bn in twenty-five years. These large amounts break down into direct costs (screening, testing and management of the disease); indirect costs (death, absence from work, reduced productivity, informal care) and complications (heart disease, excess inpatient days, foot ulcers and amputations, kidney disease, neurological conditions like blindness). The cheapest item on the bill is screening and testing – comparable to the healthcare costs in a prevention strategy. They amount to just 50p in every £1,000. Prevention is cheaper than treatment. This information is not secret, yet, all the same, its implications are ignored. We shall see later why they are ignored. For now, let us simply bear in mind that prevention is cheap but it is also a hot potato.

The total direct and indirect costs of heart disease (cardiovascular disease, coronary heart disease and stroke) in 2006 totalled £48.0bn, with £27bn of that arising from indirect costs.[15] In cardiovascular disease, the Centre for Economics and Business Research forecasts[16] that healthcare costs will rise to €17.3bn by 2020; mortality costs will rise to €5.7bn; and morbidity costs will rise to €146m. Total costs will rise to €23.1bn. This is an increase of over 22% in six years.

The Department of Health estimates that cancer incidence in England is rising at 1.5% each year.[17] Some of the financial costs of this have been calculated, for example £24.72bn will be spent by the NHS, on hospices, by families and through losses in productivity[18] with an average annual increase of over £500m.

What about the overall costs of poor health? Public Health England has done some calculations on this.[19] It looked at the financial costs to individuals, employers, the NHS, the government and to the whole economy. The total is between £147bn and £185bn – about 10% of the total wealth created in the UK each year (its GDP – Gross Domestic Product). If we include health costs for Wales, Scotland and Northern Ireland as well, this raises the cost of poor health to about 11% of GDP. We give these numbers, not to suggest there is any waste or inefficiency but in order to show that health is important financially as well as socially and culturally. If the country spent all its resources on optimising health – following the new definition of health that we suggest in Chapter 12 – we would not complain.

Societal costs

Individuals pay a price, one way or another, for their long-term conditions. In financial terms, there is likely to be a loss of earnings, a loss of promotion prospects and an earlier end to working life leading to a reduced pension. Additional living costs are likely to arise: people may need an extra room and modified housing, or they may need to use taxis or to eat specialised foods.

But there is also an impact on any community when more of its members have reached the end of healthspan. Most studies have, however, looked at the opposite phenomenon – at how a dysfunctional community increases the risk to its members of getting long-term conditions. Let us first look at this.

Suicide reflects a lack of mental health. Depression is one factor making suicide more likely. A number of studies indicate that a modifiable risk factor for suicide is 'social fragmentation' (other terms referring to the same idea are in use). Sociologists say that social fragmentation refers to the absence or the underdevelopment of connections between the society and the groupings of some members of that society on the lines of a common culture, nationality, race, language, occupation, religion, income level or other common interests. This definition is not easily converted into a readily measured quantity. Epidemiologists have therefore come up with a convenient 'social fragmentation score'. This is based on some easily obtained, simple facts about the way of life of an individual: are they single; do they live alone; have they lived there a short time; do they rent the property? If the answer to each of these questions is 'no', then the individual will have a lower score. The major advantage of this scoring system is that answers can be retrieved from the national census. This is held every decade. It would be sensible to design the census so that its questions can shed greater light on the common long-term conditions and their modifiable risk factors.

What researchers have found is that suicide rates are higher in areas with high social fragmentation scores. For example, using census and suicide data from the 1980s and 1990s, researchers were able to look at all 650 parliamentary constituencies in the UK. They found that constituencies with high levels of social

fragmentation had high rates of suicide. This was i
of the amount of social deprivation (measured by a
ing system that includes unemployment, car and hon
and overcrowding). What's more, constituencies with the greatest
increases in social fragmentation between 1981 and 1991 also had
the greatest increases in suicide rates. They suggested that suicide prevention should therefore be targeted in areas with higher
social fragmentation.[20] However, a more recent study in Hong
Kong found that social deprivation in a neighbourhood – rather
than fragmentation – was the bigger factor driving higher suicide
rates.[21] While we may ask why there is this difference between the
UK and Hong Kong, it would be wise for public policy to address
both social fragmentation and deprivation – and to collect data
more frequently than once a decade.

But social fragmentation does not only have a negative impact
on mental health. A study in Sweden ascribed risk of heart attacks
to both fragmentation and deprivation, although it couldn't dis-
entangle the two factors.[22] In Boston, adolescents in more socially
fragmented neighbourhoods were physically less active and so
more at risk of obesity, diabetes and other chronic diseases.[23]

One of the logical implications of social fragmentation for a
community is the increased separation of individuals from each
other. This separation can then lead to feelings of loneliness. This
can't be measured from sources like the census but instead requires
use of a questionnaire. The Revised UCLA Loneliness Scale[24]
asks twenty questions such as: 'I have a lot in common with the
people around me: Never / Rarely / Sometimes / Often.' Use of
this questionnaire with 325 people showed that they scored high
for loneliness if they had diabetes or did not exercise regularly.[25]
In the UK, a study of 3,200 people found that loneliness was associated with individuals diagnosed with metabolic syndrome – a
collection of symptoms (e.g. overweight and high blood sugar)
that indicate elevated risk of diabetes, and heart conditions.[26] In
Switzerland, 20,000 people took part in a survey and it was found

that loneliness was associated with poorer physical health, poorer mental health and lower physical activity.[27]

So it is possible to detect how social isolation can prompt the end of healthspan in individuals. But what about the other way around? Does an increase in a community of the number of people with the disabilities that come at the end of healthspan result in the community becoming more fragmented? On this, we must turn to personal experience and anecdote for now. Most of us have families where a parent or grandparent is the life and soul of the family: the grandad who makes us all laugh; the granny who offers a shoulder to cry on. When they die, the family may fall apart, not because of some drama about the Will but just because what the members of the family all held in common is no more. The family members may go off in different directions: a small 'community' has become fragmented. They have all lost out. The same fragmentation could easily occur within a larger community, not necessarily because a key individual has died but simply because that individual is no longer around as much – owing to their disability. They can't organise the annual Christmas party. They can't cajole everyone to join in some community event. This type of situation will be known to most of us. The effects of this loss of active members of the community may be felt for many years. The glue that holds communities together is probably weakest in big cities. Social fragmentation is almost complete. We barely know our neighbours, and so the task we have of rebuilding a sense of community is massive.

There are other ways that a long-term condition affecting one person has an impact on other people; some examples are listed here.

One of the effects of obesity is that people frequently suffer from sleepiness during the daytime as well as from interrupted sleep and snoring. This is called 'obstructive sleep apnoea'. In a survey of over 12,000 drivers in nineteen European countries nearly one in five (17%) said they had fallen asleep at the wheel in the previous two years.[28] When another 70,000 drivers were asked if they had felt sleepy when they had had an accident, it turned out that the sleepy ones were over twice as likely to have had an accident. As a result, once the European Union recognised that this type of sleepiness was one of the highest risk factors for motor vehicle accidents, it tightened the rules about issuing driving licences. This is a start, but it overlooks people who develop the condition after they have their licence. The thing about accidents, of course, is that more than person may be involved and more than one car may be involved. An indirect effect of rising obesity is that a driver's sleepiness puts us all at greater risk from accidents whether we are in a car, in a lorry or on the pavement.

Obesity also leads to reduced male fertility. This is seen most clearly among men whose sperm is used for assisted reproduction by in vitro fertilisation (IVF). When the man is in the normal range of BMI, the success rate is about 41%. But, this falls to 27% if the man is overweight and to 22% if he is obese. In other words, obesity almost halves the chances of a man reproducing successfully. While only a small proportion of all pregnancies arise from assisted reproduction, this method of reproduction is independent of the sexual prowess of the partners: its success or failure reflects the properties only of the sperm and eggs. So, male obesity is linked to fewer babies (live birth outcomes), but it is also associated with increased risk of miscarriage and the fertilised eggs do not develop as well as usual.[29] In Europe, the US and Australasia – but not in South America, Asia and Africa – male sperm counts have fallen in recent decades.[30] The rate of fall has been 1.6% a year. Between 1973 and 2011 there was a drop of 59.3% in average total sperm count. We do not know if this drop is due to factors additional to obesity: epidemiologists have suggested factors such as chemicals in plastics, pesticides, heat, stress and smoking. This is a serious issue for the people of Europe, the US and Australasia if the effects of obesity reach through to the next generation. But we also know that the risk of obesity is higher among the children of obese parents. In a nutshell, parental obesity reduces the chances of having babies and, when one is born, they have a higher chance of becoming obese.

An extreme example of the impact of one person's disability on their community is the spate of mass killings in the US by individuals whose loneliness or isolation transitions into a psychotic state. People of all ages have been killed and injured – from infants and their teachers, to school students, to politicians. The effects of these killings, however, have had far wider repercussions across society. For example, fear of such attacks has spread through the population, with the consequence that more and more people feel isolated. Their reaction has often been to seek to defend themselves from such threats by buying a gun – or buying even more guns. These processes risk a vicious cycle whereby isolation leads to psychotic episodes, to more killings, to greater isolation, and on to further killings. This cycle contains a whole range of risk factors. It is beyond belief to most of the world that the most obvious and most easily modified risk factor – access to lethal weapons – is not seen as a public policy priority in the US.

The common long-term conditions have an impact on very large numbers of individuals. But this has knock-on effects for the community as a whole and for the nation as a whole. Therefore, the loss of good health among others affects the individual: your loss is my loss.

5

Deckchairs on the Titanic

There can be little doubt that the British people have trust in, and affection and respect for their National Health Service (NHS). They may well believe that the common long-term conditions – the modern plagues – that we have described are either being managed or could be managed by the NHS. While trust, affection and respect are justified, it is not our view that the NHS offers the principal means of halting or reversing these modern plagues.

Right from its creation, the NHS answered a national prayer: please remove our fear of doctors' bills. Look at the gratitude of the mother who named the nation's first NHS baby – Aneira Thomas – in honour of one of the founders of the NHS, Aneurin Bevan:[1]

> It was coming up to midnight on Sunday 4 July 1948 and my mother, who had been in labour for 18 hours, was just about ready to give birth to me. She wanted to start pushing. But, the doctors and mid-wives looked up at the clock on the wall and said, 'Stop. Hold on, Edna, hold on.' They knew they were moments away from the start of the National Health Service and wanted me to be the first baby born into this new service. So, my mother took a deep breath and held on. That's how I was born at one minute past midnight on Monday 5 July 1948 – the first NHS baby.

Healthcare free to all at the time of need is the fundamental principle of the NHS. The NHS has also attempted to provide that healthcare directly by itself. There is an important benefit to this that is often overlooked: a greater ease within one organisation of sharing data efficiently. The NHS started construction of such a data-sharing infrastructure in the first decade of this century until a fad for 'out-sourcing' put paid to it. Construction had been slow and difficult but it became much more difficult once multiple organisations were involved. Easy access to full health information is essential to getting the most effective and efficient healthcare. But, as we shall see in Part IV, it is also essential to tackling the modern plagues.

Services for treatment and prevention

The NHS is both necessary and sufficient for our healthcare. But is it sufficient when it comes to our health – when it comes to the prevention of the common long-term conditions? The NHS is reactive more than proactive: its focus is on cure rather than prevention. So, does the NHS suffice for the task of reducing the risk of those conditions in the first place?

The job the NHS does in the prevention of infectious disease is first-rate. This is largely down to the method of prevention used – a few simple jabs and it's all over. Long before an individual comes into contact with the virus or bacterium that causes disease and risks death, a vaccination will guarantee protection, sometimes for life. Even if a vaccination programme misses out a small percentage of the population, the risk of an outbreak is massively reduced because an infected individual in that small percentage only has a low probability of passing on the infection to another unprotected individual. Very simply put, if I am protected, then you are too. This is what is meant by 'herd immunity'. Note that the allowable fraction of unvaccinated people varies from one virus to another (a hard-to-infect virus means that the allowable fraction is greater) and from one location to another (a crowded city means that the allowable fraction is smaller). Therefore, the anti-vaxxers – or their offspring – are living on borrowed time and risking the health of other people who have missed out on vaccination by oversight.

The NHS vaccinates us against some twenty-two diseases (diphtheria, tetanus, whooping cough, polio, Hib, hepatitis B, pneumococcal infection, rotavirus, meningitis type B, haemophilus type b, measles, mumps, rubella, cancer of cervix, mouth, throat, genital warts, meningitis types A, C, W, Y, influenza, chickenpox, tuberculosis, shingles).[2] This national programme of vaccinations is a tribute both to science and to a society committed to the prevention of infectious disease. This commitment is altruistic, for sure. It could well have been what Aneurin Bevan primarily had in mind when he wrote that prevention was 'an indispensable part of what we mean by civilization'. But vaccination also reflects our needs as social animals: it is in the collective interest to cut the risk that your infection may become my infection.

An important feature of the range of NHS vaccinations is that additional vaccines are continually introduced. For instance, the HPV vaccine – directed against Human Papilloma Virus – is quite new. But it is the consequences of HPV infection that is the major problem with this virus: HPV increases the risk, years later, of different types of cancer. So, here we have a situation where a jab can prevent a long-term condition and where the NHS is well placed to deliver that jab. We can see therefore that there are circumstances where the NHS is well-placed to deliver prevention of common long-term conditions.

The system for delivering this particular 'prevention service' involves a range of skills: nurses, community health workers, pharmacists, vaccine producers, general practitioners (family doctors) and public health and education workers. All need to work together if the population as a whole is to be protected from avoidable infection and epidemics. Building up this prevention service in the post-war years was a major effort, but there is still work to do as new vaccines are developed. A systematic approach called 'life-course immunisation' is being tested across the EU and is recommended by the European Commission. This approach seeks to ensure that all age ranges in all EU Member States eventually become vaccinated against the diseases that can cause both viral and bacterial meningitis and septicaemia.[3]

However, there is no sign that vaccines, or medicines for that matter, will become available anytime soon to prevent (rather than treat) diabetes, heart disease, common cancers or depression. So, what has public policy had to say about that? The answer is not much, as far as the UK is concerned.

The first time that the word 'health' appeared in the title of a law passed by Parliament was in 1848. It was a Public Health Act. More Public Health Acts followed in 1875, 1878, 1925 and 1936. Invariably the laws dealt with infectious diseases (tuberculosis above all), their prevention and their control. These were the plagues of their day. In 1945, tuberculosis was the leading cause of death for teenagers and adults up to the age of 55 in men and 45 in women.[4] With the introduction of streptomycin in 1946, mortality declined rapidly.

Yet the next Public Health Act in 1961 – when heart disease and cancer were the leading cause of death – was still focussed on infectious disease, with new rules for sanitation and for notifying the authorities in the event of an outbreak of an infection. Of course, we are not saying that politicians were not aware of this so-called 'epidemiological transition' from infectious disease to long-term conditions. Action was taken to provide resources to treat people with heart conditions or cancer and such action continues to this day. The point we are making is that prevention of these long-term conditions was not covered by legislation.

Yes, there has been legislation on infectious disease, on environmental risks, even on well-being. However, only in Wales with the 2017 Public Health (Wales) Act did legislators start to turn their attention to the leading modifiable risk factor for the modern plagues – obesity. It has taken seven decades since the epidemiological transition became apparent for us to start to legislate on modifiable risk factors. We do not believe that legislation alone will end the modern plagues but some politicians are starting to think clearly about the problems.

A contract for health

The first ever minister of public health – Tessa Jowell – effectively had in her job title the prevention of diseases and conditions. Along with Health Minister Frank Dobson, she proposed that the health of the population could be improved via a contract between different parts of society. This idea was the centrepiece of the 1998 Green Paper (a consultation document – not legislation) called 'Our Healthier Nation: A Contract for Health'. The contract was to take the form of a 'partnership' between government, health authorities, local authorities, business, voluntary bodies and individual citizens. This contract would then agree on two goals: to increase healthspan and to reduce health inequality. The priorities were heart conditions, accidents, cancer and mental health and, for each priority, a target for improvement was set.

Was this mechanism – creating a kind of contract that would underpin some form of partnership – sensible or sufficient? Perhaps it might have worked, but the problem with creating a contract is that you are driven straight away into a legalistic way of thinking. Two parties form a contract with rights and duties. If the contract is not enforced or cannot be enforced, then it is not really a contract.

These issues are not discussed in the 1998 Green Paper. However, there is this warning: 'Regulation and legislation should be the exception, not the rule – a step taken only where voluntary action will not sufficiently protect the public's health.' It is as though Jowell were saying: 'I'm against contracts, but I want a contract'. This contradiction is resolved by equating the idea of a contract with the idea of partnerships, as you can see from this quotation:

> The government is setting out a third way, between the old extremes
> of individual victim blaming, on the one hand, and nanny state
> social engineering, on the other … Our third way is a national con-
> tract for better health. Under this contract, the government, local
> communities and individuals will join in partnership to improve all
> our health.[5]

What exactly is a partnership that lacks an enforceable contract?
The answer is: not a great deal from a legal point of view. Two
partners like that are just good friends at best. They will probably agree to sit on the same committee. They may even agree a
common course of action. But, if they represent organisations, the
committee members cannot be sure that their parent organisations
will agree with any particular action.

Building partnerships is about building voluntary forms of
action. While this is certainly sensible, it is clearly not sufficient to
end the modern plagues.

Putting prevention first

A decade on, in 2008, health minister Alan Johnson presented
a government policy document on preventing heart conditions.[6]
Entitled 'Putting Prevention First' its centrepiece was not a partnership but a new service: the NHS Health Check. Jowell's contracts and partnerships were dropped. The service was to be
located within primary care (at the family doctor's surgery) and
to comprise a risk assessment for the likelihood of different heart
conditions in people between forty and seventy years. Individuals
at high risk were to be offered further services intended to reduce
their risk.

This particular service has a basic problem. Its benefits are
hard to see because the numbers of people dying from heart disease has been going down steadily for decades. On top of that
there is the problem that any benefits may emerge rather slowly
because the check is limited to people over forty – by which time

the damage may already have been done. Then there are issues with the service-based approach, which makes citizens into passive recipients: uptake will be incomplete and so many people will miss out; some family doctors are better at getting people to have a check than others; some people are more committed than others at sticking to a risk-reduction activity like losing weight.

The contract or partnership approach and the services approach are both imperfect by themselves. But, at least prevention was now on the political map and a minister had responsibility for prevention. There have been ministers of public health ever since, though they have tended to become more junior and their brief has been substantially diluted with other responsibilities such as NHS re-organisation, out-of-hospital care and primary care.

Living well for longer

In 2013, Jeremy Hunt, the then health minister (not the public health minister) published a vision entitled *Living Well for Longer: A Call to Action to Reduce Avoidable Premature Mortality*.[7] The title contains an ambiguity that the vision fails to clarify. Does 'living well for longer' refer to increased healthspan or to increased lifespan? We need crystal clarity that prevention means extending healthspan. In his introduction to this 'call to action' Mr Hunt, wrote: 'I want us to be up there with the best in Europe when it comes to tackling the leading causes of early death, starting with the five big killer diseases – cancer, heart, stroke, respiratory and liver disease'.

This vision effectively combines two ideas that need to be dealt with separately. We can see this if we ask what 'reducing avoidable premature mortality' means. It has to refer to both improved treatment and to improved prevention. Improved treatment – a new, better medicine, for example – will save someone's life and they will live longer. The medicine means that the person has avoided a reduced lifespan. Improved prevention – a new better health check perhaps – will increase the probability that people will reduce their risk of a disease through, say, increased exercise or social interactions. In this way, more people will have extended both their healthspan and their lifespan.

So, this vision rolls up clinical and non-clinical activities into one package. The minister writes: 'If we are to tackle the challenge we face, we need to make improvements across the three domains of prevention, early diagnosis and treatment.' In the long run, this may be sensible, but for now it isn't. This is because non-clinical activities have, for a long time, been and remain the Cinderella of health. Public Health has been subservient to the institutions of

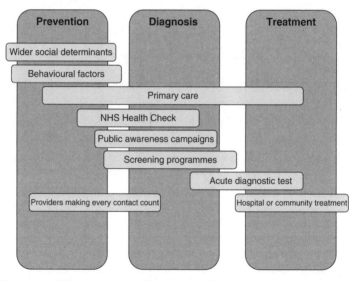

Figure 5.1 Mixed messages: 'If we are to tackle the challenge we face, we need to make improvements across the three domains of prevention, early diagnosis and treatment'. This diagram from a Department of Health policy document entitled 'Living Well for Longer' illustrates how clinical and non-clinical activities are to be wrapped up into one package. Ultimately, this is to the detriment of improved population health and of an end to the plagues of our times.

medicine. We need a laser-like focus on increasing healthspan, on preventing the modern plagues.

Budgets for prevention remain paltry; primary care increasingly acts as triage for secondary care; hospitals over-spend their budgets. The local authorities' public health budget was down by £200m for 2015/16.[8] From 2009/10 to 2013/14, spending on primary care services fell at an average rate of 1.3% p.a. and among acute hospital providers, 81% reported a deficit in 2014/15, resulting in a net shortfall of over £700m.[9] This is unsustainable. While increased funding can provide relief, a new strategy for health has also become essential. A new strategy does not mean a new financial model: mainland European funding models and the US model have been as ineffective as the UK's financial model when it comes to ending the modern plagues. A new strategy does not mean we need to 're-align the health economy': rather, we need to re-align thinking about health so as to prioritise prevention.

Among the action points in *Living Well for Longer* are public education campaigns on nutrition and exercise, plus working with the food industry to reduce sugar, calories and salt in processed food and to reduce alcohol consumption. Thus the strategy mainly comprises actions from the centre.

We can see the same government-centric approach in the 2016 plan to tackle childhood obesity.[10] This plan involves a sugar tax, plus official encouragement for primary schools to provide pupils with physical exercise and sport and to serve healthy food. The government says: 'We are confident that our approach will reduce childhood obesity' and foresees a significant reduction in the rate of childhood obesity by 2026.

Prevention in the 2020s

By 2019, this conflation of treatment and prevention was replaced by another philosophy outlined in a new consultative Green Paper called: 'Advancing our health – prevention in the 2020s'. This philosophy is summed up as follows: 'In the 2020s, people will not be passive recipients of care. They will be co-creators of their own health. The challenge is to equip them with the skills, knowledge and confidence they need to help themselves'.[11]

Stripping away the jargon, this philosophy says each of us is on our own when it comes to extending healthspan. The aim is to introduce 'a new personalised prevention model'. Although there is reference to new technologies suited to the model, this view of the problem sees no room for partnerships or contracts for health, it questions the need for service provision (the NHS Health Check is to be reviewed) and it has no memory of Aneurin Bevan's prescription for prevention as 'health by collective action [that] builds up a system of social habits'. We shall be discussing later how to use the new technologies (in data management and in modern molecular biology) in ways that do not leave citizens on their own trying to fight the modern plagues as isolated individuals.

Switching horses

These brief summaries of how governments have approached the problem of improving the population's health indicate three main strategies. These are: improved or new services; action by central government; mobilisation of action across society. One different strategy has followed another in the space of a few years. This does not inspire confidence but, rather, it suggests that every government wants to end the modern plagues, every government comes at the problem with their own ideological baggage, but no government is truly confident of what will work. The result is that no single approach is given time to prove – or disprove – itself. Politicians need greater patience – they should not be switching horses in the middle of the stream. To mix our metaphors, they are merely moving deckchairs around on the deck of the Titanic. What health requires is bold consensus long-term actions based on evidence and then modified by new evidence – not by old dogmas.

Why has so little happened? Why have we only scratched the surface of the problem of prevention? Why does it seem that we are all engaged in re-arranging those deck chairs? We could point the finger of blame at some professionals (focussing on minutiae or despairing at the limits to their influence), at some politicians (being decades behind the real world of the modern plagues), at sections of industry (having vested interests that have the side-effect of spreading those plagues) or at well-paid pundits (asserting their smug self-satisfaction of superiority over the allegedly ignorant and feckless). But we do not think the blame game is worth playing when the question is what we can do about it all.

Part II

The scale of the modern plagues leaves us with no choice but to try to end them. The first step is to understand the science that describes and explains the causes of these plagues and that proposes actions to end them. In the next four chapters we do this by describing the science of epidemiology, the complications of the long-term conditions that comprise the modern plagues, the nature of risk and the distinction between risk factors that we can or cannot modify.

6

The appliance of science

Epidemiology untamed

We have seen that vast numbers of people come to the end of their healthspan and must then endure a range of long-term conditions. This then has knock-on effects on the fabric of society. So, no-one can deny that something must be done. But panic, of course, is not the right way to go. Rather, we need to go back to first principles, make sure we are thinking clearly about the problems, work out how things have gone wrong and then suggest a way out.

The first attempt in modern times to think clearly about the causes of large scale outbreaks of illnesses – about the causes of epidemics – has to be ascribed to a modest man called John Snow (1813–58). He is often called the 'father' of epidemiology. Readers may be familiar with his story but we focus here on one part of that story – his interaction with the authorities. Epidemiology aims to understand, prevent and control diseases and conditions that affect populations of plants, animals or humans. Its method rests on observation and action. First, observe the mechanism whereby a disease or condition spreads. Then, second, seek to modify that mechanism. 'Epidemiology' literally means the study (of disease) among the people. It is a science that is a dynamic combination of research and action. Snow's story illustrates this.

Today, 'The John Snow' is a pub in London's Soho that sells a decent pint. The pub did not exist in the 1850s, but one could get a drink of water from the water pumps nearby. The trouble in 1854 was that the water might well deliver a lethal dose of cholera. But, no-one had a clue whether, when, why or how these cholera cases might arise. The eminent medical doctors of the day relied on hand-me-down hypotheses from ancient times: there was, they said, too much 'bad air'. And, certainly, London was far from fragrant.

Snow disagreed with those doctors but he had to prove himself right. As a young man, he had witnessed outbreaks of cholera in the slums of York, managed to get an education and by the 1850s was a physician at London's Westminster Hospital. He was convinced that 'bad air' explained nothing. Cholera was, he proposed, 'propagated by human intercourse'. It was 'communicated'. And the mode of communication, he insisted, involved contaminated water. He wrote:

> The belief in the communication of cholera is a much less dreary one than the reverse; for what is so dismal as the idea of some invisible agent pervading the atmosphere, and spreading over the world? If the writer's opinions be correct, cholera might be checked and kept at bay by simple measures.

He was able to test his 'simple measures' in 1854, while the eminent medical doctors could only wring their hands. Because he thought that cholera was present somehow in drinking water, it might therefore be controlled and prevented by washing hands and by avoiding water sources 'into which drains and sewers empty themselves; or if that cannot be accomplished, to have water filtered and well boiled before it is used'.

Starting on 31 August, there was a major outbreak of cholera in Soho, around the corner from Snow's lodgings. Some fifty people a day from a small neighbourhood were dying. Water pumps were scattered around the area, including one fed by an underground source that was located in Broad St close to today's John Snow pub. So, what Snow did was to draw a map. This showed where the pumps were and where the cholera cases were.

I found that nearly all the deaths had taken place within a short distance of the pump [in Broad St]. There were only ten deaths in houses situated decidedly nearer to another street pump. In five of these cases the families of the deceased persons informed me that they always sent to the pump in Broad Street, as they preferred the water to that of the pump which was nearer. In three other cases, the deceased were children who went to school near the pump in Broad Street. Two of them were known to drink the water; and the parents of the third think it probable that it did so.[1]

The map showed there was a cluster of cholera cases close to the pump on Broad Street. This was not the only observation that Snow made, but it was enough for him to take his next step. This step is what makes epidemiology a special science. With a view to ending the epidemic, he set out to get a modification of the environment in which the epidemic had emerged.

He took his case to the local government – in those days this part of Soho was under a Board of Guardians for the Parish of

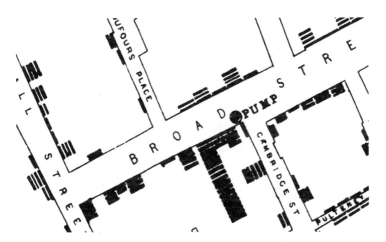

Figure 6.1 This section of a map of streets around Broad Street, Soho, London, appeared in John Snow's *On the Mode of Communication of Cholera* (1854). Each solid rectangle on the map represents a cholera death. Snow reported the clustering of cases near the pump to the local authority and it then decided to remove the pump handle.

St James – and asked for the Broad Street pump to be disabled by removing its handle so that no-one could draw water. The Board of Guardians were desperate. They had a raging epidemic on their hands. People were dying in the streets. Everyone with the money to do so was fleeing.

So, when Snow came along and offered a solution to the crisis, the Board of Guardians may well have regarded it as heretical because it had nothing to do with 'bad air'. But they must have shrugged their shoulders and thought it was worth a try.

Unfortunately, the records of this historic meeting on 7 September 1854 of the St James Board of Guardians have not been located. We can only guess what led the Board to agree to Snow's plan. Maybe they thought he was a crazed obsessive with his mad theories about water. But, all the same, his proposal was cheap, simple, quick and reversible. He wanted just one pump handle to be disabled. Residents still had access to nearby pumps. The handle could go back on again at short notice. The Guardians would be able to claim they had taken every conceivable step to tackle the crisis. So, Snow got his way and the handle came off. Thereafter, the number of cholera cases went back down to its usual level. Snow therefore seemed to have proved his case and, what's more, he seemed to have ended the epidemic.

Now, the questions that the guardians ought to have considered before backing Snow include the following:

- Should we abandon our role of guaranteeing water supplies to Broad Street residents?
- Could lack of water put residents' lives at risk?
- Do we need to get the consent of residents?
- Do we need the consent of our electorate (only property owners had the vote)?
- Should we act against the short-term interests of the company that managed the pump?

- If Snow is wrong, are we not risking increasing the suffering of the residents?
- If Snow is right, what extra costs might then arise?

These queries indicate why we say epidemiology is a special science. It is special because it leads directly to a case – often a powerful case – for changing society in some way. But such change is nearly always a highly contested issue because of the conflicting interests and values that are in play.

Snow's achievement was to drag health science out of the realm of speculation, with its reliance on handed-down texts, into the modern era of observation, hypothesis and experiment. He is honoured today by the John Snow Society which holds an annual 'Pump Handle Lecture'. We, of course, would add that the Board of Guardians should also be recognised. It was a public body that worked with the evidence to attempt to tackle a plague of times past.

Snow did not, of course, identify precisely what it was that made the water from the Broad Street pump so lethal. He speculated that it must be 'some material which passes from the sick to the healthy, and which has the property of increasing and multiplying in the systems of the persons it attacks'. Identifying Snow's 'material' required some basic scientific research. The first clue on that issue was revealed by an Italian anatomist Filippo Pacini in the same year as the Broad Street cholera outbreak. He saw under the microscope in fluids from cholera patients unusual rod-shaped bodies (later named as *Vibrio cholera pacini*). Only some years later was the significance of these bodies recognised when French biologist Louis Pasteur first proved that a micro-organism – yeast – was responsible for alcoholic fermentation and then went on to show that other micro-organisms were responsible for various diseases. This then helped establish the germ theory of infectious disease as we know it today.

Epidemiology tamed

Snow showed there was some association between water supplies, sewage contamination and outbreaks of cholera. Ever since, the search for associations of this kind has been the first thing that epidemiologists set out to find. But the second strand of Snow's work on cholera was to propose and perform a test on the effects of an experimental alteration to the environment (removing the pump handle). The efforts today of epidemiologists to perform such tests have been severely constrained. The reforming character of epidemiology has been tamed. The best term to describe this aspect of epidemiology is 'action research': observation, hypothesis and action all rolled into one.

Why has this powerful weapon for prevention of disease so often been shelved, while it is used all the time for finding new medicines, new treatments for diseases? Why is there action research for treatment but not it seems for prevention?

There is a case against action research. Simply put, it is the risk of unforeseen consequences. You cannot know all the effects of the action you propose to take based on your observations and the hypotheses to which they give rise. Those unforeseen consequences may cause harm. For example, what would be the effect on people of removing the Broad St pump handle? Perhaps it would indeed stop cholera – but it would reduce the supply of water and this might then leave people desperate for water. It is possible that the Board of Guardians and John Snow did not consider this risk.

The counter-argument to this is that the risks from unforeseen consequences can be managed. Action research can be piloted on a small sub-population and can be carefully monitored to seek to detect any unintended consequences. If there is any hint of problems, the action research can be paused or abandoned. The pilots can slowly grow in scale (more people) and impact (more vigorous action) over time, with experimental controls built in.

This is precisely how action research is carried out in the discovery of new medicines and treatments. The term 'action research' is not used. Instead this discovery work is called a 'clinical trial'. Here, the unintended consequence of trying out a new medicine is mainly the risk of unexpected negative side-effects. Let us see what happens in a clinical trial. First a chemical (termed a 'new molecular entity') is tested in the lab for possible medical use by seeing what happens to some living cells. If the hoped-for effect is observed, then the chemical is tested on simple organisms, then on a small mammal like a mouse and then on a larger mammal. If all is going well, the chemical is given at a low dose to the first humans – healthy volunteers who are paid for their risk-taking. Only if all goes well do some of the intended beneficiaries – the patients – get the chemical. These are likely to be patients for whom no known treatment has proved effective. Eventually, larger groups of patients enter the clinical trial. In all cases there is careful monitoring and long-term follow-up with third party supervision and with rules and regulations designed to minimise the chance of doing harm.

These procedures have been spectacularly successful in finding the tiny proportion of new molecular entities that can treat people who are seriously ill. Indeed, there have even been occasions when patients have argued for the rules to be relaxed. This was the case at the start of the AIDS epidemic in the US in the 1980s. Patients and their supporters organised public protests to get access to new antiviral drugs before these had been fully tested. The argument was: 'Look, the drugs we have are not effective. We are going to die soon. So, we are willing to risk taking new unproven drugs.' It is a powerful argument and, in this instance, patient power prevailed.

So, while unintended consequences are a risk for action research, whether aimed at better prevention or at better treatment, it has overwhelmingly been in medicines development that this risk has been well-managed. What is more, the rules have, in practice, been applied flexibly so that where the need is greatest and where people are desperate for help – as in treating AIDS – the rules may be bent a little.

Tobacco

Why is action research avoided for the prevention of diseases and conditions, while action research for their treatment is praised by one and all? Thinking about the story of tobacco may be useful in answering this question. Tobacco, we all know, contains the highly addictive chemical, nicotine and, when smoked, leads to our lungs being filled with thousands of cancer-causing chemicals and irritants.

Figure 6.2 A deceptive newspaper advertisement for a cigarette brand. The man smoking seems more troubled by 'trying weather' than by cancer.

The appliance of science

In 1641, Nicolaes Tulp – whom Rembrandt painted in The Anatomy Lesson – was among the earliest critics of tobacco. He said it caused lung damage.[2] But, the earliest proposals that smoking and lung cancer were linked were made by Edward Tylecote (1927) in Manchester and Frederick Hoffman in San Francisco.[3] These proposals contradicted standard medical thinking in those days. For example, the famous 1950 study on smoking by Richard Doll and Bradford Hill was set up to test the hypothesis that fumes from tarmac on the roads caused lung cancer. However, they found that, in fact, what the lung cancer patients actually had in common was that they smoked.[4] Bigger studies by them and their successors followed, which then found associations between smoking and heart disease and respiratory disease.

Had John Snow been around in 1950, we might fantasise that he would have gone straight to Prime Minister Clement Attlee, and said: 'We can save thousands of lives if we ban tobacco' and that Attlee would have agreed on the spot. Why is this fantasy? First, Attlee was a heavy smoker and so almost certainly he was a nicotine addict. Second, most of the people he knew were smokers too: over 80% of men over thirty-five smoked in 1950. Third, the lines of on-going, direct communication between actual researchers and politicians were then and still are impeded by, for example, the so-called Haldane Principle which inadvertently – and spuriously – asserts the independence of science from society. Fourth, tobacco growers in Rhodesia (now Zimbabwe) or Virginia and manufacturers in the UK and elsewhere sought to challenge the evidence. Fifth, finance ministers liked tax revenues from tobacco. In other words, there are powerful psychological, social, cultural and financial factors that resist preventive action based on observation. There are also ideological factors such as, in this case, the belief that the market knows best. This leads to the dubious prediction that market forces – Adam Smith's 'invisible hand' – will eventually end tobacco use as consumers discover its harmful effects.

These are the forces then that have tamed epidemiology. Its observations remain as acute as ever. The need for epidemiologists is evident whenever there is an outbreak of flu or when a new disease agent or environmental hazard appears. Society has to know how serious the risk is. It also needs epidemiologists to propose what action to take. For example, in the event of a major epidemic of a new virulent flu, epidemiologists have worked with public bodies to devise a containment strategy that would restrict the population's freedom of movement. Indeed, such strategies must now be developed by law at a national and local level: the Civil Contingencies Act (2004) has led government to consider pandemic influenza to be one of the highest priority risks. These risks are assessed and updated in a National Risk Register and in Community Risk Registers maintained by local government.

When a serious risk materialises, the government needs to coordinate across many ministries. Such coordination is probably advisable in the best of times but in the worst of times it is simply essential. Imagine we have an outbreak of a serious infection that may turn into an epidemic, putting hundreds of thousands of lives at risk. If the government fails to nip the outbreak in the bud by tracing all the contacts of every infected person, it is forced to try and suppress the infection. This suppression shuts down all but the most essential aspects of daily life. Every part of our society needs to work together to minimise risk of transmission of infection. Epidemiologists and public health experts need to be able to record and track the course of the epidemic in the greatest possible detail, not with a view to some future policy recommendations but with a view to steering public policy 'on the hoof'. In normal times, epidemiologists have merely observed reality. In epidemics, they must act to change that reality.

This is all made possible by legislation like the Civil Contingencies Act. So why do we say epidemiology has been tamed? Surely epidemiologists are centre stage in this flu scenario? Maybe so. But, they are only centre stage after the event, after the epidemic has taken hold, when society is in a hole. Then, and only then, are epidemiologists allowed (with oversight of course) to do what they really need to do: to perform experimental science and not be trained observers and analysts alone.

We need to say a little more about smoking because some progress has been made in this area. Between 1950 and 1998, the proportion of men over 35 who smoked fell from over four out of five to less than two in five. The proportion of women smokers over 35 was lower than men at two in five (for the under sixties) and one in five (for the over sixties) in 1950 and this proportion declined more modestly up until 1998.[5] That is still a lot of smokers, but there has been further reduction during this century. One in five adults (20%) was a smoker in 2012. However, unemployed people (39%) were around twice as likely to smoke as people in work (21%)[6] and there are regional differences (for example, in 2012, more adults in Greater Manchester were smokers (23.1%) than the England average (19.5%)).[7]

This raises two questions: how did so many people get off such an addictive substance as nicotine and why have so many remained hooked? Probably the most important factor explaining the decline in smoking is action by government to restrict the activities of the tobacco industry. Action on Smoking and Health has found thirty-two pieces of legislation on this, going back to 1693 when, as noted previously, MPs first took care of their own interests. We, the people, have had to wait a little longer. Most of the laws were made in the modern era.

This mass of legislation suggests that the public has long wanted either to kick the habit or avoid it in the first place. But government has not done the obvious thing of banning sales of tobacco. Instead there has been piecemeal reform. This suggests legislators have been facing opposition – most clearly from across the tobacco industry and the advertising industry. Even the piecemeal reforms have faced legal challenges.

What has all this got to do with the case for action research in epidemiology? Well, all this tobacco legislation in fact comprises a series of small societal experiments. If a legal measure is found to have been effective – by epidemiologists of course – and if no bad side effects emerge, then that measure will have been validated as a cause of improved health. The special feature of legislation as action research is that the action is carried out by the state. This has certainly worked to cut tobacco use but this state action has not eliminated tobacco use as such. So, state action has its limits. It seems likely that legislation elsewhere, by itself, will also only be partially effective when it is directed against other sources of risk such as sugar, junk food or alcohol.

Nor is it likely that prevention of the modern plagues will be achieved by legislation alone. The government is certainly an important actor, it has an important role to play, but, as we shall see, other societal actors also have roles to play. Epidemiologists – with their skills of observing, hypothesising and devising new experiments in action research – are just one of those actors. All John Snow had to do was to insist on meeting with the Board of Guardians and to press his case for the pump handle to go. Today, the various actors in the field of diabetes, depression and so on also need to get consensus on action. Who are these actors? They include elected politicians, for sure, but also the health improvement professionals, employers, educators, community organisations, leisure organisations, voluntary bodies, community activists and, above all, people committed to improving their own health. Part IV will spell all this out more fully.

7

When things start to go wrong

Epidemiologists – like their biologist colleagues – want to observe very carefully the rise of the common conditions that are precipitating the end of healthspan for billions of people world-wide. They don't want only to observe; they also want to use those observations to help steer us all toward ending these modern plagues. Observation by itself is not enough. Just counting the numbers won't take any of us very far because there is also a need to observe and understand the natural phenomena and the human phenomena – the biology and the sociology. The scientific approach insists that we seek to understand as many of the processes that disrupt the normal functioning of the individual as possible.

Those disruptive processes encompass not only different systems inside the individual but also other systems that we usually think of as being outside the individual – what people loosely call the environment. When it comes to diabetes, depression, heart disease and cancer, we need to understand what is going on inside as well as outside.

The exposome

This inseparability of what goes on inside and outside is captured by epidemiologists with the word 'exposome'. First coined by an epidemiologist, Christopher Wild, in 2005,[1] the word comes in two parts. The first part is from the word 'exposure'. We are familiar with 'exposure to sunlight' but plants, animals or people (all different kinds of organism) may be exposed, as far as epidemiologists are concerned, not only to solar radiation but to any force and to any material or substance. It could be exposure to ultra-violet light in a night club or diesel particles in the air. It can also be something that is harder to pin down such as 'junk food'. Or it may be a constraint, such as the absence of opportunities for physical activity. Exposures may be either good or bad for health.

The second part of 'exposome' is the ending -ome. This ending appeared first when it was tacked onto the word 'gene' to give 'genome'. Whereas a gene is a sequence of chemical 'letters' that may for example specify the sequence of amino acids of a protein, the word 'genome' is the entire set of structures of all the chromosomes in a cell. So, the ending -ome is now used to imply 'everything to do with'. 'Exposome' means 'every kind of factor to which a living thing may be exposed and that may affect that living thing in some way'. Any one factor making up the exposome may originate inside or outside the body, the organs, the tissues or the cells. For example, diesel fumes originate outside the body but can end up right inside cells where they can cause damage. Or a sugar like glucose may have entered the body in a food source and been processed. The glucose then bathes the tissues: we say that the tissues are exposed to the glucose. Epidemiologists inevitably focus on exposures where they suspect some association between an exposure and a risk of harm, and they tend to start examining exposures where the harm is greatest and the risk may be highest. Nonetheless, exposures may also be essential to health.

Wild coined the word 'exposome' in order to counter-balance an over-emphasis on genomic risk factors that had emerged after the success of the Human Genome Project. All the molecules in the cell, not just DNA sequence, can be tested for their ability to reveal processes that cause harm to health. Three technical terms indicate major sources of risk: transcriptomics, proteomics and metabolomics. All three terms end in '-omic' because the intention is to emphasise that the whole story must be understood, whether transcriptomics (looking at the activity of all the 22,000+ human genes) or proteomics (looking at the activity of all the 90,000+proteins around the body) or metabolomics (looking at the thousands of small molecules called metabolites that arise from our diet and from the activity of the proteome). But there are sources of risk that can be measured and that lie outside the cell, whether it is alterations to an organ of the body (fat deposits round the pancreas are a risk factor for diabetes) or to the body as a whole (obesity is a risk factor for a number of harms to health). Beyond the individual body are risk exposures that come from social groups (a culture of physical inactivity comes to mind) and from what we may call the external environment. We shall be discussing these exposures from outside the individual body in Chapter 12 when we shall present the exposures as elements of the needs humans have to maintain health. The idea of the exposome is to insist that there is nothing that may not be associated with harm.

What is 'normal'?

At the beginning of this chapter we referred to the 'normal functioning of the individual' as the state that exists before it is disrupted by some exposure or other. But 'normal' is not quite the right word when every individual is different. What we all have in common – what all living things have in common – is the property of seeking to keep our bodies in a more or less constant state of optimal functioning. The technical word used to describe this property is 'homeostasis' (derived from the Greek 'similar to standing still'). One of the nineteenth-century founders of modern biology, Claude Bernard, a contemporary of Darwin, first emphasised the importance of this stable internal environment. He wrote:

> The constancy of the internal environment is the condition for free and independent life: the mechanism that makes it possible is that which assures the maintenance, within the internal environment, of all the conditions necessary for the life of the elements.
>
> The constancy of the environment presupposes a perfection of the organism such that external variations are at every instant compensated and brought into balance. In consequence, far from being indifferent to the external world, the higher animal is on the contrary in a close and wise relation with it, so that its equilibrium results from a continuous and delicate compensation established as if the most sensitive of balances.[2]

Note how, for Bernard, constancy is not something static. Instead, there is an active process of maintaining equilibrium in living beings. This equilibrium can be perturbed by factors in the exposome. That perturbation is then associated potentially with ill-health, disease and death. So, to answer the question of what the 'normal functioning of an organism' is, we can say that homeostasis – maintaining equilibrium – is normal. Every individual of the same species is able to maintain its own dynamic states of equilibrium, and each of these states is unique. Every member of a species, every human being is different. We can see it or, if not, we can infer it, by looking at their genes, for example. We each have different – millions of different – variations in the DNA sequences that comprise our genes and chromosomes. No single DNA sequence is 'normal' but any combination of variations in sequences found in a living being is compatible with the maintenance of equilibrium throughout the healthspan of that living being. The way living organisms have evolved has been so that there is a huge number of potentially viable equilibria. The idea that organisms maintain equilibrium is deceptively simple because actually it allows for massive variation and complexity.

Maintaining equilibrium

Let us look at just one example of how equilibrium is maintained so as to see what a complicated business it is. Here we can only tell part of the story (because we don't know the whole story and we want here merely to provide a taster on homeostasis).

Glucose is the energy source that is used to power up every cell in our body. Its concentration needs to be kept constant at around 0.9 grams (about a quarter of a sugar lump) in a litre of blood. If the concentration is too low, you may pass out. If it is too high, it becomes toxic and your body starts to lose control over its ability to maintain constant glucose concentrations. If it is too high for too long, you will eventually come down with diabetes. So as to keep glucose concentration at, or close to, 0.9 grams per litre, the body produces two proteins (hormones) that send opposite messages to the tissues. Glucagon sends a message to release stored glucose into the blood. Insulin sends a message to remove glucose from the blood. Specialised cells within the same small organ – the pancreas – make each hormone: glucagon is made in 'alpha cells' and insulin in 'beta cells'.

When we eat complex carbohydrates (like pasta or potatoes) or simple carbohydrates (like sucrose), the digestive system eventually turns it all into glucose and this passes into the blood stream. The concentration is monitored by the pancreas. If glucose goes up, the beta cells in the pancreas pump out insulin. This stimulates all cells in the body to take up more glucose and, at the same time, it stimulates the liver to store the glucose in a different form called glycogen. Once the glucose concentration has fallen, the alpha cells start to pump out glucagon.

This action in opposite directions by two hormones is typical of mechanisms in the body to keep something in equilibrium. For the glucose control system to work, the two hormones need to be degraded since if they were stable they would simply accumulate and cancel out the effect of the other. Both insulin and glucagon have short half-lives of some five minutes. So, we can see that, as far as glucose is concerned, this is a dynamic fast-acting system for maintaining a constant glucose concentration. The concentration of glucose can double after a meal for an hour or two. But, the hormones then bring the concentration back down again. Other mechanisms for maintaining equilibrium include negative feedback mechanisms. Here the end product of a process accumulates but this accumulation starts to inhibit the process until the end product has been removed by some other process. In fact the insulin-glucagon control system is really a more complex version of a simple negative feedback system.

Living systems are full of these control loops. Virtually every reaction between chemicals in our body (metabolites such as sugars, amino acids, minerals and fats) and every activity of a tissue or organ (like the heart rate) is regulated and controlled. The control loops seek to ensure a Goldilocks outcome (not too much, not too little; not too hot, not too cold). But, in the end, the loops fail: our lives are transient. We don't all die at the same age – or, to put it another way, we each maintain homeostasis with slightly different robustness and we each have our own exposomes over the course of life.

However, when we go to the doctors they do not tell us: 'I'm afraid your homeostasis is not sufficiently robust and your exposome has an unfortunate risk profile.' Such a statement backed up with evidence cannot be made: we remain ignorant of much of the detail of human biology.

Our bodies are like a big completed jigsaw puzzle with tens of thousands of pieces. What most of the pieces are made of has been discovered, but there is only flimsy knowledge on how to put all the pieces together. On top of that, this jigsaw puzzle is not only three dimensional – it occupies space – but the fourth dimension of time has a role in that some of the pieces change in shape over the years.

If you think this analogy is over the top, think about metamorphosis. A caterpillar starts life as one jigsaw puzzle and ends up as another – a butterfly. These two forms of life have precisely the same genetic blueprint. So, under different conditions, the blueprint can be used in completely different ways. In plants, think of the amazing transformation of a deciduous tree between winter and summer. In humans, think of the plasticity of our brains. Throughout our lives, the brain is making and breaking contacts between nerve cells. From the moment we are born at, say, four kilos to our adult weight twenty times greater, we are continuously changing shape, we are growing and developing. Yet each and every shape is a state of equilibrium – of dynamic equilibrium.

Out of kilter

Our body may have its equilibrium perturbed when it is exposed, say, to a virus. The body attempts to compensate, first, with an arsenal that is aimed at specifically destroying the virus and, second, with physiological responses to help in that job. A virus infection makes us feel tired and so we conserve our physical energy, thereby enabling more energy to go towards fighting the invader. If we are exposed to starvation – the absence of nutrition – then systems are set off in our bodies to conserve physical and chemical energy. If we are exposed to too much food, leading to too much glucose in the blood, there is of course the short-term effect of releasing insulin to rebalance things but there is no long-term defence against gaining too much weight. This is hardly surprising: the biology of humans has not had time to evolve to cope with the contemporary phenomenon of excess calorie intake. However, bears have evolved so that they can double in weight over the summer and then lose that weight during the winter.

But there are limits. Infections can and do kill us. The HIV virus, for example, grows primarily in a specific type of human blood cell that is a component of our immune defences. The virus grows inside and the cell bursts open and, as a consequence, the immune defence becomes unbalanced owing to the deficit in one type of blood cell. The immune system has gone out of kilter: it struggles to replace the cells that the virus is killing, but the system eventually cannot keep up. This means the body becomes defective in its defence against any kind of infection, by bacteria or moulds or viruses. HIV leads to a person eventually succumbing to Acquired Immuno-Deficiency Syndrome (AIDS).

When it comes to a long-term condition like diabetes, the precise chain of events leading to a breakdown in homeostasis has not been discovered. This is why scientists have undertaken so many genetic studies on the condition in the hope of finding clues about that chain of events. They have identified a large number of genes that each make a small contribution to the risk of diabetes but it will be some time before we know why the presence in some people of a given variant of a gene increases their risk. And it will be even longer before that knowledge can be converted into specific new treatments. Overall though, the story is the same: in diabetes the dynamic equilibrium of constant blood glucose concentration is perturbed because the insulin and glucagon balance is out of kilter due to the body being exposed long-term to too high a concentration of glucose.

Turning to the other common long-term conditions like depression, anxiety, heart disease and the cancers, here too we are a far away from discovering the complete, precise chain of events. When it comes to cancer, things are occasionally clearer. Cancer refers to a very large number of different conditions where each is associated with abnormal growth in a particular kind of tissue in the body like the breast or the prostate. Let us look at one example – cervical cancer – where some insight now exists into the chain of events leading to the condition.

In the middle of the last century, epidemiologists were looking for clues on the causes of cervical cancer in women (the cervix is a ring of tissue separating the vagina from the uterus). They were surprised to find that this cancer was more common among women who started having sex at a younger age or who had

had multiple sexual partners. This seemed odd because cancer isn't catching. Yet the pattern they saw was similar to that of an infection – a sexually transmitted infection.

That similarity was intriguing enough to start Harold zur Hausen, a molecular biologist, speculating. What if cervical cancer was caused by a virus? He had read that, back in the 1930s, a cancer in rabbits had been associated with a member of the papilloma virus family of viruses. Was human cervical cancer due to infection by this type of virus? He was asking this question half a century later and, to cut a long story short, his guess was right and he won the Nobel Prize thirty years later in 2008 – the same year that two French scientists won the prize for discovering another virus – HIV. Sadly, the various epidemiologists involved were not honoured in this way.

It turns out that there are many types of human papilloma virus (HPV), that infection of humans is common, that only a small proportion of women exposed to HPV develop the cancer and then only after many years. This insight then led to the development of a cervical screening test for earlier detection of the condition: early detection favours better treatment outcomes. Today, a vaccine has become available which prevents infection in the first place. Cancer mediated by HPV had been conquered – once you got the jab.[3]

The HPV story shows that to get better treatment and to allow prevention as well, you first need to look for the faintest of clues using epidemiology and then you have to use your clue to help you discover the basic biology. Of course you also need imagination and you need permission to follow your hunch. The kind of clue you need is something that indicates the probable perturbation of the equilibrium within the body or a part of the body.

Can genetics help?

Today's technologies can characterise our DNA more quickly, cheaply and accurately and in more detail than any other molecule that makes up our bodies. It costs less than a set of new car tyres to get the sequence of all 3bn bases of the human genome. These advantages have made DNA the subject of intense study. The DNA sequence of the chromosomes from millions of people round the world is being determined right now. We all have different sequences from each other and we all have a paternal and a maternal copy of each chromosome.

These variations in DNA sequence allow us to determine whether all the people with a disease – let us call it Z – share the same sequence at some specific location in their genomes. If they do all share the same sequence (or if a statistically significant proportion of them do), then this provides a clue that this genomic location is associated with Z and that the particular shared sequence may have some role in causing Z. Even if that turns out not to be true, the association between the sequence and Z is useful for measuring the risk that people may get Z in the future.

Over 37,000 significant associations have been established between precise locations on the chromosomes and human characteristics, including the presence of diseases and conditions. When we say 'significant' we mean we are confident that there really is an association. However, the association may not be substantial – the characteristic may only be manifested in a small proportion of the people who have the DNA variant in question. Nonetheless, discovering over 37,000 associations is an important achievement. If all those associations were between a single base in the genome and a human characteristic and if every base in the genome had some purpose for human functioning, then there would be billions of possible associations. There is therefore probably still a great deal to discover.

To make clear the day-to-day significance of this, consider when people say 'I've got the gene for this particular characteristic' (or more precisely 'I've got variant A for condition Z'). They are wrong to think that the characteristic is the inevitable consequence of 'having the gene'. They are wrong to think they have condition

Z because they have that variant A. What they can say, however, is that, because they have variant A they are, from conception, at an increased risk of developing condition Z, compared with people that have some other variant B. The amount of increased risk is usually quite small in practice – about 1%. That would mean that for every 100 people with variant B that had condition Z there would be 101 people with variant A that had condition Z.

Of course, if a characteristic has significant associations with say 100 different variants scattered around the chromosomes, then some people may well have more than one of the variants that increase risk. That would put these people into a higher risk group.

But, all the same, this genetic risk with which we are born and which cannot, to all intents and purposes, be modified is only one source of risk. There are many others. For the common long-term conditions, a major risk factor that we shall return to is being overweight or obese. There is a crucial difference between genetic risk factors and these other risk factors. Whereas there is nothing any of us can do about the variants we have inherited in our DNA and the risks that go along with some of those variants, there is plenty we can do about other risk factors. In other words, they are modifiable risk factors.

So, things start to go wrong when risks materialise. Some risks we can do nothing about, but others can be reduced.

8

Knowing the unknown

When it comes to prevention of today's common long-term conditions, the two big scientific obstacles are, first, that we do not know in full the processes that end healthspan and, second, we do not know precisely when an individual's healthspan will end. The effect of this is that we are forced to work with probabilities, with risks. This is not especially a problem for scientists: they know their conclusions are always provisional because truth itself is provisional. But, for most of us, there is some uneasiness when the answers that we get have attached to them lots of ifs and buts.

Here we shall discuss how we use probability to make up for our incomplete knowledge, or – to be frank – how we use probability to make up for ignorance. The way to work out the probability that an individual's healthspan will end by a particular date is based on looking at the past and matching the individual with how others have done in the past. Doing this requires a 'population study' where information and samples are collected over many years from a selected set of individuals. One can say that the probabilities that are eventually calculated are just a guess, but at least an informed guess based on what has happened to real people in the population study. That guess just may enable one to take some action to prevent or delay an undesirable outcome.

How people perceive risk

The weather forecasts in Figure 8.1 show that the chance of rain is higher in Mecca than in Manchester on precisely the same day. The chance of precipitation in Mecca was calculated to be 40%, while in Manchester it was calculated to be under 5%. But, how many people in each city took with them a waterproof or umbrella when they went out? One can be confident that fewer did in Mecca.

So, what is going on? The weather forecast is based, first, on looking at a mass of information about the weather in these cities

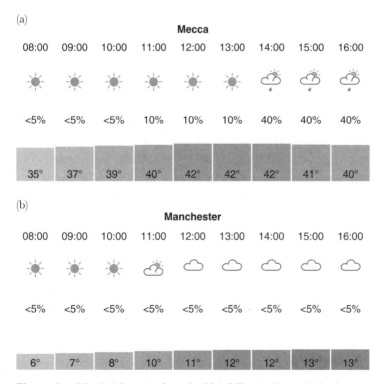

Figure 8.1 Weather forecasts from the Met Office on the same day in Mecca and Manchester. The risk of rain was eight times higher in Mecca, but people's behaviours were surely different.

and their surroundings in times past. Then, a computer algorithm finds the closest match with the actual conditions at the particular time it calculates its predictions. It assumes that what happened with the closest match in the past is what is most likely to happen in Manchester and in Mecca (we are simplifying the story). So, on the one hand, we have a careful set of calculations of the probability of an event. And, on the other hand, the good people of Manchester think they know better. They know how unpredictable the weather is there (as does the algorithm). And the good people of Mecca also think they know better: a 40% chance of rain on a hot, sunny day is nothing to worry about. Both groups of equally sensible people are assessing the probability of a drenching but they come up with opposite conclusions.

The best way to explain this difference is based on our emotions of hope and fear. The Mancunians fear a drenching more than the Meccans hope to avoid one. Of course the hopes and fears are based on people's experience of consequences: a drenching is probably a rare relief in Saudi Arabia but probably not in North West England. However, it is not just our knowledge of consequences. Sometimes people feel they must take risks as a matter of principle. Perhaps someone may want to show their fearlessness by leaving the waterproof at home. In the case of Fred Hill, his principle was his wrong-headed view of individual freedom.

Fred Hill was a motorcyclist who repeatedly refused to wear a helmet, despite the law that was enacted in 1973. He refused to pay the fine on every occasion and he therefore repeatedly ended up in jail. During his thirty-first spell of imprisonment, he died of a heart attack. His justification for law-breaking had been that he was fighting for freedom. Some MPs thought the same. Commenting on Fred, Enoch Powell MP, who was not a motorcyclist, said: 'The maintenance of the principles of individual freedom and responsibility is more important than the avoidance of the loss of lives through the personal decision of individuals'.[1] Hill's supporters – who still exist to this day – would say his assessment of risk was reasonable. After all, he died from a heart attack, not from any lack of helmet. His detractors would say he was lacking in foresight. After all, he sadly died alone in jail without his freedom. One might add that he did not understand that his risk of injury was also a risk for the National Health Service.

If our perceptions of risk are coloured by our hopes, fears, outlook on life and values, they are also affected by other factors including our state of mind (resulting in recklessness or phobias) and the large number of times that we make risk assessments knowingly, unknowingly, with or without or the facts. For example, whenever we use the future tense, there is necessarily a risk calculation being made. Consider: 'I think it will rain' or 'I think it may rain'. These imply assessments of a higher or lower probability of the event. They are not based on the Meteorological Office's algorithms, but on our experience (strictly, on our imperfect recollections of experience) alongside all those hopes, fears and so on. We lose sight of the fact that risk assessment is a serious business and, in so doing, we lose sight of the meaning of risk itself.

Working with risk

When organisations or individuals decide to treat risk seriously, they use the words 'probability' or 'likelihood'. All those other words – like risk, chance, fate, luck, odds, possibility – are avoided and great efforts are made to put a number on the probability of an event. The weather forecast gave a 40% probability of precipitation in Mecca – in other words the algorithm calculates that it will rain at that time on that day in forty cases out of 100. Nonetheless, here we don't in the main use the word 'probability'; we use 'risk' because we are almost invariably describing the probability of an undesirable event. Yes, we are mixing maths with a value judgement. So, we apologise for that. But we hope it will make things easier to understand.

In order to manage the risk of an undesirable event that an organisation has recognised, it can use 'risk management tools' that focus on two main features of the event: its probability and its severity. These tools, developed for business and institutions, help to monitor levels of risk, to avert a crisis by maintaining awareness and to manage a crisis by stockpiling the things needed to avert the consequences. They deploy what are called 'risk matrices'. These are commonly found in the NHS and are used extensively in hospital management. They give rise to a traffic light warning system:

- Green: low or acceptable levels of risk. No risk reduction action is required.
- Amber: moderate risk. Constant vigilance – but no immediate risk reduction action – is required.
- Red: high, unacceptable risk. The issue requires discussion at the highest level and risk reduction is required.

The way it works is that first an undesirable event is named. The event is then scored as low severity to high severity. So, the best guess is made of the likely impact. This score is given a number from one to five (e.g. 1 = minor, 2 = serious, 3 = very serious, 4 = disastrous but retrievable and 5 = catastrophic and irretrievable). Next, the probability of the event is scored, also from 1 (less likely) to 5 (more likely). See Table 8.1. This probability is, in principle, based on experience in the past or elsewhere and so may correspond to quantitative estimates of risk – for example a risk of under 20% gets score 1, while a risk of over 80% gets score 5. However, at least to start with, there are no quantitative estimates so the organisation starts by making a reasonable guess (e.g. 1 = almost impossible; 2 = remotely possible; 3 = unlikely but possible; 4 = quite possible; 5 = almost certain).

The risk matrix is obtained by multiplying severity times probability. Then red is set at a score of sixteen and over, while green

Probability higher					
5	*5*	*10*	*15*	*20*	*25*
4	*4*	*8*	*12*	*16*	*20*
3	*3*	*6*	*9*	*12*	*15*
2	*2*	*4*	*6*	*8*	*10*
1	*1*	*2*	*3*	*4*	*5*
	1	**2**	**3**	**4**	**5**
	Greater severity				

Figure 8.2 A risk matrix for assessing risks of differing severity and probability. A manager gauges an event to be less or more probable (1 to 5 in bold) and predicts its effects will be less or more severe (1 to 5 in bold). The size of the product of these numbers (in italics) for different events identifies priorities for action to reduce risk.

is set at eight and under. That then leaves amber for all the values above eight and below sixteen. Over time, as experience grows, all these values may be adjusted. The important thing is to keep the list of undesirable events up to date and to monitor everything going on in the organisation as carefully as possible. If use of a risk matrix helps ensure that this is happening, then the organisation can hope to minimise the number and severity of crises. The risk matrix does not provide a method for mathematically precise decision-making to reduce risk. However, it does put in place a way of thinking and acting that will achieve virtually the same result.

If the motorcyclist Fred Hill had considered probability and severity in this way, things may have turned out differently for him. In the absence of a helmet, the probability of head injury and death in a road traffic accident is high. The severity of these outcomes is indisputable. Similarly the probability of a jail term is high if you refuse to pay your fine for breaking the law and the outcome of dying in jail is severe. Of course, these were not considerations that his famous political supporters had to worry about.

Measuring risk

Risk matrices are a useful qualitative tool (i.e. not quantitative, not a rigorously derived set of numbers) for making good decisions. But, there is a large amount of quantitative data out there that relates to health and we have looked at a little of it already. How can we use that data for discovering what health risks the population faces as a whole and that individuals in the population face? Just as importantly, if measures are taken to improve health, by how much has the risk of common long-term conditions gone down?

Let us say we want to know if exposure to tobacco smoke is associated with the development of lung cancer. Is smoking a risk factor for lung cancer? This is an example of the more general question: is a specific exposure associated with the development of a specific condition or disease? We want answers to questions like this because there may be ways in which it is possible to reduce exposure to this or that risk factor and thereby reduce the proportion of people that develop a specific condition or disease.

To answer this, we need to measure 'relative risk'. This compares the frequency (or incidence) of the condition in two groups of people: those with the exposure (e.g. to tobacco smoke) and those without the exposure. If there is no association between exposure and condition then the frequency of the condition in the two groups should be approximately the same. The risk is the same in both groups. The ratio of the risks is 1.0. But, if there is an association between the exposure and the condition, then more in the exposed group will be affected than in the unexposed group. The risk is different. The ratio of the risks is not 1.0. If we express the ratio as (frequency in exposed group) divided by (frequency in unexposed group), then the value of the ratio is more than 1.0. An invented calculation of a relative risk is shown in Table 8.1. The incidence of the condition in the presence of the exposure is 5.34%, while its incidence in the absence of the exposure is 1.27%.

Table 8.1 Calculating relative risk

Exposure	Group with condition	Group with no condition	Total number of people	Incidence
Present	14	248	262	14/262 = 5.34%
Absent	2	156	158	2/158 = 1.27%

The ratio of these percentages is a number called the relative risk (4.2).

Calculating relative risk

The larger the ratio of these percentages between the groups, the more confident we can be of an association between the exposure and the condition. However, the smaller the size of the groups, the less confident we are that the people in those groups are fully representative. Statisticians get round this problem with separate calculations (of p-value or confidence interval).

The problem with the concept of relative risk is that it does not mean very much to most of us. Maybe that does not matter if you are a patient. After all, for you it is too late, you have the condition, the risk has been realised. But, it does matter – or should matter – to the rest of us. We tend to be left with a vague notion that doing something is probably bad for us because it means we might come down with something else. However, what does a relative risk of 4.2 really mean? What does it mean being 4.2 times more likely to develop a condition by doing something you enjoy than not doing it? The doubting Thomas in the public bar is already probably saying: 'You have got to die of something, so what the hell'. People and health professionals need access to simple and intuitive ways of understanding personal risk. Understanding statistics should not be the essential precondition for making good decisions about the health risks we face.

We can get one step closer to appreciating our own risk by calculating the 'absolute risk' of developing a health condition. This is the risk of developing the condition over a specific time period.[2] Ideally this should be calculated as a lifetime risk adjusted for the individual's age at the time that the absolute risk is calculated. However, it is usually calculated for five years or so because epidemiological studies are not usually supported for long enough. Note how absolute risk differs from relative risk: the latter is based simply on totting up the number of affected and unaffected individuals with or without an exposure.

The lifetime absolute risk of women developing breast cancer in the US is currently 12.4%. This means that for every American woman, over twelve in 100 will develop this condition at some point in their lives. Absolute risk is always expressed as a percentage but it is really the ratio of people who actually have a condition compared to all the people who could have had the condition. It is possible for 'lifetime absolute risks' to be calculated individually for all the plagues of our times.

It is also possible to further refine the lifetime absolute risk by including information generated by calculating a relative risk for a particular risk exposure. For example – the absolute risk of developing a particular condition is, say, 6% in non-smokers. The relative risk of this condition is found to be increased by 50% in smokers. This 50% relates to the six people with the condition, so the absolute increase in the risk is 50% of 6%, which is 3%. Thus the absolute risk of smokers developing the condition is 9%. Although not perfect, we are slowly starting to reach a position where appreciation of risk is starting to be more intuitive. Would you want to reduce your lifetime risk of this condition from 9% (roughly one in ten) to 6% if you stopped smoking? Perhaps not, but if you could reduce it even further by seeing the reduction due to other changes in behaviour, it may then become a more attractive proposition.

Another way epidemiologists can investigate and define the actual contribution of a risk exposure to the development of a condition is by calculating something called the attributable risk. This is a different way of quantifying the contribution of an individual risk factor to the overall risk of development of a disease or condition. Attributable risk is the absolute difference in incidence of the condition observed in a group of people exposed to a risk factor compared with an unexposed group. This quantifies the risk of the condition in the exposed group which is attributable to the risk exposure by removing the risk that would have occurred anyway due to other factors. Put another way, this is a way of calculating the number of cases of the condition that could be eliminated if a particular exposure were eliminated. This is probably much less useful to someone thinking about their own risk but it is a useful measure that population health professionals and politicians can use to appreciate what benefit could be gained by removing a particular exposure. It would, for example, be a good way to estimate the number of cases of respiratory conditions that could be reduced if air pollution levels were reduced in a particular area.

Measuring my own risk

Insurance companies have long needed to know what risks of illness or death their clients might have. The story goes back to Caspar Neumann, a clergyman in the Polish city of Wrocław, who looked at death rates in the city around 1690. His data was then used by Edmund Halley, an astronomer in Oxford, to make calculations on life annuities (a pot of money that pays for someone's pension). The calculations were then used by the government in pension policy. Similar calculations are used to this day, not only for state and private pensions but also for health insurance. Health insurance companies need to know how best to set the insurance premium for each client so as to leave a surplus after covering treatment costs and death benefits. Figure 8.3 illustrates the way that professionals in the insurance industry see health risks.[3]

If an actuary gets it wrong and sets a pension that is too high or too low, the insurance company either loses money or breaks the

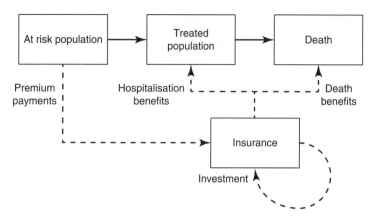

Figure 8.3 This flow diagram shows how insurance companies see health risks. They need to know how many people are likely to require treatment and what proportion will die. This then enables them to calculate premium payments and benefits.

law. This is why insurance companies have detailed questionnaires asking potential clients their age, gender, occupation, weight, smoking status, previous and existing illness, family history, age of parental death and so on.

When it comes to helping individuals extend their healthspan (as much as an individual can do this by themselves), only modest progress has been made in getting intelligible information to each of us that could reduce our own current level of risk of common long-term conditions. Over the last decade, personalised risk-prediction models have started to be introduced for diagnosis and prognosis. But they are also being developed for prevention. The models make use of research studies on populations and could also use health records from doctors and hospitals (primary and secondary care). From these data sources, one can:

• Determine whether a particular exposure is associated with the condition (the greater the association, the more reason to include the exposure as a risk factor in the model).

- Determine the size of the relative risk and attributable risk from a given exposure.
- Determine the absolute risk of the condition over a specified period of time (preferably the lifetime absolute risk) for a set of more common risk factors.

This information allows the calculation of absolute risk for a health condition observed in people stratified by a range of factors, for example the risk of a condition in smokers versus non-smokers, or the risk of a condition in women versus men. Having such data on outcomes allows a multiple exposure risk model to be created for a given condition.

Such a model then needs to be tested to see how good it really is at predicting whether a person develops the condition or not. This is done by using a proposed initial model to attribute levels of risk of the condition in a sub-sample of people where their extent of exposure to risk factors is known but their actual status for the condition is 'blinded' from the tester. Once the true status for the condition in this sub-group is revealed, this can be compared to what the initial model had predicted for them. These types of predictive models (also known as predictive algorithms or equations) can be tweaked repeatedly and refined using further sub-groups of the cohort to try and maximise the predictive power of the model. The aim is to predict the future status of people accurately – that is, without incorrectly assigning those who eventually get the condition (i.e. by predicting they will stay healthy) or alternatively incorrectly assigning people who remain healthy (i.e. by predicting they will become ill).[4]

Such predictive algorithms for specifying the differing risks people have for different conditions can be useful for shaping the advice people are given and for identifying steps to prevent the conditions themselves. Such applications are only just emerging. However, we need to emphasise that, by themselves, the algorithms – even if presented as a pretty app on your mobile phone – do not extend healthspan. They are just one tool in the toolkit that we discuss in Chapter 15.

There is no settled name yet for these types of predictive tool. We shall settle for 'risk calculators'. The JBS3 (Joint British Societies) Risk Calculator is an example of one that is used for assessing heart conditions and strokes using information about a range of risk factors.[5] It calculates the estimated age of your heart compared to your chronological age. This may prompt an individual to re-evaluate their behaviours. It also calculates lifetime risk of having a heart attack and at what age, and that too may prompt re-evaluation of behaviours. An add-on feature allows an individual to change the input information to what they think they could realistically achieve by way of changes in their behaviour. They can then see how much this would reduce the estimate of heart age and how much it would reduce lifetime risk of a heart condition or stroke. An individual may, for example, see what the benefits would be of reducing weight or cholesterol levels and of stopping smoking. The JBS3 is work in progress: additional risk factors could be included like levels of physical activity. We shall see that some long-term conditions and risk factors spread through social networks. Exploiting this phenomenon to spread healthy behaviours instead is another way in which benefits from risk calculators could be enhanced.

9

Risks that we can change

Removing a pump handle can be sufficient, we saw in Chapter 6, to end an outbreak of cholera. Using today's scientific language, we would say that eliminating a modifiable risk factor for cholera can be sufficient to reduce substantially the number of cholera cases. Notice that a risk factor does not necessarily act as a cause of the risk in question. The handle itself was not the cause of the cholera epidemic. Soho was not at risk of cholera because there were too many pump handles. The Broad Street handle was, instead, one critical component of a water management system. The way the system worked increased the likelihood of transmitting cholera bacteria from an infected individual to uninfected individuals. It was exposure to the workings of this water management system – not to pump handles – that was the problem. The system had to be disabled, modified and, of course, improved.

Risk reduction can only work by tackling modifiable risk factors. 'Modifiable' simply means that the factor can be changed by society and / or by individuals so as to reduce risk. The opposite type of risk factor is fixed, it is non-modifiable. The most well-known type of fixed risk factor is that due to inherited common genetic variation. When we are conceived with our complement of DNA sequences, each sequence includes common variants. Some of these variants decrease risk or increase risk of a given condition compared with the population average. No technology is currently in place that can modify these sources of risk: the risk is fixed at conception. Such a fixed risk factor has only indirect significance for action to reduce overall risk. Knowing about such factors does, however, have significance to the search for new treatments.

We want to look at the modifiable risk factors in our developed post-industrial society for the common long-term conditions of our day. They have been identified over the years via numerous observations. Three important ones are obesity, physical activity and social isolation. It is all too easy to look at each of these separately, when in reality they are all linked to each other. It is also all too easy to consider them as 'private' (only affecting specific individuals) when in fact they are 'public' (arising from our way of life). Public policy that focusses on just a single 'private' modifiable risk factor is doomed to failure or, at best, to yielding only marginal benefits. So, while, for the purposes of analysis, we may look at each risk factor separately, when it comes to action to reduce risks substantially we are obliged to act on all the common risk factors as though they were one. This is just as much the case where the modifiable risk factors can be assessed by measuring biochemical changes in the body, by measuring 'biomarkers' (markers for a biological process). A biomarker change may be detected as a proxy for a gross change in a modifiable risk factor and this may be a convenient and accurate way to measure what is going on. But, any single change detected is part of a much bigger story that involves the whole body, the whole exposome and the whole society.

Body mass

The most common measure of being overweight or obese is the Body Mass Index (BMI). This is the ratio of two numbers: a person's weight in kilogrammes divided by their height in meters squared. Four categories of people are then defined by their BMI measurements: underweight (BMI under 18.5); normal (BMI between 18.5 and 24.9); overweight (BMI between 25 and 29.9);

and obese (BMI of 30 and above). There are other categories such as 'moderately' or 'severely' or 'morbidly' obese. The same categories – but with different BMI values – are used to describe various groups of children – pre-school, school-age and adolescent.[1] There are some exceptions like sportsmen and women who have a higher BMI due to muscle mass rather than due to fatty tissue. To allow for these exceptions, a separate measure of the ratio of muscle to fat tissue has been developed.

BMI is useful because it is a modifiable risk factor for common long-term conditions. It's not a value judgement: it isn't a subjective score at a beauty pageant. Nor is it a diagnosis of any condition or disease. If anything, it is a proxy measure that overlaps with other modifiable risk factors like nutrition, physical activity or social inclusion in specifying our risk of common long-term conditions.

At the population level, it is valuable to know how many people have a high or low BMI – to know the distribution of BMI values in a population. It is a rough and ready way to assess the need for action to improve healthspan. For example, The Food and Agriculture Organization of the UN compared men in Brazil, China and Tunisia for their BMI values.[2] The distribution of values was similar in all three countries, with most individuals having what it called an 'acceptable' weight. But Tunisia had the most obese men, while China had the most underweight men (described as 'chronic energy deficiency'). Such comparative data allows the UN to develop public policy recommendations.

An interesting example of the variation over time in BMI values for a population comes from Cuba. In the province of Cienfuegos between 1991 and 2010 the BMI of the population was measured regularly and this gave rise to bell-shaped curves of BMI values. In Figure 9.1, the top of each bell-shaped curve corresponds to the most common BMI in the population in a given year. This top-of-the-curve BMI value was 22.5 in 1991. This went down to 20.5 in 1995 and then went up again to 24.5 in 2010.[3]

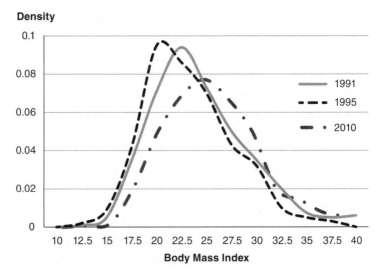

Figure 9.1 Variation in Body Mass Index between 1991 and 2010 among the population of Cienfuegos in Cuba. Note how the top of the curves moved to the left (reduced BMI) during the 'special period' (1991 to 1995) but then moved back again to the right (increased BMI). The vertical axis is given in 'density units' – similar to the proportion of the population.

What happened in Cuba to cause these large changes in BMI over just a few years? Commentators agree that it was the result of global politics. In 1989, the Soviet Union and its common market, Comecon, imploded. This meant that subsidised exports of consumer goods and oil to Cuba stopped and the country suffered a severe economic recession. President Fidel Castro called it the 'Special Period in Peacetime'. There was an average loss of 5.5 kg in body weight so that BMI plummeted to 20.5 in 1995. At the same time, there were rapid declines in diabetes and heart disease. But, during the Special Period, Castro also introduced reforms in industry, agriculture, car usage, diet and healthcare.[4] These reforms worked, but by 2010 BMI had risen even higher than it had been before and diabetes and heart disease deaths also grew. This episode has important lessons for public policy in Cuba and elsewhere too.

Over the decades in Britain, by contrast, there has been an unrelenting increase in BMI. Data from the UK's National Obesity Observatory show big drops in the fraction of the population with healthy weights and big rises in the fraction that are obese.[5] For example, nearly half of British women had a healthy weight around 1992 but 17 years later in 2009 only a third had a healthy weight (47.6% against 36.8%). Men fared little better. Moreover obesity jumped in that time period by 12% among men and 8% among women. The Health Survey for England 1993–2014 backs this up. It found that, between 1993 and 2014, male and female obesity rose from 14% and 17% to 25% for both men and women over sixteen. The prediction of the International Obesity Task Force is that, by 2050, obesity will affect 60% of adult men, 50% of adult women and 25% of children.[6]

Being overweight or obese is by no means only a British issue: it is increasingly a global one. Every country is affected to a greater or lesser extent, especially in North and South America, in northern and southern Africa and across Europe.[7] In North Korea, where our media report starvation, over one in six (17.4%) girls are overweight.

Can you catch obesity?

In 2015, England's Chief Medical Officer declared an obesity epidemic: the UK obesity rate reached one in four people.[8] As we have already noted, for there to be an epidemic, three criteria need to be satisfied: a certain proportion of the population should be affected; typically the condition should be due to a virus or bacterium or parasite; the condition should pass from person to person.[9]

When it comes to the proportion of the population affected, obesity clearly scores as an epidemic. For influenza, an epidemic means one in 500 is affected. For meningitis, an epidemic means one in 6,666 is affected. So, one obese person in four must qualify as a major epidemic.

The World Health Organization of the United Nations agrees with the Chief Medical Officer. It says humanity is facing a 'global obesity epidemic'. It began sounding the alarm in the 1990s: 'At the other end of the malnutrition scale, obesity is one of today's most blatantly visible – yet most neglected – public health problems. Paradoxically coexisting with under-nutrition, an escalating global epidemic of overweight and obesity – "globesity" – is taking over many parts of the world. If immediate action is not taken, millions will suffer from an array of serious health disorders'.[10]

But is obesity a disease? The European Bioinformatics Institute near Cambridge says it is 'an eating-related disorder in which excess body fat has accumulated to such an extent that health may be negatively affected'. This is close to what we would say: obesity is a modifiable risk factor for various health conditions. In extreme cases, where symptoms have emerged, 'morbid obesity' can be said to be present. Of course sometimes a risk factor can also be a disease (for example diabetes is a risk factor for kidney disease). But, obesity alone is compatible with a long period of what many affected individuals consider to be normal life. Despite this, it is nonetheless reasonable to consider that there is an obesity epidemic because the risks from prolonged obesity are life threatening. It is akin to the pump handle in Broad Street: the handle was part of a system of water management that constituted the major risk factor for cholera. Obesity is part of a system of inappropriate nutrition, exercise and social isolation.

The third criterion for an epidemic is that it can pass from person to person. Is obesity contagious? Contagious is a word with the same origin as 'contact'. This may refer to physical contact – from a simple handshake to full intimate contact. Or it may refer to contact solely by communication: I can contact you if I communicate by phone or by Facebook.

Can contact by communication be a mechanism whereby obesity can spread? This question was first asked in the 1990s,[11] so that there is now empirical evidence for obesity spreading in social networks. The longest running study of human health was set up in 1948 in the town of Framingham, Massachusetts in the US. Researchers repeatedly collect from the participants many kinds of health and social data – for example, Body Mass Index, family information and friendships. Analysing data collected from 1971 to 2003, the researchers saw that when two people perceived each other as friends, if one friend became obese during a given time interval, the chance nearly doubled that the other friend would become obese. Among pairs of adult siblings, if one sibling became obese, the chance that the other would also become obese increased by 40%. If a spouse became obese, the likelihood that the other spouse would become obese increased by 37%.[12]

They also found that obesity is clustered in communities. For example, the risk that the friend of a friend of an obese person would be obese was about 20% higher than expected. The risk was also higher for a friend of a friend of a friend. The term we use to describe these relations between friends is 'degrees of separation': my friend has one degree of separation from me, while their friend has two degrees of separation from me, and so on. By the fourth degree of separation, the risk of obesity had fallen to normal levels. Simply put, this means that you are not influenced by someone you don't know at all. People of the same sex had relatively greater influence on each other than those of the opposite sex. The spread of obesity that was seen in the network of friends and family couldn't be explained by other possible causes such as the spread through networks of attempts to quit smoking.

This spread of risk of obesity through social networks has great significance for the rise of 'globesity'. It implies that blaming the individual for being overweight is wrong. We should explore whether the risks that are associated with obesity are also spread in this way. Could it be that diabetes, heart disease, cancer and depression / anxiety also spread through social networks?

There is growing interest in using social networks to improve health. Efforts in this direction have provided positive results for preventing tobacco use and alcohol misuse, for improving sexual health and well-being, for reducing the risk of diabetes as well as for improving treatment of diabetes.[13]

How exactly does the contagion of obesity spread through social networks? Researchers in Sheffield have identified three social processes that seem to explain the role of social networks in the transmission of overweight and obesity.[14] The three processes are called social capital, social contagion and social selection. 'Social capital' refers to the sense of belonging and the social supports that influence our weight and our behaviours related to weight. 'Social contagion' refers to a process whereby the network in which people are embedded influences their weight over time. 'Social selection' refers to the processes whereby a person's network might develop according to his or her weight.

Let us explore one of these a little to see how weight is influenced by 'social capital'. Basically, this term refers to the strength among members of a social network of things like trust, mutual help and cooperation. There is already evidence that where people in a community cooperate well, you find a lower risk for infectious diseases like tuberculosis and sexually transmitted diseases as well as overall improved health status. Could the same be true in reducing risk of obesity across the community?

What researchers did was to look at 48 states in the US where there was data on BMI and data on social capital (measured by looking at things that vary from place to place like community organisational life, involvement in public affairs, volunteerism, informal sociability, and social trust). And what they found was that where there was less social capital there was more obesity and also more diabetes.[15]

Physical activity

In 1769, a physician, William Buchan, in typical Scottish Enlightenment style, published a health manual to educate the general public. The manual's long title is a summary of the contents: 'Domestic Medicine, Or, A Treatise on the Prevention and Cure of Diseases by Regimen and Simple Medicines with Observations on Sea-Bathing and the Use of the Mineral Waters'. The treatise suggests using cow dung, urine, oyster shells and eels, but it also has advice on prevention: it advocates sea-bathing, eating a varied and healthy diet, breathing plenty of fresh air and taking exercise. The book was so popular that there was even a copy aboard the HMS Bounty, which Christian Fletcher's mutineers took with them to Pitcairn Island.

If exercise was already recognised as important in pre-industrial Britain, then today the evidence is clear and the need has become critical. In the UK and worldwide, physical inactivity is one of the major risk factors for health conditions, for disability and for premature death, according to the World Health Organization.[16] Higher levels of exercise extend lifespan by three years, and reduce mortality due to cancer by 15%, due to heart diseases by 40%, and due to all causes by 30%.[17]

In the UK and elsewhere, top health officials publish and update recommendations on how much physical activity we all need.[18] But in the UK, only a minority of doctors are even broadly familiar with the recommendations.[19] In the US, four out of five adults fail to achieve recommended levels of physical activity.[20] A large survey in England found that one person in five undertook no physical activity, that less activity went along with lower incomes and poorer education, that this reduced activity was already apparent in teenagers, and that the activity gap between rich and poor continued to grow up to the age of 85.[21]

Attempts have been made to reduce physical inactivity with economic incentives, mass media and social media campaigns or 'nudging' people (e.g. with signs saying 'Use the stairs'). Sometimes neighbourhoods have been redesigned. But all these have had only limited success over the longer term.[22] This limitation does not mean that economic incentives, media campaigns, nudging and so on are not valuable tools. The fact that they work in the short-term suggests that the tools can work in principle. But something is missing that would allow them to work for the long term, for the whole of people's lives. One factor that is missing is social cohesion, as described below.

Social isolation

University students on a US campus were invited by researchers to volunteer online to attend sessions on a short fitness course. They were randomly assigned to four groups. The 'control' group was left to get on with it. Students in the 'comparison' group could compare their performance records with others. Those in the 'support' group were able to encourage and support each other person to person. In the fourth 'combined' group, students could both compare themselves to others and support each other. At the end of the course, which group attended the most – and the least – number of sessions? As you might predict, the combined group did the best. They stuck at it. And those who were left to their own devices in the control group – those who were most socially isolated – did the worst. They attended fewer than half the number of classes attended by the combined group. For the record, among these young educated men and women, being able to compare your performance with others was more effective in improving attendance than being supported by others. Just knowing how others are getting on can be enough to get these students going – at least in the short term.[23]

This kind of research points to the harmful effect of social isolation in undermining our commitment to fitness. Support from other people and knowing how other people are getting on is crucial to our ability to turn a commitment into performance, to turn our hopes into reality. Social isolation leads to us dropping out. Similar outcomes occur when people quit smoking: if they are isolated, they are more likely to fail.[24]

Evidence that social isolation is a risk factor for common long-term conditions comes from research where efforts are made to provide a number of people with support from their community in the shape of friends, family, neighbours, local faith groups and so on. Most of this research has focussed on people already diagnosed with a long-term condition. Where this support is made available, the patients do better in managing their condition than those who have no organised support. It is precisely because people do so poorly without this kind of social network support that this research has been undertaken. One tool that is being tried out at the moment is the mobile phone app. This is a minimalist social network: if you use the app, say, to control your weight, you know that you are not entirely alone. You have contact with a computer program and you can usually contact an adviser – a real person – as well. Whether such minimal contact can end the modern plagues is open to question but it may work for some individuals. We suspect that it is not enough to neutralise pressure going the other way – pressure such as social network effects that spread increases in the common modifiable risk factors or pressures that come from our way of life in a developed post-industrial society.

Our way of life

Our way of life has caused – or failed to prevent – social isolation. Whether earlier ways of life were actually so much better in preventing social isolation or in sustaining social cohesion is not really the point: industrial and pre-industrial societies have plenty of their own problems. This isolation is not forced on society because they are so few people. Quite the reverse: most people live at high density in large cities. So, the social isolation has social origins, not geographic ones. Our way of life is moulded by the way that goods and services are produced, distributed and exchanged. This mainly involves large private or public organisations – the big firm or the government body – that transiently brings people together who have a wide range of skills. This then tends to mean they live over a wide area in predominantly private houses or flats. That in turn means they need to travel a long time over long distances to and from work. The consequence is the physical separation of people; the consequence is social isolation. Then, because work tends to be sedentary and travel tends not to be by foot or bike, the levels of physical activity with this way of life are low. This in turn elevates the risk of obesity – along with the ready availability of energy-dense processed food that can be rapidly prepared at the end of a busy day.

All of us know all this well enough. What we know less well is that this way of life is not fixed or inevitable or unmodifiable. Our way of life is a modifiable risk factor for the various ways of death that are most likely to befall us.

It is no longer controversial to say that our way of life risks major climate change. Such change is also a modifiable risk factor – for drought, floods, famine, exotic diseases, destructive weather and ultimately for extinction. So, changing our way of life in order to prevent a climate disaster is, today, a common ambition. Some may lack that ambition, but that's another issue.

It is also, surely, a common ambition to reduce the level of risk from the factors that shorten our healthy lives. Diabetes, depression, heart disease and cancer all have modifiable risk factors in common. They can therefore be prevented or delayed in precisely the same way: by reducing the levels of those common risks. And, those risks – high body mass, low activity, social isolation – all arise, to a substantial degree, from our way of life. In other words, the leading risk factor for the modern plagues is our way of life.

Part III

The failure of public policy to end the modern plagues means it is time for a re-think. By going back to basics in modern biology and philosophy, health can be redefined in a positive form. This new definition replaces the widely held negative view of health as the absence of disease. Health is defined as the condition wherein human needs are optimally satisfied. As a consequence, the maintenance of health – in other words the prevention of ill health – means taking action to satisfy optimally our human needs. This definition then leads on to a novel paradigm for public policy that transcends the classical positions of Cicero and John Locke.

10

Biological relativity

Up to this point, readers will have seen that an advanced post-industrial society is plagued with a set of common long-term health conditions which, together, have social, economic and political impacts. Readers will have seen how public policy responses over the decades have related to this and how the weakness of the responses has failed to end, or even begin to end, the modern plagues. These public policy responses have arisen from some of the recommendations made by epidemiologists and so readers have learnt a little about this discipline and the constraints under which it has worked, as well as about the risk factors that are the epidemiologists' stock in trade. There have also been allusions to the societal barriers that restrain public policy change.

If public policy has failed, then there can be no stronger case for reforming it. And, if tinkering with public policy has also failed, then there can be no stronger case for progressive reform. The case for such reform could rest on moral or political arguments. But our case rests on reason and science – on the consequences of humans living as social beings as a part of the natural world.

Biology and determinism

At school, we are led to believe that we learn about the world by chopping it up into different subjects. It starts with three main subjects – reading, writing and arithmetic – and then, in secondary education, with a dozen or so subjects. These subjects mirror the way universities and researchers saw fit to chop up the world in an earlier decade – or even century. Subjects are clustered into either the sciences or the humanities. This clustering has been so rigid and has lasted such a long time that the Cambridge scientist and writer C. P. Snow observed that society had two cultures – the sciences and the humanities. His 1959 book, *The Two Cultures*, argued that the breakdown of communication between the two in modern society was a major hindrance to solving the world's problems. Snow wrote:

> A good many times I have been present at gatherings of people who, by the standards of the traditional culture, are thought highly educated and who have with considerable gusto been expressing their incredulity at the illiteracy of scientists. Once or twice I have been provoked and have asked the company how many of them could describe the Second Law of Thermodynamics. The response was cold: it was also negative. Yet I was asking something which is about the scientific equivalent of: 'Have you read a work of Shakespeare's?'[1]

Six decades later, we still chop up the world into the humanities and sciences and we then sub-divide the sciences first into physics, chemistry and biology. We are dimly aware that this is unsatisfactory because we assert that all three of these science sub-divisions serve humanity in some sense. And that, of course, begs the question: how can science serve humanity unless it also has a clear understanding of humanity and the humanities? The same is true for the sub-divisions of the humanities: the two need to work in tandem. This, obviously, is not to suggest that everybody needs to know everything.

There was not always a division between science and the humanities: Aristotle bridged the two cultures between philosophy and biology when there was no dividing line. But, as civilisations acquired ever-greater knowledge and understanding, specialisms were defined and the specialists defined separate vocabularies and interests.

C.P. Snow recognised that this fragmentation was becoming counter-productive. Today, the re-integration of 'subjects' has become essential: we are moving from a world dominated by analysis (drilling down to see how something works) to one where we need synthesis (re-assembling the bits of knowledge). In framing the questions that researchers ask, in carrying out an investigation ethically and in using the results of an investigation, we recognise today that we should work together not only across the two-culture divide, but also across the subdivisions of the humanities and the sciences.

There has been some success in achieving this. For example, in human biology research, both legal and ethical questions abound. Across all the natural and human sciences there is a coming together of funding organisations: in the UK, the once-separate funders of different branches now work together in one organisation called UK Research and Innovation. There is a similar coming together across the EU. One of the buzzwords in science today is that it should be 'cross-cutting': we are all trying to draw the threads of human knowledge together.

We are doing this not because we are turning into New Age mystics marvelling at the sublime unity of the Universe but because discovery and innovation is more fruitful across the old boundaries.

The case for overcoming divisions, boundaries, silos – call it what you will – is especially pressing in biology. A plant or an animal or a humble bacterium is an integrated living system that must maintain an internal balance and a balance with its environment. That means that the divisions we make in the study of living systems – between ecology, proteins, social science, genetics, behaviour, biochemistry, epidemiology, clinical medicine and so on – do not reflect reality.

That is not to say there is no value in dividing up a larger subject into smaller pieces. It is the foundation of the analytical scientific method. This involves holding constant all the variables in the system under study except the one variable whose behaviour we are investigating. We examine the world one thing at a time – one variable at a time. We seek to reduce a complex situation to a simpler one. This is called the reductionist method and it has served us well. But the next step has to be to put the variables all together again – as they are in the real world. An error we can make in doing this 'synthesis' is to treat one variable as the sole key to understanding the system. We have slipped from reductionist analysis to determinist synthesis. We have jumped dangerously to conclusions. It is dangerous because it is likely to be an avoidable over-simplification of reality.

It's in his D-D-D-DNA

There is one variety of determinism that has been especially harmful for biology and for its application in improving the health of human populations. This is 'genetic determinism'. It's a common expression nowadays to say that something is 'in your DNA'. 'DNA' is the title of a top-ten song by a British girl group called Little Mix. Here is a taster:

> It's in his DNA, D-D-D-DNA
> It's in his DNA
> And, he just takes my breath away
> B-b-b-breath away
> …
> He's from a different strain
> That science can't explain[2]

Little Mix are coining a metaphor whereby some boy has an innate property that makes the girls breathless and that this property is down to the boy's DNA. Of course, Little Mix is jesting but, all the same, the popularity of this DNA metaphor points to the penetration into mainstream culture of a misconception, a determinist misconception, from biology. To say that a human attribute is 'in the DNA' comes very close to what genetic determinists claim. Such claims are over-simplifications when used to suggest that genetic difference explains variations between people in their performance of tests that claim to define intelligence. In the best known examples, the problem goes beyond mere over-simplification. It is mere assertion – plus scientific fraud.[3]

Genetic determinism is wrong because it over-simplifies biological systems: it promotes just one kind of molecule – DNA – into the privileged position of specifying the properties of the biological system. Determinism itself has deep roots in the human wish to simplify problems – consider the supernatural determinism that inspires the Book of Genesis in the Abrahamic religions. The roots of genetic determinism are more recent. The French Enlightenment philosopher René Descartes suggested that mathematics would predict the man from the sperm that begat him (he overlooked women and their eggs). Three hundred years later, the physicist Erwin Schrödinger, held that 'hereditary material' accounted for the events in space and time which take place within the spatial boundary of a living organism. However, despite the roots of genetic determinism being so distinguished, there is no escaping the fact that we really are not just our DNA – or even our D-D-D-DNA.

More recent varieties of genetic determinism are no less flawed. *The Selfish Gene* by the zoologist Richard Dawkins is the most influential science book of all time according to a poll taken to celebrate the Royal Society science book prize. Dawkins later wished he had used a different title.[4] But the fact is that the title sums up his main idea very neatly. This idea is that the genes of an organism are in a privileged position so that their principal function is to ensure their own survival in a biological system. Genes that are passed on are the ones whose evolutionary consequences best ensure their replication, rather than, necessarily, best ensuring the life of the organism. This view overlooks the fact that all the domains of a biological system are essential: if you take away any one of the domains, then the organism, the species, becomes inert matter. Dawkins' oversight has wider significance because his book is so influential and so easily misunderstood. The book is taken to conclude that human selfishness is inevitable. His readers have 'misheard' the statement that 'genes are inevitably selfish' with the statement that 'humans are inevitably selfish'.

The limitations of DNA, of genes, of genomes is illustrated by the case of a US scientist Craig Venter who, in 2010, wanted to construct a completely artificial living species in the lab. He cleverly assembled an artificial genome – a DNA sequence that he thought would do the trick. However, to get a viable organism, Venter was obliged to take the cells of an existing living organism, remove its own genome (its DNA sequence) and replace this genome with the one he had made himself.[5] The media loved it. '"Frankenstein" lab creates life in a test tube', proclaimed a British tabloid, saying: 'A controversial geneticist has "gone towards the role of a god" by becoming the first person to create "synthetic life"'.

This is the face of genetic determinism: synthetic DNA = synthetic life. Venter had not created 'synthetic life' but, rather, he had failed to. He had not usurped any god. He had simply introduced synthetic DNA (that he had made using well-established methods) into a cell where that foreign DNA could enter the cell's metabolism and be controlled by it so as to act as a template for a set of proteins. He had thereby actually disproved genetic determinism. Introducing foreign DNA into a living organism has been going on in genetics labs since 1928.[6] Moreover, in the natural world, different kinds of bacteria have been doing it between each other for millions – perhaps billions – of years. The origin of the whole science of molecular biology comes from exploiting this natural phenomenon.[7]

Presumably, none of this was known to the ethicists and philosophers who saw fit to comment on the publication of Venter's unremarkable experiment. A philosopher proclaimed the experiment was a 'defining moment in the history of biology and biotechnology'. An ethicist opined that Venter 'is creaking open the most profound door in humanity's history'. Thus one of our two cultures was commenting on the other in blind ignorance of the facts.

No privileged position can be assigned to genes in establishing a living system. The DNA of which genes are made works with a large number of proteins, with small molecules and large ones, to constitute the coordinated system that we recognise as life. The environment of a cell or an organism or a person elicits changes within the living system. Those changes work to minimise the risk to loss of viability of the system.

A simple transmission belt of 'instructions' from our DNA to our bodies just does not exist. Look once more at the butterfly. It starts the life cycle as an egg, developing into a caterpillar, then a chrysalis and then a flying insect. At all stages it has, as far as we know, precisely the same set of DNA 'instructions'. The point is that the organism does not just get DNA instructions to change its form. It also gets instructions from elsewhere. These come from other molecules like proteins inside the insect and from the insect's environment. Living beings – organisms – are the product of combined multiple causes, functions, mechanisms, purposes, histories, systems. There is no spark of life, no metaphysical prime mover, no mono-causality whether in life or health or disease. Chicken and egg – or butterfly and egg – arise together.

When it comes to the transmission of traits from one generation to the next, DNA is of course an essential component of the organisation of the organism to achieve this end. But transmission of traits does not only occur via inheritance of DNA sequences. It can also occur epigenetically, in other words by proteins that can create subtle modifications (called 'epigenetic signatures') of specific 'letters' in the DNA sequence. These epigenetic signatures are somewhat like the accents on letters that we see in some French words (e.g. 'garcon' would be pronounced differently from 'garçon'). An accent modifies pronunciation, while an epigenetic signature modifies the activity that can be elicited from one or more genes. The proteins are only able to modify specific DNA letters when they receive the right signal to do so from other cells or from outside the body. Epigenetic signatures can be transmitted from parent to child and it is thought that this is one way that the offspring of obese parents acquire an increased risk of obesity. Note that an obesogenic environment (an environment that favours individuals becoming obese) can also perpetuate obesity across the generations. So, genes are not the only way that traits may be transmitted down the generations. It's not just in the D-D-D-DNA.

Biological relativity

If genetic determinism is wrong, or at least a gross over-simplification, then what is really going on? The best way of understanding this currently is with the theory of biological relativity. It shares an idea with Einstein's theory of relativity. Einstein said there is no privileged time or place in the Universe: we live in a space-time continuum. Prior to this, people had said that there must be a privileged place, a centre of the Universe. Over the millennia, this was variously placed in Athens, Beijing, Rome and elsewhere. More recently, we have thought that this privileged place was the Earth or the Sun or our galaxy.

The theory of biological relativity proposed by Oxford physiologist Denis Noble says much the same: there is no hierarchy in biological systems, no level in its organisation that has precedence over any other level.[8] This denial of a hierarchy is exactly what comprises the denial of determinism – of, for example, the genetic determinism which we (in line with Noble) traced back to René Descartes. Different rules and behaviours, says Noble, exist at one level that cannot be predicted from the way another level behaves.

Noble identifies a number of these levels. While we can illustrate these levels with arrows going from small to large, size is not what matters:

Atoms → *Molecules* → *Organelles* → *Cell* → *Tissue* → *Organ* → *Organ system* → *Organism*

The size of the smallest level – the atoms – is a trillion times less than the biggest organisms like a whale. In between are the molecules (like DNA – made of atoms), the organelles (little factories that make, say, proteins), the cells, a tissue (clusters of cells that make up, say, muscle tissue), an organ (comprising different tissue types as in a heart) and an organ system (a heart and all the arteries and veins). Finally we have the habitat and the wider environment.

These are huge variations in scale. However, as we said, size is not what matters. The feature of these levels of organisation that we are focussing on is the ability of each level of organisation to have its own properties – properties that are not specified by any other level. This does not mean, of course, that the different levels do not 'speak' to each other: channels of communication are two-way and multi-channel. They are the channels that enable homeostasis. Figure 10.1 illustrates how, in living systems, causality (shown with arrows) occurs both from the small to the large and from the large to the small.

A clear example given by Noble of a property existing at one level of organisation within an organism is the electrical rhythms of

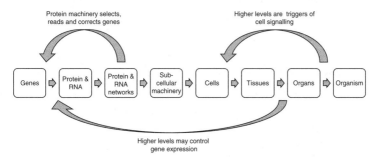

Figure 10.1 Causality in living systems (shown with arrows) occurs both from the small to the large and from the large to the small.

the heart. These rhythms arise from the operation of the Hodgkin cycle – named for Cambridge scientist Alan Hodgkin. To operate, the cycle requires just two protein complexes (a complex is a cluster of different proteins) to be present in a cell membrane (the thin layer that separates the inside and outside of a cell – think of a balloon where a rubber membrane separates helium inside from air outside the balloon). One of the protein complexes is called a sodium channel and the other is a potassium channel. These enable only sodium or only potassium to move in and out of the cell. The sodium and potassium are electrically charged (they are ions) and so when they move across the membrane, an electric current flows. However, each type of ion can only move if the corresponding channel is 'open'. The channel is open or closed depending on the voltage difference between the two sides of the membrane. And this difference is dependent on the difference in concentration of ions on both sides of the membrane. These properties of the proteins lead heart muscle cells to have rhythmic fluctuations in electrical current and in ion concentrations inside each cell. And, the changes in ion concentrations permit muscle molecules to contract and then to relax.

This Hodgkin cycle goes on all by itself. It is not dependent on any DNA sequence except for the purpose of replacing the proteins of the channels that 'wear out' over time. However, this does not mean that the Hodgkin cycle or any other biological process is entirely autonomous. The speed of the cycle can be varied by other levels of the organism: the outside environment for example may increase or decrease the speed. But the rhythm itself – the beat – goes on. It is better to think of biological processes as being 'relatively autonomous' – able to perform a particular task, using opportunistically whatever tools are available to get the job done but able to achieve robustness. In some cases, this robustness can be achieved through redundancy – through having more than one system that can undertake a particular process (rather like the way we carry a spare tyre in the car).

Another level of organisation with its own 'rules' exists for social animals (including us humans). By forming groups, the animal can reduce the risks of predation (consider flocks of starlings at risk from hawks or a shoal of sardines at risk from sharks) or can improve food security (consider colonies of termites and ants with their fungus gardens) or can improve mating prospects (consider the swarms of male and female mayflies that all take their sexually mature form simultaneously).

The success of the animal group hangs on most of the individuals following the same rules of social behaviour: the starling that fails to follow its neighbours in flight is more likely to be killed. Sticking to the rules is often aided by communication, whether it is vocal (the twittering of starlings) or chemical (the pheromones of ants). The same purposes – safety, food, reproduction – can be seen in humans forming groups. However, our capability of communication is far superior and has enabled us to choose to form many types of groups as long as we have successfully communicated it to others. The purposes of such groups include all the purposes that animal groups have, like safety, food or reproduction, plus any other purpose. This superior communication capability comes with at least one inherent problem: we may collectively set purposes whose risks to the group outweigh benefits to the group. However, setting the purpose of improving population health surely has greater benefits than risks. In conclusion, the theory of biological relativity implies that human social organisation is part and parcel of the other levels of organisation seen in our species – from atoms upwards. Social development may appear to sit outside the rules of biology, but that is mere human vanity.

Omics

So far in this discussion we have used the phrase 'levels of organisation'. We agree with Noble that this phrase is not fully satisfactory:

it suggests there is some kind of hierarchy with different levels of organisation having differing importance. This suggestion contradicts the idea of biological relativity. We would substitute the phrase 'domains of organisation'. We would also note that the specification of levels or domains is a heuristic device: it allows us to begin to understand the functioning of what is, in reality, an integrated system whose components do not respect the boundaries implied by the use of words such as levels or domains.

The biological research community is, today, trying to escape from hierarchical thinking. For example, a word has been coined by geneticists to reflect their growing recognition that DNA is more than a simple string of genes. The word coined was 'genomics': the study of the genome, of the entire sequence of all chromosomes, of the variations in the sequence and of the chromosome as a whole. 'Genome' is a compound of 'gene' plus a contraction of the word 'chromosome'. The word was coined when new technologies meant that we were able for the first time to study everything at the same time, as it were. DNA was no longer analogous to coding as in a computer program. A new narrative emerged where DNA had become a complex object that could be used and modified by the cell in different ways in different environments.

This way of thinking caught on rapidly and researchers started adding the suffix of '-omics' onto virtually any biological topic of interest. Over 140 usages have been coined including a couple of academic jokes (for example, unknomics was said to be the study of all that is unknown).

'Omics' implies not only a methodological approach but also a conceptual one, where the basic concept is that biology – or life – is non-hierarchical. Some uses of the suffix 'omics' are more hierarchical than others. For example 'genomics' restricts its vision to DNA and the molecules with which DNA directly interacts. A less hierarchical coinage comes from the network theorist Albert-László Barabási. He coined the word 'diseasome' to describe the totality of diseases and how they arise. His model for this diseasome comprises three 'networks'. Each network comprises a 'level': levels of interacting molecules, of interacting disease, and of interacting people.[9] A fourth 'environmental network' has also been proposed.[10] Barabási argues that human diseases are not separate from each other: they are associated with one another in a 'disease network'. But that network is associated with a social network that confers risk of disease and a network of molecules whose activities are modified by the other networks. However, there is a problem. Barabási's three networks coincide with different broad methods of analysis. This is probably not just a coincidence: the same coincidence exists for most of Noble's levels of organisation. Are we, perhaps, confusing a level of organisation in the real world with the type of tools we use to examine each bit of that world? Biological relativity says our living planet is one whole integrated system. But to understand it, we are forced to use a range of tools so that we can describe it one slice at a time. We are driven to experiment by use of the reductionist method. The slice under examination we may then call a 'network' or a 'level' or 'domain'. But, as we have already suggested, we are doing this for heuristic purposes, to help us get a handle on the problem. The living planet is an integrated whole and one could say that each network or level of organisation is actually a slice of what we might – for heuristic purposes of course – call 'planetomics'.

Do we humans break the rules?

The theory of biological relativity applies to all species. In every case, the individual member of the species, like the species as whole, has no level of organisation that takes precedence over any other. This means we shall not be able to explain or modify a phenomenon using evidence from just one level. This restriction applies just as much to humans.

We may think we can modify biological processes by acting on just one level of organisation. Occasionally we are right, as with vaccinations where one injection may provide lifelong protection against an infection by us tweaking one system in our bodies – the immune system. But our efforts to modify biological processes involving many levels of organisation – like weight gain – are far more problematic when we only modify one of them. Take the diets that people use. These go from A to Z – from the Alkaline Diet (avoid foods deemed acidic[11]) to the Zone Diet (get in the zone with your athletic performance[12]). Wikipedia lists 84 of them. A current fad is the Palaeolithic diet. It has been claimed to be 'scientifically proven', but the National Health Service was distinctly unimpressed by the science.[13] It summed up the problem: 'The cavemen had no car.' In other words, a healthy weight is not simply the product of a healthy diet. In Palaeolithic times, diet was inseparable from physical activity – we had to gather our vegetables and hunt our meat. And we staved off hunger by sharing. These two levels within social organisation – work and food – have, in modern societies, become largely separated from each other and from other aspects of social organisation.

Perhaps we should not worry too much about this or that diet. The ability of our bodies to maintain their homeostasis allows us to cope with the excesses of most food fads. But when the social impact of a fad is part and parcel of the problem of the modern plagues, we cannot let it pass.

11

Natural prevention

In 1859, Charles Darwin published *On the Origin of Species by Means of Natural Selection, Or the Preservation of Favoured Races in the Struggle for Life.* His ideas about evolution make the book fundamental to understanding the living world including human society and they underpin the theory of biological relativity that we have just discussed.

The book is best-known by a shortened title – *The Origin of Species.* However, we want to draw attention here to the words 'preservation' and 'natural selection' in the full title because they are closely allied to the notion of 'natural prevention' that we now explain.

His terms 'preservation' and 'natural selection' are effectively synonymous. He writes: 'This preservation of favourable variations and the rejection of injurious variations, I call Natural Selection'.[1] He prefers the latter term because 'selecting' implies simultaneously preserving one variant and rejecting others. Moreover it brings to mind breeders like Darwin himself (he bred pigeons) who select a particular individual with traits deemed to be valuable for preservation (for propagation) while they reject other individuals.

Darwin explains the 'struggle for life' as the key process that explains how a new species arises from existing individuals:

Any variation, however, slight and from whatever cause proceeding, if it be in any degree profitable to an individual of any species, in its infinitely complex relations to other organic beings and to external nature, will tend to the preservation of that individual, and will

139

generally be inherited by its offspring. The offspring, also, will thus have a better chance of surviving, for, of the many individuals of any species which are periodically born, but a small number can survive.

Darwin's concept of 'struggle' is not so much the titanic clash visualised by Hollywood between two fierce beasts red in tooth and claw, but rather one individual's 'infinitely complex relations' with other species – be they animals, plants, bacteria, moulds or viruses – as well as with the natural environment as a whole. He specifically includes in this idea of struggle the 'dependence of one being on another', citing as an example mistletoe's dependence on the apple tree. This plant grows on the boughs of trees such as the apple, taking some of its nutrition from the tree's sap.

For us 'natural prevention' comprises the biological (including behavioural) processes in all species that prevent an individual and its progeny from succumbing to any disease or condition, and so give it a better chance of surviving. The biological processes are the processes of Darwinian selection that preserve 'favoured races' i.e. that enable the birth of progeny that will succumb less frequently to a given disease or condition. This requires progeny to have had transmitted to them traits that favour the maintenance of homeostasis when the disease or condition would otherwise have disrupted homeostasis.

We now give a few illustrations of the ways in which natural prevention works. These ways surely arose from the processes of natural selection and we suspect that 'natural prevention' is merely another way of expressing the idea of natural selection. However, when it comes to our own species this correspondence between prevention and selection is less immediately apparent, as we shall show.

Bacteria

Bacteria prevent successful infection by a virus (called a phage) in two steps. First, the bacterium uses proteins called modification enzymes to modify its own DNA with epigenetic signatures, as we mentioned previously. Then it uses other proteins called nucleases, which digest any DNA that lacks the epigenetic signatures. So when a virus attaches to the cell and squirts into the cell its own DNA which lacks any epigenetic signature, that DNA is immediately digested by the nucleases. This then stops the phage in its tracks: its DNA has been digested and destroyed. The bacterium is thus able to prevent a lethal infection. This prevention method arose through natural selection.

Plants

Plants have four basic ways to prevent harmful effects from pathogens (viruses, bacteria and moulds):

Physical protection. Leaves and individual cells may be covered in waxy materials that bar the entry of pathogens.

Chemical protection. Soap-like chemicals may coat the plant and these can kill some pathogens.

Localised active protection. A leaf cell detects a pathogen and mounts a defence by releasing certain proteins that destroy the pathogen. If this fails, then the cell is sometimes able to tell its neighbours to commit suicide so as to deny the pathogen the 'food' of living cells that it needs.[2]

Plant-wide active protection. Here an infected leaf releases chemicals that diffuse to uninfected leaves where they signal those leaves to start preparing localised protection.

Animals

Animals share with plants the use of physical and chemical protection methods. Think of the hide of a rhinoceros or the poisons exuded by some frogs. We tend to think of these in the context of preventing a predator from killing the animal, but this too is a form of prevention where the aim is to reduce risks to life from the animal's exposome (see Chapter 7).

In some species, natural prevention has occasionally taken the form of self-medication.[3] Fruit flies preferentially lay their eggs in high-ethanol food to reduce the risk to the progeny of infection by parasitic wasps. Wood ants incorporate into their nests antimicrobial resins from conifer trees so as to prevent microbial growth that would harm individual ants and the colony as a whole. Monarch butterflies infected with a parasite preferentially lay their eggs on anti-parasitic milkweed to reduce the risks to progeny of high levels of parasite growth. Chimpanzees, bonobos and gorillas swallow leaves that help to wash out (to purge) intestinal parasites and may choose to eat leaves with anti-parasitic properties. One study suggests that house sparrows and finches add high-nicotine cigarette butts to their nests to reduce mite infestations. If this suggestion is correct, then clearly natural prevention can sometimes work very quickly. To be certain that these are all prevention behaviours, scientists have to demonstrate that the behaviour increases fitness. The mechanism of transmission of the behaviour between generations may be genetic, epigenetic or learned.

As in plants, many animals also have active protection systems. Among the higher animals these systems constitute the 'immune system' that has developed over the last 500m years. Immunologists make a distinction between 'innate' and 'adaptive' immune responses. The innate immune response comprises a range of highly effective biological processes that are directed with more or less equal intensity at virtually any bacteria, viruses, fungi or parasites that enter the animal's body. Adaptive immunity is both more subtle and more deadly in defeating the invader.

The distinction between the two immune responses is a bit like two different ways of defending a castle in medieval times. Innate immunity would correspond to pouring boiling oil off the ramparts in the hope of scalding the enemy. Adaptive immunity would correspond to a sniper with a crossbow who can take out the king, his knights and their horses.

Adaptive immunity is the prevention mechanism that is elicited when we are infected with, say, the measles virus. The mechanism is only activated when the virus has got past any physical protection systems and has entered the body. The mechanism is directed just at that virus. The first time the measles virus enters the body it can take a week or more for the mechanism to become effective at killing the virus, but on the second occasion, the mechanism is often able quickly to remember what it did on the first time and so launch a rapid attack on the virus.

It is worth pointing out that there may be some advantage in social animals having an immune system which is occasionally slow to overpower an infection, which may fail to prevent some illness. The advantage is a reduction in the risk of cross-infection and of predation of uninfected animals. For example, if in a herd of wildebeest, one of them becomes infected, its immune system will respond and this in turn will cause the animal to feel 'under the weather'. It will lag behind the herd: it will be isolated. This confers an advantage on the herd since it is less likely to be cross-infected by the sick wildebeest. Moreover, the isolated animal cannot escape predating lions. And, by the time the lions have devoured the carcase, the herd is far away and safe. Feeling under the weather when carrying an infection may not be something that natural prevention selects positively, but nature is blind to the mechanisms of a species' survival: all that counts is the result.

Humans

Humans use the same methods as other animals for prevention of disease. There is no evidence to suggest that human innate or adaptive immunity is much better or worse than that of our fellow great apes. What is different is the human ability to modify our exposome. Perhaps human migrations to different environments or perhaps the discovery of clothing or of fire were the first expressions of that ability. Gorillas have modified their exposome by colonising both the low and the high lands of the Congo basin, while humans have modified theirs by colonising every continent. The highland gorillas avoided exposure with thicker hair than their lowland counterparts while humans discovered clothing and fire in order to avoid exposure.

No wonder we think we are smart. But we are not infallible. We have created new risks to our health precisely because we are smart. Take the problem of nutrition. We evolved alongside our primate cousins so that we could cope with poor nutrition, at least for a time. But, then we jumped ahead so fast that natural selection – natural prevention – could not possibly keep up: we discovered that agriculture could provide a surplus of food. That surplus meant, on the one hand, that trade was possible and, on the other, that we might eat too much and so create one of the risks of the modern plagues.

Natural prevention in this situation should have weeded out individuals more prone to obesity and its consequences. But there just hasn't been time for this process to work: it is slow compared with our human ability to achieve change. Perhaps this 'weeding out' is at work here and now: overweight and obesity are known to be associated with reduced fertility. Therefore, obese people who also have a transmissible predisposition to obesity may have a reduced ability to transmit this trait.

In other situations, natural prevention has worked for humans as they changed their exposome through adopting pastoralism (keeping cattle). Exploiting every possible food source is an important driver of natural selection. In birds, it explains, for example, the variety among the beaks of finches that Darwin observed in the Galapagos Islands.[4] There were beaks best for big nuts and beaks best for small nuts. Among humans, the advent of pastoralism created a new lifelong food source: cows' milk. But only a minority of people were able fully to exploit this new food. Those who couldn't were at greater risk of under-nutrition.

All babies can easily digest their mothers' milk because they make an enzyme that digests a type of sugar called 'lactose'. This same sugar is present in cow's milk. But when babies are weaned, they stop making the enzyme, they can't digest milk any longer and they get cramps, bloating, diarrhoea and flatulence.

Infants who carried on making the enzyme would be at an advantage because they would benefit from drinking cow's milk. Such individuals existed in small numbers in all human populations. They had inherited from their parents genetic or epigenetic variants[5] for lifelong enzyme production and they could pass on this trait to their progeny. These individuals thrived so that, in modern populations with pastoral ancestors, their descendants with the trait persisted while those without the trait were rejected by natural selection. Thus natural prevention has been at work over a remarkably short time – 10,000 years or so – to reduce the risks of under-nutrition in populations where cows' milk had become readily available.

A similar story may explain variation between human populations in the amount of amylase they can make. Amylase is an enzyme that breaks down starchy food and it has been found that populations with a high starch diet like the Japanese have on average 6.5 copies of the amylase gene, while populations with a low starch diet like the Yakut of Siberia have about five copies.[6] If we assume that more amylase is made in people with more copies of the gene, then it is conceivable that natural selection underlies population variation in copy number. Natural selection might work by parents with a higher copy number raising more children more successfully because they have better access to the energy in the starch. However, this observation of a difference between Japanese and Yakut people could simply reflect random clustering of higher or lower numbers of copies in the different groups.

There is some evidence that populations in different parts of the world have different average levels of risk of heart disease and diabetes. These differences have been correlated with different frequencies of genetic variants between those populations. This has led some to hypothesise that populations at higher risk of heart disease or diabetes have genes that are better adapted to ways of life preceding our contemporary one with its sugary diet and low levels of physical activity.

It just so happens that the populations allegedly better adapted to past ways of life are people of colour. This is therefore an inflammatory hypothesis that cannot be proved one way or the other. It is intrinsically unlikely to be true because our contemporary obesogenic way of life is new to all humans, a way of life that is only a few decades old. None of us have had enough time to benefit from the comparatively slow processes of natural prevention which might preserve traits that confer resistance to the modern plagues. Or to re-state this, the other way round, virtually all of us are adapted to former ways of life perhaps as hunter-gatherers, perhaps as pastoralists. It is hard to say. All we know for sure is that the invisible processes of natural prevention – that is, of natural selection – are at work on us all right now.

Systems Prevention

If humans were the same as all other species, then there would be no alternative to doing nothing about the modern plagues. We would all have to sit it out and wait for natural prevention to take its course (as it has done in broadening our diets). Medicine would fare little better: to combat gut parasites we should have to wait until natural prevention had taken its course and we had perhaps learnt the same purging behaviour as seen in the great apes.

However, humans have acquired two unique traits: a capability for advanced communication and the advanced consciousness that rests on this capability. Because we are also a social species, these traits confer on us substantial collective survival capabilities that are manifested in our forms of social organisation, our ideas, reasoning, cultures, arts, technologies and sciences. Overwhelmingly, our purpose is (or we believe it is) to improve our lives. This inevitably puts our health at the heart of our activities, either explicitly or implicitly. Indeed, in some way or other, what drove the emergence in Africa of our capabilities for advanced communication and consciousness was the struggle of our ancestors for health and life and against their opposites.

Our crucial advantage over other species has been our increasing potential to short-circuit natural prevention. We use our powers of reasoning to plan how to improve our lives and in so doing, we transcend natural prevention. Securing our food supply via agriculture to prevent under-nutrition is an early and clear example of transcending natural prevention.

Short-circuiting natural prevention can help satisfy human needs. But it has a different, darker aspect. It could, after all, be taken to mean practising eugenics. This is the conscious selection by some social actor, like the government, of some individuals as being suitable parents and the rejection of other individuals as unsuitable. Eugenics is beyond our scope, but let us be clear that short-circuiting natural prevention does not mean practising eugenics. This is because eugenics would not be successful in ending the modern plagues (as well as being objectionable). There are three reasons. First, eugenics can only reduce simple genetic risk (e.g. arising from a single gene variant), while the genetic risks of the modern plagues are complex (involving hundreds or thousands of genetic variants). Second, only a small fraction of the total risk of each of the modern plagues can be attributed to genes, so that even if miraculously all of the genetic risk were removed, the overall risk would still be high and the modern plagues would go on. Thirdly, prevention by eugenics – or any other method – of today's common long-term conditions would be a matter of delaying the inevitable: some other long-term condition will get every one of us eventually.

Saying humans have the ability to 'short-circuit natural prevention' is not fully accurate. Natural selection has conferred on humans advanced communication skills and consciousness. It is these attributes that facilitate consciously made natural prevention. We may call such prevention 'man-made' rather than 'natural' but this is mere conceit since we are still children of nature. The attempts that are made by societies today at improving population health are labelled simply as 'prevention' – without the word 'man-made'. This reflects the generally haphazard efforts that societies have made. People have not ruminated together to list systematically what all the needs are for human health in the context of our total environment and then planned how to meet those needs optimally and systematically. Societies have engaged in crisis management and have obtained mixed results. We can surely do better than this: society needs a systematic approach to prevention and we suggest it be called 'Systems Prevention'.

We use this term because it brings to mind 'systems biology' – the term used by researchers today to emphasise the interconnectedness of all biological systems with each other and their total environment. This idea of inter-connectedness also underlies the terms biological relativity, natural selection, the exposome, homeostasis and, of course, Systems Prevention. Each term focusses on different aspects of this inter-connectedness. While natural selection focusses on long-term change over the generations, homeostasis focusses on transient change within the lifespan. The exposome focusses on the totality of risks to the maintenance of a given condition of homeostasis. Systems Prevention focusses on the mitigation of those risks to the individual human and to the human population. Biological relativity asserts inter-connectedness and explicitly rejects the error of reductionism while emphasising the power of the reductionist method.

The distinction between natural prevention and Systems Prevention is not simply the difference between unconscious and conscious activities. It is also the distinction between fortuitous outcomes and the evidence-based, rationally planned outcomes that can arise in a species such as ours with advanced communications and consciousness.

A brief history of Systems Prevention

The first public health messages

The emergence of the hunter-gatherer way of life during the Palaeolithic era saw a change in our species' way of living. Using fixed permanent dwelling places like caves and providing the group with food by dividing up the work between hunters and gatherers helped meet two needs that are vital for health: better shelter and more reliable food supplies. This new way of life was probably accompanied with a rising level of consciousness as evidenced by symbolic representation in carvings, ornaments and cave art. We can see in Figure 11.1 how a group of hunter figures are cooperating to kill deer.

The painting displays a society in which people (probably men) cooperated in shooting arrows at deer. So much is clear. It implies a way of life with consciousness (the painting), innovation (bows and arrows) and cooperation (four human figures working together). These features surely contributed to the improved survival of the group through better nutrition. But we can only surmise that this outcome was pre-planned rather than fortuitous. Improved hunting also provided more pelts and hides for clothing and again we cannot be certain that this outcome was pre-planned. It seems unlikely that there was no pre-planning: someone had clearly invented bows and arrows and disseminated the technology and someone had recognised they could get more food and clothing with less danger by working together.

Whether in Europe, Africa, Asia or Australia, cave art is often interpreted as the work of pre-historic hippies exploring

Figure 11.1 This mural from the Barranco de Valltorta Horse Cave (Castellón, Spain) shows men hunting deer around 10,000–9,000 BCE. The painting has a public health message: men have to cooperate to satisfy the vital need for nutrition.

the subconscious. However, a plausible explanation is that some of the representations are prehistoric propaganda transmitting public health messages to ensure that work was done to satisfy the prerequisites of health. So, cave art may be an early step toward transcending natural prevention.

The first inklings of Systems Prevention

With the invention of agricultural society ten thousand years ago, towns and cities became feasible. But their high population densities increased the risk of infectious plagues. The most common were what we now call cholera (where *Vibrio cholera* bacteria spread via human faeces in water or food), typhoid (where *Salmonella typhi* bacteria spread in much the same way) and bubonic plague (where *Yersinia pestis* bacteria enter the body from fleas borne by rats).

The word 'plague' comes from the Latin 'plangere' meaning to lament or wail: that is all the ancients could do when a plague struck. The only ways to reduce the risk of infection were to escape the city or pray to the gods. But the new towns and cities also developed somewhat better methods of prevention and sometimes this was conscious. The Old Testament, for example, tells us that anyone with leprosy remains unclean as long as they have the disease and that they must live outside the camp away from others [1, Lev. 13.46]. Moreover a duty is prescribed to expel from camp everyone with a dreaded skin disease or bodily discharge [1, Num. 5.2]. This was conscious prevention.

Archaeologists have found structures like gutters and drains in ancient cities of the Indus Valley, Egypt, Crete, Incas, China, Greece and Rome. The organisation of water management was quite sophisticated: public officials in Athens and Rome were charged with supervising management, though the poorer parts of town were usually overlooked. While water management reduced the risk of some diseases spreading, what may have largely been on the mind of the city fathers was pride in their city and wanting to combat the smell and taste of 'bad water'. They were doing the right thing for the wrong reason. Improving population health was a haphazard affair.

Democratic Athens was an exception. While most still sought health via the gods (Hygieia, Asklepius and half a dozen others),

Hippocrates (460–370 BCE) developed a new theory of disease that insisted on natural causation and explicitly excluded divine intervention. When discussing epilepsy, he wrote:

> I am about to discuss the disease called 'sacred'. It is not, in my opinion, any more divine or more sacred than other diseases, but has a natural cause. Its supposed divine origin is due to men's inexperience and to their wonder at its peculiar character.[7]

He thought that the new towns in Sicily that Athenians were constructing should be located for health reasons away from malodorous swampy ground where the air was a source of a disease-conducive 'miasma' (bad air).[8] Again, the right thing was done for the wrong reason: prevention was haphazard.

In the later years of republican Rome, Cicero had a brilliant insight. His book, *On the Laws*, makes a brief comment on 'salus', the Latin word for health or welfare, good, salvation or felicity. He wrote: 'Salus populi suprema lex esto' which is usually translated as 'the health of the people should be the supreme law'. Cicero is a whisker away from proclaiming the supreme importance of Systems Prevention, as we shall see in Part IV.

12

Health is what we need

Up till now we have avoided the basic question of what 'health' actually means. In Chapter 1 we criticised the conventional idea that health is the absence of disease – because it is not a positive definition. It tells us what we don't want – not what we do want. The inclusion of 'well-being' in the World Health Organization's definition of health, while well-intentioned, still leaves us with a negative since 'well-being' so easily reverts to meaning the absence of its opposite. However, the 1986 Ottawa Charter specifies 'peace, shelter, education, food, income, a stable eco-system, sustainable resources, social justice, and equity' as being 'prerequisites' and the 'fundamental conditions and resources' for health. This is certainly positive, but it is just a list. It lacks structure and systematisation. It is more like a slogan than a coherent narrative. However, it does introduce the idea that health has to be defined by its preconditions in much the same way as homeostasis is defined by the dynamic equilibrium of processes that interact.

We believe that the simplest positive definition of health is the title of this chapter: health is what we need. This has two meanings, of course. First, it means that our species has a requirement to be healthy. This is virtually a slogan that one might hear on a public demonstration demanding reform. But the second meaning has a deeper significance. It is claiming that the state of good health is defined by the state in which we find ourselves – as individuals and

153

as a population – when certain needs have been optimally met. In other words, health is the optimal satisfaction of human needs resulting in the maintenance of homeostasis. Our definition is not inconsistent with recent attempts at a new definition of health 'as the ability to adapt and self-manage'.[1]

But, what precisely are the needs that should be satisfied? Before we come to that, we should first seek to avoid possible misunderstandings. If health is 'the optimal satisfaction of human needs', this of course does not in any way imply any possibility of an eternal human lifespan: we all die even if all our needs are satisfied. Nor does it imply any possibility of an eternal health-span: we all remain susceptible to some injury or infection for which there is no vaccine, or to some long-term condition that ends our years of health. Satisfaction of human needs does not stop health being a transitory phase of our lives. However, it does delay the end of the transition from health to disability. It delays this ending of healthspan by reducing the risk of contracting long-term conditions. Optimal satisfaction of needs is not a 'precondition' for health (as the Ottawa Charter perhaps might put it): it is, rather, the state that enables us to be as healthy as each of us can possibly be. Attaining that state is an unending task for society and the ways of attaining it are a matter for debate and experiment. There is no fixed, eternal recipe because our environment changes, our understanding changes and we change.

Political philosophy of needs

We have borrowed from a political philosopher the definition of health as the state where there is satisfaction of human needs. During our preparations for writing this book, we came across Lawrence Hamilton's *The Political Philosophy of Needs*.[2] He argues for a rehabilitation of the concept of 'human needs' as central to politics and political theory. Others have focussed instead on issues of justice and welfare and, in his view, this has had a deleterious effect on political practice because it has tended to exclude important issues like the satisfaction of human needs, political participation and democratic sovereignty. His view may well be right but there is also, in our view, the evidence which demonstrates that human needs arise from biology. To ignore that evidence is to put our species in peril.

His argument is that human societies exist in order to satisfy human needs better via their various public and private forms of organisation, and that the ever-present challenge for societies is the better alignment of society's organisation with needs. Hamilton identifies three categories of human needs: vital needs, social needs (which he refers to as 'particular social needs') and agency needs. For us, these categories of need each refer back to distinguishable levels of organisation as defined in the theory of biological relativity (see Chapter 10). Unless these categories are all satisfied, we are incapable of 'full human functioning'. He defines vital needs as 'the general ineluctable [i.e. inescapable] needs that are unproblematically associated with individual health'. Hamilton specifies that human needs should be met adequately or sufficiently, but we suggest that a better word is 'optimally'. While 'optimal' has well-characterised parameters for needs like nutrition, for other needs there is no societal or even scientific consensus on how to measure those needs: they are matters of debate and experiment.

Hamilton goes on to specify some general 'inescapable' needs:

- The required daily calorie intake.
- Adequate shelter.
- Sufficient clothing.
- Periodic rest.
- Exercise.
- Social entertainment.

When he says these needs are unproblematic, he means that the evidence for them being vital needs is not in dispute. While we accept this in general, that does not mean we should not specify the needs in greater detail so as to align with what is actually possible in our societies today (see below).

'Social needs' are those felt in everyday experience yet seen to be of private concern. His examples are an efficient train service; a car; and a television. Hamilton's third category comprises 'agency needs'. The word agency has the same root as to act and so 'agency' in this context means the opposite of powerlessness. If what we say or do has no impact on others, we lack power and so we lack agency. The full human functioning that is Hamilton's goal for each of us requires us to have agency. He identifies three aspects of this agency:

- Autonomy (the goal of having greater control over everyday decision-making with a view to our full human functioning).
- Intersubjective recognition (when people have 'respect' for what each does).
- Active and creative expression that leads to a sense of achievement and accomplishment.

This categorisation of needs and the examples in each category are intended as a starting point for debate across society. They are not intended to be eternal truths. They are open to improvement and to adaptation to change. It is instructive to ask: what do we need in order to have this debate? The obvious answer is that we rely on satisfaction of vital needs (how can you debate if you are starving?), of social needs (how can you get to a debate without a bike or bus or train?) and of agency needs (what point is there in debating if your voice is not heard?).

Vital needs

Required daily calorie intake

When it comes to nutrition, we would note that it is not just a matter of getting the right number of calories (as Hamilton suggests). But let us discuss calories first. The required daily calorie intake in order to maintain constant weight is, on average, 2,500 calories for men and 2,000 calories for women. These values can vary depending on age, metabolism and levels of physical activity, among other things.

We have seen how obesity is at epidemic proportions in many countries, but we should not neglect its opposite – thinness. This is defined by a Body Mass Index value beneath the normal range. It is linked to poorer health and reduced life expectancy. Over 5% of UK children are thin. Data from the England National Child Measurement Programme found thinness in 5.2% of girls aged 4–5 and 5.88% of boys. Data from the UK Millennium Cohort Study indicated a prevalence of thinness at 4.59% at age 3, 4.21% at age 5, and 5.84% at age 7. While some are 'naturally' thin,[3] thinness rises with social disadvantage.[4] Social disadvantage was measured from the average deprivation of the neighbourhood where each child lived, from their household income, and from the social class and education of the mother.

Other essential components of our diet include molecules that the human body cannot make itself like vitamins, minerals and certain fats; protein; water (with or without additives) and the much-loved roughage. It's really a very short list, yet we make such a fuss about food and get so much pleasure from seeing it, smelling it, tasting it and eating it – especially when we simultaneously satisfy this need with that for social entertainment.

Adequate shelter

It is all too evident that the absence of adequate shelter – homelessness – is lethal. The NHS reported in 2011 on data showing that homeless people die thirty years younger than the national average.[5] But, Hamilton considers that shelter should be 'adequate'. What does that mean? Adequate shelter in the Stone Age often meant a cave but, today, we can consider using risk as the test of adequacy. The World Health Organization says that inadequate shelter combined with overcrowding increases the risk of transmission of infectious diseases (examples might include acute respiratory infections, meningitis, tuberculosis, typhus, cholera and scabies). Researchers in New Zealand found that the risk of meningitis (a lethal infection) doubled with the addition of two extra adolescents or adults to a house with six rooms overall.[6] Such results can guide public policy. The Public Health Action Support Team in the Department of Health has developed a checklist to help guide risk reduction.[7]

cold	chemicals in the home	hot surfaces and materials
heat	indoor air pollutants	domestic hygiene, pests etc.
falls (accidents)	noise	inadequate provision for food safety
damp and mould	electrical hazards	contaminated water
carbon monoxide	entrapment or collision	inadequate lighting
radon	explosions	poor ergonomics
electromagnetic fields	un-combusted fuel gas	crowding and space
lead paint and pipes	entry by intruders	asbestos and man-made mineral fibres

What was considered adequate in the past may no longer be so. For example, we did not know for a very long time just how dangerous asbestos can be in our homes. Adequacy is generally a matter of evidence, of debate and even of protest. This idea is probably better captured by speaking of 'optimal shelter'.

Sufficient clothing

The risks that arise from insufficient clothing are straightforward: they are simply the likely consequences of getting too cold, too hot or too wet. There is also the risk of poor hygiene if we have no change of clothing or no means of washing and drying clothes. As for the long-term conditions that are the focus of this book, risk of depression and anxiety may well rise if we have insufficient clothing. To the best of our knowledge, this has not been researched.

Periodic rest

Sleep deprivation is a well-known method of torture, but what is the relationship between how long we sleep and our risk of the common long-term conditions? Research indicates a U-shaped relationship between sleep duration and risk of diabetes and some types of heart disease.[8] The diabetes risk was lowest for people sleeping seven or eight hours a night but rose significantly when sleep was either shorter or longer. The implications for public policy are far-reaching. It is not simply a question of people having a bed. To get our sleep, our working hours need to be managed, our transport needs have to be met and our homes need quiet.

Sleep also needs to be at the right time of the day: night work has been shown to increase risk of diabetes and dementia and there is suggestive evidence that the same is true of heart disease and breast cancer.

Periodic rest means more than a good night's sleep: we also need a break during the other sixteen hours of the day. For example, women who work over 45 hours a week have their risk of developing diabetes raised by over 50%.[9]

Exercise

Our way of life has been and continues to be transformed when it comes to physical exercise. Sedentary work is replacing more active types of work, whether paid work in manufacture and distribution or services, or unpaid work in the home. Cars have displaced walking. Yet physical exercise is not recognised as a vital need for all. The National Health Service recommends it but we do not all have guaranteed access to exercise. In some areas of the UK, people over 60 get free access to swimming pools – though, bizarrely, often not to other exercise facilities. This age-based restriction ignores the evidence for England and Wales that diabetes, for example, is diagnosed in more people aged 20–59 (35%) than those aged 60–69 (26%).[10]

The link between exercise and reduction of risk of common long-term conditions is strong. For example, exercise improves the insulin sensitivity of skeletal muscle for up to two days. The loss of this sensitivity is one of the symptoms of diabetes. A large US study found that individuals who exercised had over 40% fewer days of poor mental health than matched individuals who did not exercise. The American College of Cardiology/American Heart Association advises adults with raised blood pressure to have over two hours of moderate to vigorous physical exercise a week so as to reduce risk of cardiovascular disease.

The usual argument against recognising this vital need for exercise is based on money – the cost of provision. There are two counter-arguments to this: first, the cost of doing nothing in terms of lost productivity and increased medical costs; second, our ability now to estimate individual risk thereby allowing priority to be given to higher-risk individuals.

Social entertainment

Solitariness or social isolation is the absence of social entertainment. Think of *The Adventures of Robinson Crusoe* by Daniel Defoe, where

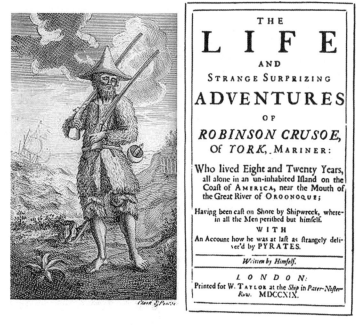

Figure 12.1 Cover page of the first edition of *Robinson Crusoe* by Daniel Defoe. In the book, the eponymous hero and Man Friday discovered a 'singular satisfaction' in not being solitary. Social conversation is a vital need for our species.

Crusoe is shipwrecked on an uninhabited island (Figure 12.1). He eventually linked up with Man Friday and they learnt to communicate. 'Besides the pleasure of talking to him, I had a singular satisfaction in the fellow himself,' Crusoe recounts. Even if he persisted in the fantasy of his own superiority, he was able to meet his vital need – and Man Friday's vital need – for social entertainment.

What is the evidence of damage due to being isolated for a prolonged period? This state is imposed on prisoners in solitary confinement and often results in a mental health crisis. Observers in the US found that:

> The most extreme punitive confinement – super-maximum isolation – most heavily taxes limited coping competence, and

leads, literally, to points of no return … prison cells become filled with prisoners who have withdrawn from painful reality and quietly hallucinate. Their symptoms, their torpor, incoherent mumbling, restless sleep, and waking nightmares are difficult … for casual observers to spot, and non-casual observers are unwelcome in punitive segregation facilities.[11]

Loneliness is similar to solitary confinement but is not quite so extreme. In both younger and older people it has been linked to depression, stress and anxiety.[12] In older people there is also a link to the common long-term conditions of obesity, diabetes and heart disease.

Social needs

Consider the 'man on the Clapham omnibus'. Maybe we can see him as a Victorian in his serge suit with a starched collar and a hat sitting on a bus going from Clapham Common to the City where he earns his keep. He needs that bus and the well-made roads that it goes along. He needs that suit, hat and collar. All those things need to be in good order if he is to put food on the table in his home and pay his bills. This is what is meant by 'social needs': those needs that are preconditions for the satisfaction of our vital needs (like nutrition) and which arise from the reality of social life at one time in one place. He feels those needs in his everyday experience yet most of them are seen to be a private concern.

The same kinds of needs exist today for all his descendants. If those needs are not properly met, then vital needs are imperilled. Whether these social needs are solely a private concern or also a public concern is a matter for society to debate, decide on and act. However, any debate about a need should at least consider the health impact of a decision. Indeed the decision should be considered to be a health decision since health comprises the satisfaction of needs.

Health is what we need

In today's advanced post-industrial society, social needs are changing fast and widening in scope. Just over a decade ago, Hamilton saw televisions as such a need. But already we can see the case for smartphones substituting for TVs or at least becoming a more ubiquitous need. Whether having a smartphone is solely a private concern depends in part on whether owning one is essential for serving a vital need such as finding a job to put food on the table or preventing social isolation. If a smartphone is essential to meeting such vital needs this can, first, be proved with the right research and then society can decide if and how mobile access to the internet should be facilitated for all.

It may be, for example, that the infrastructure which supports smartphones should be what society seeks to guarantee. There is indeed currently a debate around this very question, although the terms of the debate are not related to health. Some types of infrastructure have readily been recognised as both 'health' related (sewers and drains) and a public concern. Enabling transport infrastructure, by contrast, has been a bit of a political football. Yet it is clear, even before the Clapham omnibus came along, that everyone needed to get from A to B to satisfy vital needs. Hence transport policy has always been health policy. With the advent of cars, new risks emerged in the transport infrastructure (e.g. the International Agency for Research on Cancer states that particles from diesel fuel are associated with lung cancer and respiratory diseases,[13] and of course raising carbon dioxide levels is raising global temperatures and the associated disease risks). In New York, there is an annual Fit City Conference where architects, planners, designers, landscape architects, developers, transportation professionals and public health professionals seek to implement the Mayor's 'Active Design Guidelines' explicitly to counter the risks of the common long-term conditions through improved urban design.[14] Whether guidelines will do the trick for those inhabitants, time will tell. If time is at a premium, then something more vigorous may be necessary.

Agency needs

It is not hard to argue that satisfaction of agency needs – autonomy, inter-subjective recognition and creative expression – should contribute to health. The reality and the sense of powerlessness implied by the failure to satisfy agency needs makes people feel of little value to society or to their community. They feel uncared for. This negative self-image then soon leads to negative behaviours whereby people do not take care of themselves in a way that prolongs their healthy years. Getting robust observational evidence for this in populations is hard because there are many factors involved. For example, we have mentioned 'social entertainment' as a vital need and suggested that its opposite is social isolation. Yet social isolation is so close to powerlessness, to the lack of satisfaction of agency needs, that to unravel the two is not a simple matter.

One environment where we may see the effects of deficiencies of needs satisfaction is in prison. Prisoners in the general prison population lack autonomy (though there may be a modicum of inter-subjective recognition and even some creative expression), while prisoners in solitary also lack social entertainment. We have seen already how solitary confinement is associated with torpor, incoherent mumbling, restless sleep and waking nightmares. For the general prison population, the issue is whether their health – particularly as regards the common long-term conditions – is better or worse during or before and after incarceration. Recent research suggests:

> Prisoners globally are characterized by complex and multifaceted health problems. Although imprisonment confers its own unique health risks, health usually improves in custody, where stable accommodation and regular meals are provided at little or no cost, illicit drugs are less readily available, and high-intensity health services are routinely provided. Unfortunately, these health gains are often rapidly lost after return to the community, where many ex-prisoners experience poor health-related outcomes, including

poorly controlled disease, elevated rates of life-threatening drug overdose, preventable hospitalization, and mortality.[15]

Risk of suicide is another measure that may cast light on deficiency in agency needs. We saw in Chapter 3 how a social fragmentation score has been developed based on marital status, single and short-term occupancy and renting. This score predicts risk of suicide. However, it fails to unravel which of the agency needs or vital needs contributes the greatest risk. We are left with an interesting hypothesis from political philosophy that is crying out for research investigation.

The health benefits of creative expression are easier to come by. Arts therapy (drawing, dance, drama and music) is known to promote 'well-being'. It is also useful in helping cancer patients with anxiety, people with dementia, ex-military with post-traumatic stress syndrome and others with a deficit in mental health. But are these benefits solely due to being creative? Are other needs not being simultaneously satisfied to some degree: exercise, social entertainment, autonomy and inter-subjective recognition?

Figure 12.2 Optimal satisfaction of human needs for health. The diagram summarises the idea that the state of being healthy exists when three types of need are all satisfied – simultaneously and optimally. Such satisfaction minimises the modifiable risk factors for the common long-term conditions.

Closing comments

Hamilton's ideas provide a coherent set of ideas with which to define health, to improve the health of the population, and to end the modern plagues of diabetes, depression, heart disease and cancer. Importantly they improve the terms of debate by prioritising policy change over legalistic approaches. By this we mean that the tendency to declare that health is a human right leads ultimately, if implemented, to arguments in court between lawyers, whereas health as the satisfaction of human needs leads to continuous research and reform. While the law is one tool in the toolkit for tackling the modern plagues, it is by no means the only one. Workers in the biological sciences and the social sciences know there is an urgent job to be done. It requires commitment by society to do this as we shall show – not just commitment from lawyers or legislators.

Figure 12.3 Community activist and self-styled 'gangsta gardener' Ron Finley is helping improve healthspan in his Los Angeles neighbourhood by working with others to grow fresh vegetables on the sidewalk. His aim is to end the 'food desert' that has been permitted to develop there.

Above, we characterised Hamilton's needs as running parallel to the levels of organisation of biological systems that the theory of biological relativity perceives. However, there is an additional important parallel. Hamilton's needs also correspond to the modifiable risk factors that we described in Chapter 9 for conditions like the modern plagues. This is obvious when it comes to the needs for appropriate nutrition and exercise. It is eye-opening when it comes to the other vital, social and agency needs. Similarly, there is a correspondence between these human needs and the idea of the exposome that we introduced in Chapter 7. If epidemiologists talk of the exposome as the blanket term for sources of risk to health, then when philosophers discuss the satisfaction of human needs they are, at least in part, referring to the minimisation of those risks.

Finally let us deal briefly with the counter-argument, which runs as follows: 'I know better than anyone what my needs are. I don't want anyone to tell me what they are. I can look after myself'. This blunt opinion is perhaps dealt with best through a blunt answer. The words of South Central Los Angeles community activist Ron Finley, known as the 'gangsta gardener', serve this purpose. He said recently: 'Health is your environment – all of it'.[16] His insight is based on his actions in seeking to improve the lives of one of the most deprived communities in the US.

Part IV

We live in a time of plague – of the modern plagues of diabetes, depression, heart disease and cancer. Current approaches to tackling these plagues are inadequate. There is a need to go back to basics. Part III brought us to the conclusion that society should implement 'Systems Prevention'. In this final section, we turn this concept into a plan for action to put society onto the road to recovery. It involves testing and constructing the 'Health Society'.

13

Thinking outside the box

We have seen that the modern plagues are introducing rising systemic risks to society. We provided evidence that public policy has failed to halt and reverse those plagues and failed to address the risks. These failures arise fundamentally from a general lack of awareness and acceptance of inter-relatedness in human society – as in biology – and from an absence of recognition that health is the condition where there is optimal satisfaction of human needs. To correct the failings and solve these problems, society needs to transform public policy. Why do we say that public policy should be transformed? Surely it is health policy that is the problem? To answer this, let us explore what is meant by 'public policy'.

Public policy and its transformation

Public policy entails considering and using one or more of a long list of policy instruments. Among these instruments we can mention: public expenditure; economic penalties; economic incentives; linking government-controlled benefits to behaviour; formal regulations and legislation to control behaviour; voluntary regulations between governments and non-state actors (public policy thinkers use the word 'actor' to refer to individuals who have or seek some measure of power in a society and who engage in activities that can influence policies and outcomes); linking public service provision to behaviour; legal penalties; public education and advertising to highlight risks in behaviour; providing services and resources to help change behaviour; providing resources to tackle illegal behaviour; funding organisation to influence attitudes; funding scientific research and advisory committees; organisational change; providing services directly or via non-governmental organisations; providing a single service; or setting up new markets in goods and services.[1]

The principle underlying public policy is easier to identify in states with a written constitution or similar document. The preamble of the US Declaration of Independence proclaims the idea that 'All men are created equal, that they are endowed by their Creator with certain unalienable Rights, that among these are Life, Liberty and the pursuit of Happiness.' The preamble of the French Constitution lists some principles for public policy including, for example: 'The Nation shall guarantee to all, and particularly to the child, the mother, and the aged worker, protection of health, material security, rest, and leisure.'

By contrast, states like the UK without a written constitution appear to have no settled point of departure for national policy. However, appearances can deceive: an unwritten constitution leaves plenty of room for unspoken – and therefore uncontested – assumptions and lines of reasoning. That is the case in the UK where policymakers so easily and unthinkingly fall back on dimly remembered aphorisms in dimly remembered languages. In particular, policymakers may cite Marcus Cicero (106–43 BCE) as providing a purpose or a paradigm for public policy as a whole. Cicero proposed a constitution for the Roman Republic to enable the administration of public policy. He asserted: '*Salus populi suprema lex*'. We may translate this as: 'The health of the people comes first'. However, the first two words – *salus populi* – have also been translated as the welfare or well-being or security of the people or as simply 'the public good'. If translated literally, the words *suprema lex* mean 'supreme law', but Cicero intended this to refer to a higher level of laws than those made by mere mortals.

The aphorism has been cited approvingly by well-known political and moral philosophers through the ages. Discussing the nature of government, English Enlightenment philosopher John Locke (1632–1704) wrote that the aphorism 'is certainly so just and fundamental a rule that he who seriously follows it cannot dangerously err'.[2] Hobbes (1588–1679) in *Leviathan* and Spinoza (1632–77) in *Tractatus Theologico-Politicus* also approved of Cicero's aphorism. In the UK, *Salus populi suprema lex* is the motto of Lewisham, Eastleigh, Harrow, Lytham St Anne's, Tipton, Mid-Sussex, West Lancashire, and the City of Salford and its boroughs.

For Locke, Cicero's prioritisation of health is a 'fundamental rule'. Despite this importance, the rule is today rarely discussed. The fundamental rule is taken by policymakers as read. Such complacency is now unacceptable. The rule needs amending and updating by specifying a positive definition of health as optimal satisfaction of needs and by explicitly asserting that achieving this kind of health is the purpose of public policy as a whole. In other words, a twenty-first century paradigm to underpin public policy should state: 'Optimal satisfaction of the human needs that define health is the supreme purpose of public policy.'

The World Health Organization in Europe has moved in this direction. It wants to see health as a responsibility for the whole of government and for the whole of society.[3] This position has been endorsed by the Local Government Association in the UK.[4] This is close to the words we use about 'the supreme purpose of public policy'. However, we insist that health needs an explicit, positive, evidence-based definition as optimal satisfaction of human needs. Without that, there is no explicit guide to action by all actors (as defined above) across a given society: there is likely only to be crisis management.

More profoundly, we would argue that health-as-needs is already what public policy is actually about but none of us have recognised it yet. Public policy has always attempted to satisfy the needs that constitute health but, because no-one knows this, the attempts are confused and partial while the results are contradictory and partial. To put it another way, what we call Systems Prevention comes to human societies along with our advanced communication skills and consciousness. But those societies do it very badly while they remain unaware of the fact that they are doing it. This is a bit like a game of football where no-one knows any of the rules. Occasionally a ball may go into one or other net. It's a goal but not as we know it. As a consequence, the game seems pointless to players, referees and spectators. In this analogy, the rules of football are our human vital needs, social needs and agency needs. 'Health as needs' is everything that we do as a species. By contrast 'health as the absence of disease' means that the totality of our needs as humans is banished to philosophical debate or theorising. 'Health as needs' is the same thing as 'public policy' – health is the heart of public policy. But we just don't know it yet. We need to step outside the box.

Let us look inside the box at Britain's institutional framework for prevention of disease. We'll examine Public Health England, the Health and Safety Executive and the National Health Service Health Check system. Bear in mind that other institutions and organisations, public and private, cater knowingly or unknowingly for health as satisfaction of needs.

Public Health England

The lead organisation in England for the protection and improvement of public health is not the government as such. The mission 'to protect and improve the nation's health and to address inequalities' has been handed over to an 'executive agency' – Public Health England. While the money is allocated by the Treasury (the finance ministry), management of the money and of the staff is said to be independent of government. Many governmental departments have one or more such executive agencies. The Department of Health and Social Care has two: one for public health and one to regulate medicines and healthcare products.

Critics of this way of organising things say that it leads to loss of accountability to Parliament. This is certainly a weighty objection. Supporters assert that executive agencies increase 'efficiency'. For Public Health England, however, the test of efficiency cannot be solely a financial measure. The test is also whether the mission is being accomplished. Has the population been protected from the modern plagues? Has there been any improvement? Have inequalities in health been reduced? Because the evidence says not, it is then easy to scapegoat Public Health England and harder to pin blame on the government that out-sourced the mission to the agency.

This executive agency has three main activities: health protection; health improvement; knowledge and information. Protection is aimed at infectious disease and hazards like chemicals. Improvement involves public education, the screening programmes, and reducing health inequality. Knowledge and information refers essentially to observing, as well as possible, the health of the country plus associated research. So, in relation to the plagues of our times, we can see that the agency observes their progress broadly and educates the public to a degree. These are both valid and necessary activities. But the question is whether that is enough to accomplish the mission.

Perhaps the most successful of the agency's activities is the programme for screening the population for diseases. In addition to screening all babies for a variety of conditions, the UK National Screening Committee is responsible for programmes in early detection (or very high risk) of aortic aneurysms (a potentially lethal bulge in a big artery coming from the heart), bowel cancer; breast cancer; cervical cancer and blindness due to Type 1 diabetes. However, early detection of disease is absolutely not the same thing as prevention in good time.

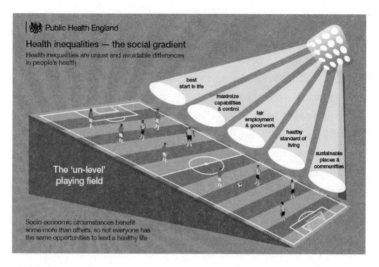

Figure 13.1 Diagram from Public Health England illustrating a 'social gradient' causing health inequalities as an 'un-level' playing field. The floodlights identify vital, social and agency needs that, if optimally satisfied for all, would level up the playing field.

Smoking cessation has been a partial success story. Education by Public Health England and charities, alongside lobbying of government for regulation, has reduced smoking prevalence as we described previously. The agency is also responsible for tackling health inequalities. As Figure 13.1 shows, it has made a fist of defining the problem.[5]

Health and Safety Executive

The Health and Safety Executive is an 'executive non-departmental public body' of the Department of Work and Pensions. This is much the same as an executive agency except that it is overseen by a committee, rather than a minister. But, unsurprisingly, the minister appoints the committee in the first place.

The Health and Safety Executive's mission is to encourage, regulate and enforce workplace health, safety and welfare, and to research the risks in the workplaces of England, Scotland and Wales. It has been the object of noisy criticism. For example, before winning a General Election, David Cameron, as Leader of the Opposition, claimed that the executive had demanded that children wear goggles to play at conkers.[6] This is a popular game where one child holds a chestnut, or 'conker', while the other tries to break it with their own. The truth was that a well-meaning head teacher had decided children should wear safety goggles to play conkers. Subsequently, some schools appear to have banned conkers on 'health and safety' grounds or made children wear goggles. This was not a case of 'Health and Safety gone mad' but of politicians, media and a handful of teachers losing the plot.

Its evidence-based regulations cover workplaces in thirty-two employment sectors, from air transport to professional diving and from laundries to nuclear power. When it comes to today's common long-term conditions, the executive has produced a number of useful documents. One gets the feeling that they would like to do more. What are the effects on health and safety of practices like zero-hours contracts, low pay, poor working conditions and non-optimal periods of rest? What regulations might it issue to minimise risks to healthspan?

NHS Health Check

We described the NHS Health Check programme briefly in Chapter 5. When launched, it focussed on just one of the modern plagues – risk of heart disease – and so it took no account of the inter-relatedness of biological and social processes, let alone of health as satisfaction of needs. Its appropriateness and benefits have been continually challenged.[7] Some evaluations have identified significant but modest reductions in modelled risk for cardiovascular disease and individual risk factors.[8] An evaluation in 2016 of 140,000 subjects found a small absolute reduction of two cases in a thousand in modelled risk for cardiovascular disease.[9] Another evaluation found that the Health Check resulted in an extra 9,000 years of life for those who got checked, and predicted that minor reforms could more than triple this gain.[10]

In the long term, it may well be sensible to make prevention of common chronic conditions a specific responsibility of family doctors (primary care). But when surgeries are over-stretched treating the unhealthy, there is a need to think carefully whether this is the right way to ensure that the healthy stay that way. On the other hand, until a better way has been found, it is imperative that the principle of the NHS Health Check is maintained – the principle that society should act consciously to prolong healthspan for all. Reform is needed. In the short term, there is a need to stop the NHS Health Check system taking the path of least resistance and turning into a screening method for earlier diagnosis. And then it needs to move away from a service model where the citizen is solely the passive recipient of the wisdom of others.

New directions: Precision Public Health

We saw in Chapter 5 how government ministers every few years lay out new directions in prevention with greater or lesser success. Some public health researchers have suggested another new direction that they call 'Precision Public Health'. The idea behind it is to use the latest data gathering and analysis methods to manage public health. To some extent, the idea comes from going beyond the conventional – from thinking outside the box. The word 'precision' is borrowed from biomedical researchers who have developed new medicines to treat people with diseases that have been defined with greater precision. This precision comes from detailed molecular analysis of diseases.

Precision Public Health is seen as aiming to measure, with greater precision, the risk of someone acquiring a disease or condition. One definition refers to 'technological advances that enable more precise descriptions and analyses of individuals and population groups'.[11] Another speaks of 'applying emerging methods and technologies for measuring disease, pathogens, exposures, behaviours and susceptibility in populations; and developing policies and targeted implementation programmes to improve health'.[12] We think these aims, while commendable, do not have the right focus. What the information technologies should be focussing on is not so much the measurement of risk of a condition but measurement of the decline in risk arising from action on prevention. There is nothing more encouraging when trying to lose weight than to see the number of kilos going down on the bathroom scales. This is a crude and imprecise measurement of just one modifiable risk factor. Better measures of such modifiable risk factors require data from large studies on populations where there are ongoing experiments to test new risk-reduction strategies. In other words, better measures require Systems Prevention.

How we started to think outside the box

We have not yet even hinted at our personal starting point that led us to the idea of Systems Prevention and its application. This starting point may well leave the reader bemused. However, it is worth recounting since it indicates that our views are rooted in experience. A major activity which both authors have undertaken for many years goes by the name of 'biobanking'. That was our starting point.

Biobanking refers to the activities that many researchers in biology (including medicine) undertake in order to collect and manage biological samples. For example, a study of the genetic risk factors for a condition like diabetes starts with the collection of blood samples from which the biobank extracts DNA, storing this material for later use. Data on the people who provided the samples are also stored. This activity of collecting samples and data may take years and, indeed, it may never stop.

Back in 2002, the UK Medical Research Council asked us to construct a national network of biobanks to manage DNA samples and data that had been collected with the long-term aim of developing new medicines. This MRC DNA Bank Network would, in the first phase, manage 100,000 samples that had been deposited by researchers on a dozen common long-term conditions. The network was a world first.[13] Almost any researcher in the world could get access to the samples from the dozen collections deposited in the bank. The network made sense scientifically, ethically and financially and the idea has been picked up across Europe, in China and elsewhere. But there was a stumbling block to scientific progress: the collectors disliked any loss of their own control over what they saw as their own, personal academic and intellectual property.

This was one of the factors that caused the demise of the network. Nonetheless, biobank networks are needed for experimental aims in both human healthcare (medicines development) and for human health (prevention). As we pondered out next step, we felt we preferred to think about biobanking as infrastructure for prevention because medicines development biobanking is organisationally trickier owing to substantial private pharmaceutical sector involvement. Our preference was not actually all or nothing: both medicines development and prevention would benefit from a new national biobank network. An international network would be even better.

These thoughts became more concrete when we discussed them with our epidemiology colleagues after being encouraged to 'think big' and 'think outside the box' by our university. We all wanted to leverage the then imminent partial devolution of health funding from central government to Greater Manchester. Health improvement had to be a top priority because the conurbation has some of the worst health statistics in the country. Eventually, a 'big idea' emerged: the concept of a 'Health Engine' (Figure 13.2).

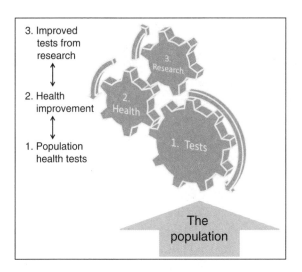

Figure 13.2 A sketch of the Health Engine: how we started to think outside the box. Repeated testing of biomarkers are seen to drive improvements in population health and to enable, via research, the improvement of testing and thus of health.

A sketch of the Health Engine: how we started to think outside the box

We envisaged three interlocking 'cogs' in this engine. The first cog – 'population health tests – establishes risk profiles for the common long term conditions among the individuals comprising the population in question. This cog then drives the second cog – 'health' – to reduce the substantial risks. These two cogs then enable research to improve tests of various kinds that would drive increased effectiveness of the first and second cogs. In essence, this Health Engine was a proposal to make epidemiology an experimental science again – as it had been when Snow got the pump handle removed (Chapter 6). The engine relied on infrastructure to manage data and samples.

While our Health Engine idea aimed at driving prevention, similar ideas being tested in the US were focussed more on research for new treatments. For example, Leroy Hood, an eminent US molecular biologist, launched a 'Wellness Project'. He wanted 'patients, researchers, physicians, and the entire health care community [to] join forces to transform the practice of medicine to make it more proactive than reactive – and, in turn, less expensive and more effective.' Precisely how they were to 'join forces' was unclear. But we agreed with his basic analysis: 'Unsustainable cost increases threaten the global health care system, and further progress is stymied more by societal than technological factors'.[14]

We took forward Hood's notion of 'joining forces' – of various actors in society working together. But, we wanted to place this firmly in the context of prevention – not treatment and not medicine. We recognised from John Snow's experience that government was one of the actors. And we recalled the hope for 'stakeholder engagement' that had driven the policy ideas of Tessa Jowell, Britain's first public health minister. However, we wanted to make an argument for change based, above all, on scientific evidence (see Part III).

14

The road to recovery

Our society has to take up Systems Prevention consciously if it is to prevent the common long-term conditions, to substantially improve the health of the population, and to recognise that health is the optimal satisfaction of human needs. We saw that, in reality, only a handful of small UK governmental organisations are explicitly tasked with prevention of the common long-term conditions. This is not enough: taking up Systems Prevention seriously means transforming all of public policy resulting in societal reform. We call this reform the construction of a national Health Society. This Health Society is the socio-political expression of the concept of Systems Prevention.

The Health Society is one where people and organisations work to ensure that the vital needs, the social needs and the agency needs of the population are optimally satisfied. Health stops being only a battle to extend lifespan and becomes the raison d'être of society, the reason why our species evolved as a mutually dependent, social animal. Society exists for the purpose of health (of the optimal satisfaction of needs), and public policy is the mechanism for implementing that purpose. We are aware, of course, that others have views on what society is for, views based on opinion, speculation, dogma, self-interest or an interpretation of the past. Ours is based on evidence from biology, including human biology.

The three pillars of the Health Society

The Health Society can be represented as a structure, as in Figure 14.1 – a 'temple of health' with three pillars. At the base, is the pressing crisis of diabetes, depression, heart disease and cancer. Holding up the Health Society roof are three pillars and a frieze.

The pillars specify three areas where change is needed – in institutions, in communities, and in the development and deployment of technologies. The frieze bears the text of the principle that public policy needs to adopt: 'Optimal satisfaction of the needs that define health is the supreme purpose of public policy.' Each of the pillars is linked to the other two via the frieze: in other words,

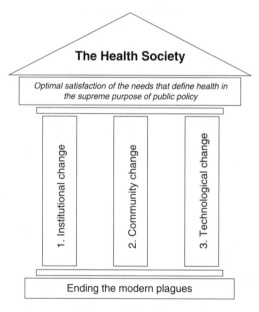

Figure 14.1 The three pillars of the Health Society. These pillars comprise change to our institutions, our communities and our uses of technology. Such change can end the modern plagues and realise the Health Society with its motto that 'the optimal satisfaction of the needs that define health is the supreme purpose of public policy'.

the changes that are needed need to be instigated in a joined-up way. Piecemeal change is not enough. So, for example, just introducing a technological change like improved data management will not end the high prevalence of diabetes. This condition, the other modern plagues and their modifiable risk factors are all rooted in our way of life (in deep-seated social habits, in a set of cultural, social, political and economic practices and their rationalisations). Public Health England calls it 'modern life'.[1] And, you can't change a society's way of life with a smartphone app.

The weaknesses of piecemeal change are illustrated by societal efforts to stop tobacco use. Over the decades we have seen measures introduced one by one: but just one in two hundred smokers quits each year. It would take very little for this decline to turn around and become an increase. Consider the numbers of men getting lung cancer and dying from it. These numbers have declined since 1990, while the numbers of male and female survivors have increased with better treatment.[2] However, this improved situation could easily lead to new nicotine addicts disregarding the risks of tobacco. This would echo the emergence of anti-vaxxers who disregard the risk of measles after years of decline in the disease due to vaccination. To make tobacco use (or vaccine avoidance) a thing of the past, we need to change our way of life, since this includes widespread ignorance of the nature of risk.

Joined-up reform is what we need. That means it has to be concurrent with more than one strand of work going on in parallel with other strands. Someone has to connect it all up together. This networking role surely falls to national and local governments. No other organisations in society have the capacity or can have the capabilities that are required for this coordination role. Government needs to do several things: put its own houses in order, give a lead, give direction, coordinate and give support to others. It is a tall order, so the rest of this chapter deals with just this Pillar One of the Health Society.

Institutional change:
Pillar One of the Health Society

National Risk Register

How do you move an entire government so that it consciously acts to satisfy optimally those vital, social and agency needs that we listed in Chapter 12? The place to start may not seem obvious; it may even seem pointless, minor or irrelevant. Actually, it is fundamental.

In 2004, Parliament enacted the Civil Contingencies Act, a law which lays out how government should deal with emergencies. These emergencies include situations that threaten to damage human welfare if they involve, cause or may cause people to lose their lives through illness, injury, homelessness or disruption of health services.

To implement the law and guard against these risks the government published in 2008 a National Risk Register.[3] This, for the first time, aimed 'to encourage public debate on security and help organisations, individuals, families and communities, who want to do so, to prepare for emergencies'. Previously, risks were a state secret: assessments were held confidentially within government. Now they were to be publicly identified.

The key to the usefulness of the risk register is that anyone and everyone can be called in by government to ensure joined-up and effective risk reduction actions. The register is the responsibility of the Cabinet Office in 10 Downing St. It sits at the heart of government but responsibility currently rests with a minister who has no statutory footing or recognition and is unpaid: the Minister for the Cabinet Office. Actual work on the register has been done by a junior minister: the Minister for Government Resilience and Efficiency. To an outsider, this looks like an arrangement where everyone and no-one is fully responsible, an arrangement ideal for inaction. Explicit responsibility for coordinated action on prevention should be assigned to the Deputy Prime Minister – along the lines of the proposed European Commission Vice-President for Health and Well-Being.[4]

Three categories of risk make it into the register: natural events, major accidents and malicious attacks. Among the natural events, there are four types: severe weather, flooding, human disease and animal disease.

On human disease, the register is careful to note that its list is not exhaustive: 'The examples have been chosen to give an impression of the range of possible diseases that would have a significant disruptive effect, but are by no means exhaustive.' Its examples are, first, pandemic influenza and, second, new and emerging infectious disease.

So, where are the modern plagues? They were certainly under-way in 2008 but they were seemingly invisible to government as a national risk. This invisibility was challenged in 2014 by the government's head doctor, Chief Medical Officer Prof Dame Sally Davies. She wrote: 'Tackling obesity in the whole popula-tion is an accepted public health priority. However, I advocate recognising obesity at the level of a "national risk"'.[5] She argued that tackling obesity had to be a national priority in order to pre-vent its consequences 'overwhelming our health and social care resources and reducing England's productivity'. The same risks face Scotland, Wales and Northern Ireland. Those consequences include all the common long-term conditions, all the modern plagues.

Despite this recommendation, obesity has not been included in the register. Changes to it are made after consulting with expert groups, government departments, devolved administrations, agen-cies, academic institutions and industry. Chief Medical Officers are not overlooked. But, so far, the obesity recommendation has been.

Here are some responses we can imagine from a minister or civil servant:

'It's not a matter for the Risk Register.' Sorry, but it is – according to the Chief Medical Officer.

'We are keeping it under review.' But what, then, are you waiting for? The collapse of the healthcare system?

'Obesity is not really an emergency.' But, by that argument, risk of flooding in a low-lying town is not an emergency either. After all it's only a risk. It hasn't actually materialised. The whole idea of a risk register is to avoid the event by lowering the risk.

'The risks we identify are based on those recognised by the World Economic Forum in its annual global risks reports. The forum does not include obesity.' This is true. On the other hand, this would ignore the fact that the forum does include risks of common long-term conditions (chronic diseases). It specifies the risks as 'rising costs of long-term treatment and [threats to] recent societal gains in life expectancy and quality'.[6]

Putting the modern plagues and key modifiable risk factors on the National Risk Register would oblige all ministers to say what they will do to reduce the risks both to their workforce and across their departmental responsibilities.

Community Risk Register

The 2004 Civil Contingencies Act established Community Risk Registers alongside the national one. Each region and community has its own risk profile prepared by a local forum of public bodies (including health services), the voluntary sector and business. The forum puts nationally identified risks into a local context. In Greater Manchester, for example, industry is represented by the city's airport, Network Rail and one of the power companies.

This engagement with business and the voluntary sector is an aspect of Pillar Two of 'community change'. There is no reason why other stakeholders shouldn't participate in the forum. For example, more local employers and leisure organisations could sit in the forum. Moreover, there is no reason why risks should be excluded just because they are not on the national register.

However, this broader approach to risks is inhibited by the language we all use. Take Greater Manchester again (we're not picking on this great place: anywhere would do, but our university is in the city). The local register talks of responses to 'incidents'.[7] While one person's diagnosis with diabetes or heart disease or cancer might indeed be an 'incident' for them, we don't use this word to describe the slow, relentless advance of these diseases across the population. Imagine if the river running through Manchester – the Irwell – were seen to be slowly and relentlessly rising. That would be considered a risk that had to be reduced. And, indeed the local plan says: the 'local authority [is] working to manage the risk of flooding by ... continuing to invest in maintaining and improving flood defences'. But the slowly and relentlessly rising prevalence of long-term conditions is, perversely, ignored by the risk register.

A worrying feature of risk management in Greater Manchester is that concerted and coordinated action is not guaranteed across local government. This may be due, in part, to the parochialism of each of the ten local authorities that are combined – not unified – in the Greater Manchester structure. The risk register is maintained by a forum, but no-one can tell anyone from a different part of Greater Manchester to do anything. Other parts of the country suffer the same weakness. This creates a new risk: the risk that risks are not reduced consistently. One might think that a decade of cuts would promote the cooperation that enables consistency. But cuts also create a fear of cooperation.

When it comes to a risk factor like obesity, reform of a wide range of public policy is needed. This includes health, housing, education, transport, planning, leisure, sport, food, employment and industrial policy.

Take housing policy as an example. This has been shown to have a significant impact on health and health costs. The National Health Service spends a fifth of its clinical budget on trying to cure illnesses caused by unemployment, poverty, bad housing and environmental pollution.[8] The Audit Commission calculated that for every pound society spends on providing housing support for vulnerable people, society saves nearly two pounds in reduced costs of health services, tenancy failure, crime and residential care.[9] The National Housing Federation estimated costs to the NHS for treating ill-health resulting from sub-standard housing at £2.4bn p.a. in 1997.[10] In a 2016 report on inadequate housing in Europe (including London and Liverpool), researchers found that 11% of the 27.8m UK dwelling stock had substantial inadequacies whose repair would cost £39bn but whose total direct and indirect health costs amounted to £27bn a year.[11] Repairs would pay for themselves in 18 months, thereafter releasing that £27bn for other health purposes. The report in 2020 from the Centre for Ageing Better and Care & Repair England reveals that over 2m over-55s are living in a home that endangers their health or well-being.[12]

A Deputy Prime Minister

One might argue that the right person to lead the work of ending the modern plagues is the Minister of Health and Social Care. But we don't think so. Prevention is not a medical issue and other ministries also have responsibilities in prevention.

The focus of the Department of Health and Social Care is on diagnosing, treating and caring for people with any medical condition. Yes, it has a responsibility for continued health of all its own employees, but given the scale of the task carried out by the NHS, it is not surprising that it only undertakes a limited amount of prevention. There is also the matter of mindset: looking after the sick is very different from working with the healthy to keep them that way. Each individual with ill-health requires personal attention but that is not necessarily the case with the healthy. And, then, in practice, people go to see the doctor to report on some symptoms or change in symptoms, not to report the absence of any symptoms. A doctor may sometimes have the chance of tucking in some words of advice on maintaining health, but prevention has to entail much more than that.

In the Health Society there will be a role for medical staff in maintaining health – the role of data-sharing, as we shall discuss. It may also be reasonable for the Department of Health to manage the Health Society Professionals that we propose (Chapter 17). However, these professionals may sit more effectively within the Department of Housing, Communities and Local Government because much of their work will be community-based work. In fact, prevention needs to be on the agenda of virtually every department of government. This is what the World Health Organization advocates when it calls for 'health in all policies' and health as a responsibility for the whole of government. We go a step further when we say that health-as-needs *is* the agenda.

The Deputy Prime Minister (DPM) is, we suggest, the right post to have direct overall responsibility for coordination across government to ensure that it tackles the modern plagues. This DPM would ask the following questions of every minister (and local authority): what are you doing to improve the health of the population including employees of your department and what are you doing to achieve agreed targets for the curtailing of the common long-term conditions? The DPM would in effect be running regular sessions of COBR – the meetings held in Cabinet Office Briefing Rooms when there are emergencies.

The DPM could set targets for the reduction of prevalence and incidence of diabetes, depression, heart disease and cancer (and of any other disorders with high prevalence and with modifiable risk factors). Alternatively – or additionally – there is a need for targets in modifying risk factors such as obesity and physical activity. Targets need to be based on evidence from Public Health England and its sister organisations in the other nations of the UK. The DPM would be responsible to Parliament for hitting those targets and so would need to lean heavily on the various ministers.

To get the ball rolling, the DPM would need the recommendations of a Royal Commission on the modern plagues. Of course, this raises the risk of the whole matter being kicked into the long grass. But our country needs to have a consensus on the best way forward. Some of the work to be done is experimental in character and so this research could start immediately. Moreover, while the Royal Commission may define best practice, that doesn't mean that some good practice shouldn't be implemented now. Good practice is about always getting better. Let us not make the best the enemy of the good. For example, the NHS Health Check is good practice, even if it isn't best practice.

One issue that the Royal Commission could address is that of re-designating the responsibilities of governmental departments so that they align with the needs of the Health Society rather than with the whim of the party in power. This would mean having ministries named for the vital, social and agency needs that we have outlined.

An immediate issue is that of getting every minister to take responsibility for prevention among their staff and contracted employees. An evidence basis for this is already in place, owing to the work of Sir Michael Marmot in the Whitehall studies.[13] Beginning in the 1960s, he looked at the health of a population of middle-aged men, all employed in stable jobs on different grades in the Civil Service across different departments of government. The first study showed that the lower the grade, the higher the risk of death from all causes. But, the statistics showed that this was not simply down to income, and a second study then tried to find out what was going on. One of its key findings was that people were more stressed in the lower grades and this stress was associated with disease. Here then is an immediate task for all ministers.

However, it is not enough for government departments to have responsibilities. They also need to work with other national, regional and local stakeholders. National stakeholders include the relevant professional bodies like the medical Royal Colleges, the

Confederation of British Industry, the Trade Union Congress and a range of national charities and community organisations. The DPM will have a big coordination job on their hands. They will be ensuring the optimal satisfaction of the needs that define the health of every citizen.

Department of Education

To achieve a society where health is understood as the satisfaction of our vital, social and agency needs will require within education not only curriculum change but also a change in the role of the school in the community.

Schools and colleges should ensure that students and staff understand that health is a product of nutrition, physical activity, work–life balance, our way of life and our engagement and involvement with other people. They should understand the nature of risk and the specific risks associated with non-satisfaction of human needs and with smoking, excessive alcohol or drugs. In the curriculum, there should be greater emphasis, especially in secondary education, on optimising and maintaining personal, physical and mental health, alongside sex education. This involves not only questions of nutrition, exercise, rest and reducing anxiety, but also of developing the necessary social habits.

Schools often act as a community hub for their catchment area. There is interaction with parents and the facilities may be open for community use. However, students, parents and teachers themselves are an under-utilised resource for community development and community health improvement. The school is a potentially excellent place for identifying and motivating Health Society Champions who reach out to their community and to their own family, including family members who may be resistant to new ideas. This will need support from Health Society professionals, of course. Student Health Champions might be rather like class monitors or prefects. They might monitor the nutrition available in the school and its neighbourhood, or help to develop a two-way relationship with the local community to raise levels of physical activity. One can imagine this might be attractive to not only school sporting heroes but also to young people who want to help others – perhaps the elderly.

Such changes require coordination across the school community, with best practice shared nationally and encouraged through the Department of Education, and with local government providing higher-level coordination. This may spark off a debate about school autonomy. However, the debate would be one between satisfying differing types of need. On the one hand, there are the needs whose satisfaction is the basis of academic excellence. On the other hand, there are the needs whose satisfaction is the basis for extending the healthspan of students and staff. Finding a balance between these needs serves the interests of young people and their community better than focussing solely on academic excellence.

Business, energy and industrial strategy

'Health-as-needs' is in fact the basis for a coherent and long-term industrial strategy to lift national productivity out of the doldrums in which it languishes nowadays. We have already described the absenteeism and the 'presenteeism' that are the result of common long-term conditions.

Some good employers have a concern for the health of their staff. For example, a report commissioned by government on mental health at work cites Thames Water as an example of an employer that leads from the top. The company explains this: 'At Thames Water, the Board of Directors are accountable for staff well-being. Its Executive Team review company absence figures and trends and for all work-related illness cases an executive review is undertaken triggering conversations with local managers about each case. Occupational Health are brought in to find the cause of illness and to learn from every individual case what the issues are, crafting solutions to support each individual and promote any wider business learning'. The Royal Bank of Scotland is also cited for its 'holistic bank-wide approach to wellbeing focussing on mental, physical and social wellbeing'. Today the only legal requirements are for the prevention of work-related accidents and 'health and safety'.[14]

Things are more advanced in Japan where employers are required to run an annual health check for employees: the employees are required to participate and to agree to see a doctor if any test suggests that they should do so. The tests are supervised via the Ministry of Health, Labour and Welfare (an interesting combination of responsibilities). Younger workers get a basic check called the Kenko Shendan as shown in Figure 14.2. This involves

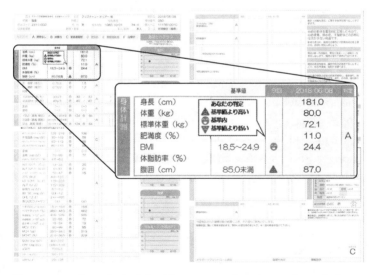

Figure 14.2 Part of a basic health assessment form for employees in Japan. All employers pay for the annual assessment of their employees in a system overseen by government. On the left is a form listing some forty tests. On the right is shown the first section of the form recording basic information such as age, height, weight and Body Mass Index.

providing biological samples and getting an X-ray and an electro-cardiogram. Older workers get a more thorough check – a 'dry dock' check – called Ningen Dokhu.

Introduced in post-war Japan to deal with rampant tuberculosis, the focus of the health check today is on the common long-term conditions. The Ministry imposes penalties on employers when too many of the employees are obese: the workforce and the company thereby share the mission to maintain the health of all. One way employers help reduce obesity is via a 'Table for Two' programme where calorie-controlled meals are served in the workplace canteen and the 'excess calories' are donated in financial form to alleviate malnutrition in low-income countries. In this way, human altruism provides positive benefits both to the donor and the recipient. Evidence of good practice elsewhere has been brought together by the World Health Organization. This often involves governmental and community stakeholders working together.

The history of football provides a clear example of the way employers used to care for the health of their staff. Many of today's professional clubs started out as works teams (restricted, admit-tedly, to fit young men, and all too often with a tendency to link sport to alcohol and smoking). A nostalgic blog called 'Game of the People: flying the flag for football as it should be played' laments the 'demise of the corporate sports ground'[15]. The opening sen-tence reads: 'If you flew across South London, Kent and Surrey in the mid-1970s, you would have looked down on acres of sports grounds comprising rugby, football and hockey pitches. Many of these grounds, with their excellent facilities and perpetual odour of horse liniment, were owned by banks, insurance companies and old boy networks.'

Charity may start at home, but corporate responsibility starts at the workplace with the health of the men and women, young and old, who work for the corporation directly or indirectly. Encouragement by the Department of Business of such corporate responsibility would act to improve productivity. The department could coordinate this and support regular health checks for staff, regular training and development sessions about maintaining good health, establishing Health Champions (see Chapter 15) and reaching out to the local community. Where catering and canteen services are provided by an employer, these need to be nutritionally assessed and 'Table for Two' programmes introduced.

Treasury

The British finance ministry is called the Treasury and its minister is called the Chancellor of the Exchequer. It has significant control over government income and expenditure. Construction of the Health Society means that the Treasury will have to start making financial decisions based in the first instance on the needs associated with the health of the population. Needs of one or other interest groups that conflict with this may have to be disregarded. This is clearly a controversial matter. Society can only come to a consensus when there is democratic and transparent examination of a particular controversy. The very process of seeking a consensus is an element of satisfying one of the needs associated with our health – our agency needs. This is one of the ways that the Treasury can contribute to the construction of the Health Society.

One controversy that could bear democratic and transparent examination today is the way that society measures its overall progress. This has been done for many years using a measure called Gross Domestic Product (GDP – the total monetary value of goods produced and services provided in one jurisdiction in one year). But some critics have pointed out that GDP treats serious illness as a positive.[16] However there are alternative measures to GDP such as the Genuine Progress Indicator,[17] the World Bank's measure of 'comprehensive wealth' or New Zealand's 'well-being budget'.[18] Some (but probably not all) economists would welcome democratic and transparent examination of these issues. A number of countries, including the UK, have established measures of happiness or well-being. For example the Office of National Statistics regularly calculates 'Personal and economic well-being in the UK'. It found in 2019 that high levels of anxiety had increased by 1.7% in a year.[19] The issue that the Treasury should be addressing is if and how taxing and spending can reverse this sort of increase.

Housing, Communities and Local Government

We have identified housing as a vital need. It deserves close attention because of that, but also because it is not like the consumer goods on which conventional economics is based. The key property of goods (like a bottle of Coke) is that they are consumed. They vanish and so need replenishing. Yet houses do not vanish – they may just decay over the generations. Treating housing as a conventional 'market' has led to high levels of homelessness and, simultaneously, high numbers of empty or under-occupied homes. This is a double market failure: a flawed analysis of housing and a host of problems for those without shelter. Those problems are urgent because homelessness leads to and is associated with curtailed healthspan and lifespan.

If provision of housing can satisfy one vital need, then the quality of housing can satisfy a number of other needs. For example, US research suggests that the health of adult and child residents improved after their flats had been renovated using 'green' and healthy principles.[20] Respiratory illnesses reportedly declined substantially. The French Agency for Food, Environmental and Occupational Health and Safety estimated the socio-economic cost of indoor air pollution to be €19bn a year from premature deaths, healthcare costs and production losses. The Health and Environment Alliance in Brussels has gathered evidence suggesting that unhealthy buildings raise the risks not only of respiratory disease but also of heart conditions, cancer and anxiety / depression.[21]

A gym in every basement and a games pitch on the roof of every block of flats would help reduce the risks of all the common long-term conditions. Such improvements to housing are inevitable: the Intergovernmental Panel on Climate Change states that there is no way around a 'rapid and far-reaching' transformation of the buildings sector so that global warming does not exceed 1.5°C and so that health is protected.[22]

Other departments

We cannot think of one ministry that might have no responsibility in seeking to satisfy the needs that define health. Even if the primary responsibility of a ministry may seem to be unrelated to health, it nonetheless has a responsibility to ensure a healthy workforce. For example, the Ministry for Defence has a primary responsibility to keep the peace and prepare for war, but it can do neither efficiently when 61,000 of its workforce in the armed forces are overweight.[23] The Department of Work and Pensions would like to see fewer disabled people whose healthspan has ended. Its choice is either to hide the levels of disability by administrative measures or to work with other ministries to increase the average age of disability onset. Those other ministries will include Health and Social Care, Environment, Food and Rural Affairs and the Ministry of Transport.

The optimal satisfaction of the needs that define health could be the thread that runs through every part of government (including its agencies and executive bodies), providing a coherent and necessary narrative for all public policy. It just requires us to think systematically about prevention.

15

Community change

To get sick Britain on the road to recovery, we need to change, not only at the 'top' of society, but also at the 'bottom'. Pillar One was about top-down change and now we turn to Pillar Two, to bottom-up change.

A community is generally thought of as all the people that reside or work – or are homeless or workless – in a specified geographical area. It also includes the groupings and organisations there, whether it is workplaces, schools, places of worship, clubs or shops, cafés and restaurants. For us a community is a little more abstract: it is a group of people who come together and interact (physically, virtually or both) for a common purpose. At one extreme, it could be Manchester City football supporters coming together from across Europe and beyond to support their team. Or it could be a darts club team in a pub. It is that coming together of people, that network formation, which goes toward our definition of community because this is the precondition for the change necessary to end the modern plagues.

A wide range of factors inhibit a potential community from coming together: community divisions are based in the perception of insuperable differences. This perception – or misperception – encompasses differences in matters such as income, wealth, leisure activities, culture, political views, customs, ancestry, ethnicity, sexuality, gender, religion and even complexion. You name it. The distance we live apart can become an impediment to community formation, though usually living in adjacent local authority areas, wards, constituencies, school catchment areas, postal codes and so on is not a major issue.

These divisions make change more difficult, in part because they seem to justify individualistic approaches. 'Our health is simply a personal problem', we may say 'and it's hard enough for me as an individual to maintain my health, let alone anyone else's'. However, this reasoning does not hold water because, as we have shown, 'network effects' spread through communities including both the modern plagues and their risk factors. In other words, the idea that 'my health is your health' is true in a pragmatic sense, as well as at the deeper level of health defined as the optimal satisfaction of human needs.

The need that people consciously grasp least well is probably their agency needs. We are all conscious of our vital needs for food, shelter, exercise and clothing. Perhaps a minority are not consciously aware of the need for 'social conversation', but most of us are. Even Trappist monks break their oath of silence and allow themselves an hour or two of conversation each day. When it comes to our social needs, we are acutely conscious when, say, on our way to work, they are not optimally satisfied – when the train is running late or there is a traffic jam.

When it comes to agency needs, we may even deny they exist. Yet the very concept of community rests, at least in part, on meeting those agency needs. A good community is one that provides the environment where its members can each express themselves actively and creatively. That expression is self-evidently aimed at other people and it elicits appreciation. The need for autonomy can be satisfied by participating in the community's decision-making processes. Its decisions become my decisions. Note that this participation meets not only individual needs but also the community's need for engagement. These ideas are all summed up in the expression: 'It takes a village to raise a child'. The saying comes from the peoples of Somalia, Uganda, Tanzania, Kenya, Rwanda, Burundi, Mozambique and Congo. According to Hillary Clinton, it is a lesson that children teach the rest of us.[1]

So far we have defined the word 'community' in quite a broad way and have indicated the needs that require satisfaction at a community level to improve health. What we are saying is that organising a Fun Run in your community is all well and good but, by itself, it will not have lasting benefits for health. Health in a community comes not just from exercise but also from meeting our agency needs. At this point, our critics will say that we have glossed over the wealth and income inequalities that reduce healthspan. In our defence, we would note that communities are, for the most part, not well-placed to deal with these inequalities directly. It is the institutions of society – our Pillar One – that are better placed to do so.

Other critics will say of us: so far, so vague. Will we please be more explicit? In one sense, that is not possible: communities have to find their own way. This is because they are so very varied in character and function. Furthermore, if a community is not permitted to find its own way then it falls at the first hurdle of meeting the agency needs – those needs essential to health – of the members of the community in question. On the other hand, while communities must find their own way, the larger society needs to provide the framework. Pillar One has a critical role to play to enable community change. One role is organisational, the other is financial. Organisationally, communities need to learn from and work with each other – they need a network that should be supported by government, directly or indirectly (say via local government). Financial support to set up community activities is also important, and in communities where deprivation is higher this support is likely to be needed for longer. Of course, many community initiatives exist already. In Wigan, for example, there is a set of agreements between the council and the population with joint pledges on health and well-being. The aim is to combine local culture and pride with health.

Reforming the National Health Service Health Check

One component of the national institutional framework that we say should contribute to the construction of the Health Society is the NHS Health Check. This service is delivered to citizens to provide individual advice on prevention of one or two of the modern plagues. This strength is also its weakness. While the original government aim in 1997 was to bring all stakeholders together to improve population health, this was lost when the Health Check system was set up a decade later.

It now needs to be found again. The way to do this is by changing citizens from passive recipients of a service – the Health Check – into active citizens motivated via the Health Check to act to improve population health. Let us call this reformed health check the Health Society Check, so as to give it a name. The trick is to enable a change from passive recipient of the NHS Health Check to active agent for the Health Society Check. The way to achieve this is to split the check-up into two phases. The first phase provides the various tests on health. The second phase starts with delivery of the results of tests. When an individual first comes for their check-up, they get a one-to-one service much as now – but with two tweaks (see below). They get their confidential results back at a second meeting. However, this is not a one-to-one meeting: it is a joint meeting with nearly all the individuals who had been measured in the same week (or some other convenient period of time). The purpose of this second meeting is to explain the nature of risk to the group and to identify a 'Health Society Champion'. In any group of people there is always a live wire: someone who wants to help others, someone who is committed to their community. If, as luck would have it, there are no live wires one week, then existing Health Society Champions will be around to fill in.

The first 'tweak' in the Health Society Check is that individuals are invited to consent to participate in health improvement research. Consent means that the individual is ready to be approached by or on behalf of researchers for purposes such as completing a questionnaire or joining in some activity. Some may be content to give their consent indefinitely. Others may want opportunities to change their minds. Consent also means that the individual is content that securely stored data and materials from the individual are made available only for ethical research purposes by ethical researchers. The most common concerns in this regard are for anonymity and against access by, for example, insurance companies. In brief, consent requires that people trust the Health Society Check. That trust has to be earned and then it has to be maintained. That requires continuous reviews and external inspections by relevant professionals (like ethicists, lawyers and researchers) as well as by participants.

Research participation is absolutely essential to the construction of the Health Society because although the aim of this society is clear – the optimal satisfaction of the needs that define health – the best way to get there and to stay there is far less clear and is bound to change as society changes. Only research can discover what the best way is at a given time. The need for research participation for health improvement is recognised by the World Health Organization[2] and by national public health agencies.[3]

The pathway to the Health Society is one that has to be found, to be discovered as we go along. The initial steps are clear, but, of course, we can't see over the horizon. On that path, there will be a need to conduct tests on small groups so as to innovate for all. The tests may be of new biomarkers (see Chapter 16) or new forms of action by any or all the stakeholders. In general terms, the research would be on the molecular and social determinants of risk and risk reduction and might encompass the fields of biomedicine, epidemiology, computing and the humanities (education, social sciences, economics and geography). Some research would involve 'real-world' experiments. Individuals and groups would be able to participate, for example, in experiments to improve social cohesion and community involvement – to meet agency needs – with a view to reducing risk of the modern plagues. The individual and their community become both the subject and the object of research aimed at improving population health. This turns on its head an old concern that if you know you are a participant in epidemiological research then this confounds the results of the research since your knowledge affects your behaviour.[4] Real-world epidemiological research – research with action – actually hopes that your behaviour will indeed change because of your knowledge. What was a statistical problem has become a practical solution.

The second tweak is this: some individuals are not invited to the second meeting. Why is that? Unfortunately, a proportion of people who come for a health check actually need or may need treatment. Such people are likely to be identified from the test results and so will instead be referred to see a medical nurse or doctor for more detailed examination. If this reveals a clinical condition, then the individual obviously becomes a patient.

Who gives the Health Society Check at the first meeting and who runs the second meeting? To answer these questions we need to see how the Department of Health describes the working of NHS Health Check (Figure 15.1).

Today's NHS Health Check

Figure 15.1 shows a man eligible for the NHS Health Check, who has taken up an invitation from a family doctor. The nurse measures his weight, height and blood pressure, takes a blood sample (to measure cholesterol and, sometimes, blood sugar) and checks his age, ethnicity, alcohol use and so on. The data is stored electronically in the 'primary care record'. Data analysis helps the nurse to decide [a] should the man go and see the doctor (indicated by the

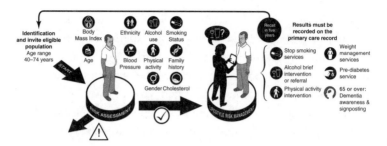

Figure 15.1 Department of Health diagram showing the steps involved in getting an NHS Health Check. Note how the results of this service are used to provide more services.

triangle with the exclamation mark) or [b] should he be offered some service like a smoking cessation clinic or [c] should he simply be recalled in five years' time.

In the Health Society Check, by contrast, the person is over 18, has consented to research participation and the blood sample is used for a range of tests. These tests can't all be done on the spot, and even if they could be, the aim is not solely to provide the participant with information but also to aid research on risk reduction. The key professional in this process is the person asking the questions. We shall call them a 'Health Society professional' (HSP). There may be a better title, but HSP will do for now. This HSP has the skills of a Health Check nurse plus some new ones. These are based on the social sciences and they include skills in organising and motivating individuals and groups plus skills in community development. A forerunner to this HSP may be seen in the 'health coaches' that have been proposed to work in primary care.

So, when participants are recalled to get their test results, they come to a meeting convened by the HSP (or HSPs). The job of the HSPs is not only to explain the test results to each participant, but also to work with the group. This work involves explaining that the best way for each of them to improve their risk profile is for participants to work with each other to reduce the main modifiable risk factors for the common long-term conditions (nutrition, exercise, social isolation). Participants are encouraged to form groups based on common interests. It doesn't matter what this interest is, as long as it is a social activity – perhaps going to the same church or being a fan of the same football club (nationally, we have no shortage with some 20,000 clubs[5]).

What the HSPs are doing is establishing 'buddy systems'. These have been shown to improve the effectiveness of smoking cessation.[6] But the buddy system should also work to achieve other health goals. However, whereas buddy systems have involved very small groups of people, the Health Society buddy system includes the possibility of recruiting brand new people – not just people who have had a check-up. This is because the goal that the HSPs set for the participants is to put health on the agenda of the social group to which they belong. If, say, three people are all fans of one football club, then the HSP will suggest that one of them take the lead in this work and become a 'Health Society Champion'. This champion will stay in touch with the HSP for advice, help and support in getting health onto the fan club's agenda.

What does being 'on the agenda' mean? It means that the improved health of the fans is to be considered at every meeting of club fans or their committee. Obvious opportunities for health improvement exist in a football club: running round the pitch, using the club's training facilities (with the club owner's agreement and, then, their support), perhaps having a football hero come along to occasional training sessions or handing out awards for excellent progress. It will be up to the champions and their friends to think of what would work in their club or organisation. It may need to start less ambitiously if the club is for playing darts or bridge – or doing macramé. Clearly the HSPs will need to learn to work with all kinds of Health Society Champions and their interests. They will need to give encouragement to the shy or the socially isolated.

Let us deal with some objections to this.

What if no buddy group can be formed because no-one at the second meeting shares a social activity? Well, the HSP will know from previous groups of a champion who would be happy to meet new Health Society recruits.

What if no-one at the second meeting has any social activities at all? In that situation, the HSP would need to use their skills to persuade as many people as possible to form a buddy group there and then.

What if people are 'too busy' to do anything to improve their health, perhaps because they work long hours? These people are very valuable precisely because of that: they offer a way into the workplace. If they are willing to become champions then they can work with the HSP to persuade the employer to have regard for the health of their employees. If they are not willing to become champions, then they can be put in touch with another employee who has had a health check to see if there is anything the two of them can do – with the support of the HSP.

What if some people at the second meeting are just plain anti-social? The HSP can still suggest things they can do as individuals to improve their health – but leave the door open to working with others later. This is not a perfect solution, but as the Health Society takes hold, peer pressure will slowly overcome the social barriers that some people experience.

What about the people who turn down the invitation to the first meeting – or the second meeting for that matter? They are 'anti-health'. This is a tough nut to crack. Some possible solutions are: repeat invitations; the long-term effects of peer pressure; advice from their doctor next time they come into the practice; a diplomatic home visit by the HSP.

Only one in ten people go to Health Checks. What about the other 90%? This is precisely where the HSPs and the champions come in. Risk-reduction activities need to be open to all – to family, friends and neighbours. The HSPs and champions lead the way in the construction of a Health Society for all. If you are a Health Society Champion in, say, a football fan club you could reach out to the local community to join the club not only for their health's sake but for the sake of the local team. It is hard to imagine that a football club director would not welcome more fans. But the same goes for any social organisation. It will not be as easy around the workplace, but there is nothing to stop employers reviving workplace-based exercise activities and facilities. There is no reason why friends and neighbours of staff could not use those facilities too, especially if they were shared with other bodies such as local government.

It will be important for HSPs and Health Champions in one neighbourhood to meet with their opposite numbers in nearby areas. First there will be a need for mutual support and encouragement. Second there will be a need to exchange experiences on what works and what doesn't. Third there may be a need to offer people greater flexibility. Fourth there will be a 'succession' issue – finding new champions when one drops out or a new HSP emerges elsewhere in the locality. Fifth, the geographical area that one club covers may not coincide with the area covered by a given HSP since the latter is likely to follow NHS boundaries or local authority boundaries.

It will also be important for HSPs to be well trained. This training should include an understanding of the modern plagues, of risk and risk-reduction, of using questionnaires, of taking blood samples, of interpreting test results, of individual and group psychology, of social dynamics, of local government, employment and third sector structures and practices, of inter-agency work and so on. It probably needs to be a degree course and it would benefit from advice from the relevant national organisations as described in Pillar One. Such a training course would surely appeal to quite a few existing practice nurses and auxiliaries.

Day to day, the HSPs will be working with groups and individuals to help ensure optimal satisfaction of the needs that define health whether those needs are vital ones like appropriate nutrition, rest and exercise or agency needs where people are especially isolated. Such work is not at all 'medical' in the conventional sense. Health Society Professionals will be a new profession. They will want their own national organisation and all we can say at this stage is that their organisation will need to be cross-cutting so that it can interact with all three pillars of the national Health Society.

How to measure success?

An obvious measure of success in building the Health Society and ending the modern plagues would be a national increase in healthspan. South Korea has gone down this path and set a national target of achieving 75 years healthspan for its population.[7] However, even if this target is useful for national policymakers, it means little to individual citizens. They want a speedy and personal measure of success. One such measure comes from regularly calculating the individual's own risks of being diagnosed with the common long-term conditions at some time in the next few years.

Let us say I am told I have a 20% risk of getting diabetes in the next five years: there is a one in five chance that I will get it in that time. Now let us say that a year later, the risk has not materialised, I do not have diabetes and, what's more, I have acted successfully to reduce my risk to a one in ten chance that I'll get diabetes in the ensuing five years. On the face of it, nothing has changed from a medical point of view. I am still well. My healthspan has not ended. Only my calculated risk has changed – my risk of an event that has not materialised. If I fully understand what my risk measurements mean, I shall be encouraged to continue or encouraged to work harder when I discover that there has been a change in risk. If I don't understand what risk means and if that risk of diabetes materialises, I will be likely to become disillusioned with the Health Society.

It is therefore important both that risk is understood by all and that measurement of risk – especially of declines in risk – is as accurate as possible. The more precise the measurement, the greater is its value to each of us who are seeking to extend our healthspan. However, most of the data we have today is not on falls in risk, but on increases. For example, we know how risk of diabetes goes up when we put on weight and health professionals have to use that data to guess – yes, to guess – what would be the effect of losing weight. A guess is a risk estimate with a big margin of error. So, guessing is unsatisfactory – although it's better than nothing. Really what is needed is a very large population study where different groups of people are undertaking different activities to reduce their risks and where they can be followed for many years. In other words, what is needed is the construction of the Health Society – in order to get the Health Society! We need to use the limited tools that we have today so as to get better tools for tomorrow. The Health Society makes us both the object and the subject of research – in much the same way as the people at risk of cholera on Broad Street were the subject and the object of removing the pump handle. We are all simultaneously potential participants in and potential beneficiaries of this societal experiment.

Other measures of success should be based on the extent to which the vital, social and agency needs of individuals and communities have been optimised. Which communities, which socio-economic groups have shown least improvement and therefore require extra support, help and advice? An overall 'Health Society Index' would be a useful tool to inform debate and change.

A pilot Health Society

We shall next be looking at the technological change needed to construct the Health Society. However, before we do that it is now reasonable for us to indicate how we can get the ball rolling in Britain. A pilot project would give some assurance that all the components work together and should begin to indicate that the Health Society is where we need to go as a society. But a pilot project needs to be visible to all so as to help future national roll-out. That means having some sort of national stakeholders' committee to observe the work in the pilot scheme, to ensure that local solutions are feasible elsewhere, and to enable future rapid roll-out nationally. It is worth recalling that the roll-out of the NHS in 1948 was helped by the fact that Aneurin Bevan already knew of the experience of the Tredegar Medical Aid Society in South Wales. Founded in 1890, by 1925 this 'pilot NHS' was providing health and dental care free at the point of need to 95% of Tredegar's population. The wartime Emergency Medical Service also helped.

But what are the criteria that this pilot should meet? Here are ours:

- A single strategically minded authority that controls its own budget (including for the NHS).
- An innovative authority tackling failures to satisfy human needs like shelter for example.
- An area with poor indices of population health and, thus, a suitable candidate for innovation.
- An area with an extensive network of community organisations.
- An area with organisations (e.g. major football clubs) committed to improving population health.
- Forward-thinking local employers (e.g. the Co-op).
- Primary and secondary healthcare systems moving toward greater integration.
- Commitment of the local authorities to the NHS Health Check.
- A health improvement research base in local universities.
- At least some of the infrastructure requirements of the Health Society (e.g. full electronic health records for all inhabitants).

From our own knowledge, some of these criteria may be met by Greater Manchester, Southampton, Tayside and Torquay.

16

The tools for the job

If we had to, we could start to build the Health Society without any technological change at all. The transformation of public policy via Pillar One and implementation of community change via Pillar Two are just about sufficient to start the work. It would be a rough and ready Health Society, not so much the 'temple of health' that we mentioned in Chapter 14, but rather a health shack. The technological changes we describe here will provide stability and will promise continuous improvement to the structure of the Health Society. That is why we need them. There are just two changes and both involve rolling out two existing technologies on a bigger scale. One technology is the development and deployment of 'risk biomarkers'. The other is improved data integration and management. Both are part of the infrastructure that will support the Health Society and national prosperity as part of the 'foundational economy'.[1]

Risk biomarkers

The needs that define health – vital, social and agency needs – are often discussed in a socio-political context. However, in a scientific context, they can be dealt with as if they reflected the absence or presence of risk factors: factors that contribute to the likelihood of one or more conditions or diseases. If our vital need for nutrition is not optimally satisfied, for example, then this will raise the risk of deficiency diseases or long-term conditions. Vitamin C deficiency raises the risk of scurvy, while excess calorie intake raises the risk over time of diabetes, and so on. So to measure an abstract concept like 'needs satisfaction' we may be able to show that estimation of a molecule like Vitamin C or a physical quantity like weight gives some indication, directly or indirectly, of whether a particular need is being met. This is important both for public policy purposes and for each individual. When the indicator of needs satisfaction is a biological molecule of some sort – a molecule linked to metabolism in some way – we call the indicator a 'biomarker'.[2]

Detecting a change in a property of a biomarker – say a change in concentration in our blood or urine – will indicate either a change in the risk of some condition or disease or will contribute significantly to a clinical diagnosis of the presence of some condition or disease. These two outcomes from detecting a change are actually on a continuum: the key difference is whether the conclusion from making measurements is that we are healthy or not and whether we need to pay attention to prevention or get treatment. To distinguish between these uses of a biomarker, we talk of 'risk biomarkers' and 'diagnostic biomarkers'.

The distinction is not hard and fast. For example, a protein called PSA is present in the blood of adult men. If the concentration of PSA is low, then studies suggest that the risk of prostate cancer is low. But, above a certain threshold, a higher concentration indicates a higher risk of the presence of disease. There is ongoing research on what is the 'real' normal threshold and on whether PSA is more or less reliable than other prostate cancer risk biomarkers. Despite this, PSA is, for now, a risk biomarker and a diagnostic biomarker for the most common type of cancer in men. Of course, the risk factors for prostate cancer also include non-optimal nutrition (obesity) and non-optimal physical exercise.

Much effort has been made to identify biomarkers. They are attractive to study because a change in, say, their concentration may indicate a person-specific direct cause or effect of the disease or condition under study. No wonder therefore that the effort to find biomarkers has largely focussed on diagnostic biomarkers (including therapeutic biomarkers that can tell us whether a given therapy or treatment is working). But the Health Society is about prevention – about reducing the risks of conditions and diseases before the risk materialises. The Health Society means we need to be able to measure a change in a biomarker that reliably indicates a decrease in risk. To do this, researchers have to follow the health of a population where a good number of people are involved in risk reduction activities. How many of these people have an extended healthspan and what biomarker changes correlate with that extended healthspan?

If researchers can find these particular risk biomarkers then they can help everyone track the success (or failure) of their risk reduction activities.

Finding risk biomarkers

Risk biomarkers may be useful for measuring increasing or decreasing risk. Increases and decreases in risk are not necessarily a simple mirror reflection of each other, as one can see from this simple example. An adult is overweight and obese if Body Mass Index (BMI) is 25 or more. As people's weight gets too high, biological processes get underway that eventually lead to diabetes. But what if some of them lose weight? Do all of, or some of, or none of those biological processes go into reverse? If they all go into reverse, do they do this as a faithful mirror reflection of what happened when the processes got underway? No-one knows. To find out, as we noted briefly before, you have to start with a large population of people who are losing weight – or trying to lose weight – and follow their health for many years. If say, 10,000 such people slim down to BMI of 20, do they get diabetes at the same baseline frequency as people who have always had that BMI? Or do the slimmers get diabetes above baseline? Or perhaps, below baseline? No-one really knows.

Shockingly this ignorance exists across the board. It is not just when we use BMI as a risk reduction biomarker. It is true of all the risk and diagnostic biomarkers. Just as bad, no-one has looked for biomarkers that are specific to risk reduction. Researchers have just assumed that if the concentration of something goes up and this is associated with increased risk, then it can't be a bad thing if its concentration goes back down again.

To find risk biomarkers, researchers look at proteins, metabolites, RNA and DNA. All except DNA can vary in their concentration as a consequence of biological processes like growth or disease (i.e. the impact of the exposome). All four can be modified in their molecular structure by different biological processes. So, there are many millions of variations and modifications that can be measured and which may associate with any biological process in our bodies including the process of reduction of risk of the common long-term conditions.

The issue is which measurements are easiest and cheapest to take and which give the most precise and robust results? When it comes to the discovery of risk biomarkers, one wants to look at a biological sample that is as easy to obtain as possible and that contains molecules that are chemically stable and that can be characterised in large batches by a single quick and cheap method. These criteria are probably best satisfied by using blood samples and characterising its DNA for epigenetic modifications.[3] This combination is good not only for discovery of new risk biomarkers but also for population-wide testing.

What is meant by 'epigenetic modifications' to the DNA sequence? We described this briefly in Chapter 10. Here we give a little more detail. A chromosome is a single very long molecule, along which are strung nucleotide bases that are rather like many beads on a long string. There are four kinds of these 'beads' – A, C, G and T. A given DNA sequence is a specific combination of beads on the string. The living cell is able to interpret the various combinations to help it build the right proteins at the right time. This building process is tightly controlled. One of the control systems involves enzymes that can subtly modify the structure of some of the nucleotide bases – the beads – so as to fine tune the building process. For example, the nucleotide base C (cytosine) can become Me-C (methyl-cytosine). The study of this kind of modification of the DNA sequence is an important part of what we call epigenetics.

When an epigenetic modification occurs at a particular location in a chromosome, the cell will understand this as a signal that it should increase (or decrease) its activity in making protein from a nearby gene. This change in activity then has far-reaching consequences on the cell and indeed on the living being for better or worse. The epigenetic modification may, for example, be a consequence of someone gaining weight. Since we know that obesity is a risk factor for the common long-term conditions, it follows that we could assess risk for these conditions by looking for certain epigenetic signatures. Doing this could then end the need to weigh people.

The cost of checking for epigenetic modifications is rapidly decreasing. The data could be collected by the National Health Service Genomic Medicine Service[4] and would identify virtually all the modifications that have taken place and so allow the risks to be assessed of virtually all diseases and conditions that modify the epigenome.

While we have placed emphasis on the potential of epigenetic risk biomarkers, it would be wrong to place all our eggs in one basket. So, we should at least make passing mention of one more source of biomarkers (the microbiome) and also the potential of wearable monitoring devices.

The microbiome of a particular environment in our bodies refers to all micro-organisms (bacteria, viruses, fungi and others) that live side by side in environments such as the gut, mouth and skin.[5] There are some 100,000bn organisms in the gut. Normally they live in balance with each other and in harmony with their host, often contributing to host homeostasis. The numbers and types of micro-organism can change when risk of diabetes and heart disease are elevated by weight gain or clogged arteries. So, this then provides biomarkers for such risks. Since every micro-organism contains its own unique DNA, this DNA – extracted from stools and then sequenced – allows the relative numbers and types of micro-organism present to be estimated. The method has the advantage that the source material is obtained non-invasively.

Monitoring devices allow the continuous measurement of the body's physiology and activity. They can measure temperature, heart rate, breathing or how far we have walked or run in a given time. These quantities are, in effect, biomarkers. Their measurement has two benefits. First, the data can help the individual know if their physiology and activity is in the normal range. Second, the data can be shared in a group and so introduce the well-known 'buddy effect': friends who act together on an issue – say weight reduction – can compare notes and are more likely to be successful. If researchers are collecting all this data from existing wearable devices and the new ones that are becoming available, then it is likely that new insights will emerge on our vital needs.

Biological samples

Finding risk biomarkers is a bit like finding signs of life on Mars. Yes, you need to move a Mars Rover round the planet's surface, but first you have to get to the planet. Neither stage is easy. Similarly, finding risk biomarkers by testing blood samples means first getting hold of – and keeping – the samples. This may sound simple enough, but no country has yet been able to do it for their population as a whole. Nowhere is ready to start delivering the Health Society.

Every day, large numbers of blood samples are collected from patients receiving primary or secondary healthcare. But the samples are thrown away after testing. They are collected because a clinician wants to rule out or establish a diagnosis of some disease or condition by performing a few clinical tests. Once testing is complete, the sample is destroyed. It needn't be this way, however. In Beijing and Shanghai, for example, samples like this are now stored indefinitely. As a result, these samples can be used to hunt for new risk biomarkers or to assess individuals for their risk of conditions for which they have no symptoms. In other words the samples can be used to aid prevention. Note that health information about each individual over the years is also needed to make sense of risk biomarker data.

In the NHS Health Check, participants provide a blood sample that is tested for its cholesterol level: if it is too high this indicates an elevated risk of heart disease. A test may also be carried out for a protein elevated in diabetes. The test results are stored in the health record of the individual, but the sample is dumped. Yet it could give lifetime genetic risks, current epigenetic risks and enable discovery of new biomarkers.

There are two reasons why this does not happen. First, participants are not routinely asked if they would consent to the use of their samples in research. Second, appropriate long-term storage facilities – biobanks – are not funded as part of the health check system. There are plenty of biobanks in the UK – the total capacity is huge – but the two big problems are fragmentation (insufficient coordination between biobanks to get the most out of the samples they hold) and focus (most collections focus on new treatments not on better prevention).

The biggest publicly owned facility is the UK Biocentre in Milton Keynes but currently the collections that it holds are not integrated. The biggest single collection of people's samples and data is the publicly owned UK Biobank in Manchester: half a million volunteers provide both information and various sample types including blood. The health of these volunteers has now been followed for well over a decade. The experimental design is excellent for the discovery of certain risk factors that may relate directly to causality. For example, much scientific interest has centred on lifetime genetic risk, since this can help specify steps in a disease process where new drugs might be effective. Thus, the design of UK Biobank is primarily to support discovery of new treatments. Prevention was not a primary consideration when the project was being planned.

A complete national biobanking system for the UK could be constructed quickly: there are no technical barriers; there is plenty of experience on how to organise the nuts and bolts; industry backs the idea.[6] The principal barrier is that there is not the drive and the coordination to get all the people and organisations working together. A unitary system for managing human samples is essential to the Health Society but it is also increasingly necessary for the development of new medicines.

Health data

In a perfect world, risk biomarkers would track the risks to health across the population. This biomarker data would be all that is required to guide the actions needed to improve individual and population health. While such perfection may be a future ambition of the Health Society, in the meantime, we shall have to make do with other risk data to guide us – other data that is not so cut and dried.

This data on individuals falls into three broad categories: healthcare data, socio-economic data and epidemiological research data. Individual healthcare data refers primarily to patient records from family doctors and hospitals. Individual socio-economic data is collected from surveys and through the national census every decade. Epidemiological research data only covers a tiny fraction of the population currently but it tackles a large number of questions and is important for discovering new associations between biomarkers and health.

The key problem with patient records is, just like with sample management, that the record systems are fragmented in various ways. For example, they may be on paper or electronic and terminology is not standardised across the board. Paper records take time to find and are difficult to search, to correct or to analyse. Electronic records in different places use different programs and the programs can be incompatible. When people move house, it takes time for their records to catch them up and some records get left behind (e.g. records from previous local hospitals). This may mean a new doctor being ignorant of a patient's long-term conditions, medication, allergies or risk of serious drug adverse reaction.

So, while the NHS is a healthcare system that could deliver equitable and high quality healthcare to the entire population, it cannot achieve this without, among other things, the right data management infrastructure. The NHS does not have this infrastructure. As a consequence, the problem of inequality in healthspan and lifespan that was described in the Marmot Review (see Chapter 2) is less likely to be solved. The right data management system is a fully integrated system that standardises all health data for all the population, that supports the training and work of both Health Society professionals and Health Society Champions and that enables oversight and assessment of the Health Society in all its aspects.

Construction started in 2003 of a system for national healthcare data management (i.e. not all health data). NHS Connecting for Heath was established within the UK Department for Health in 2005 to oversee private contractors while they built and delivered a single centrally run electronic patient record system across some 30,000 general practices and 300 hospitals. However, most of the contractors failed to deliver on time or to budget. This is often the case with infrastructure projects, but a new government decided in 2010 to pull the plug on the project and to adopt a piecemeal approach. Most hospitals now keep electronic records, but they are essentially standalone and are not usually integrated with primary care data, let alone linking hospitals together. Yet such integration is recognised by everyone, including the pharmaceutical industry, to be essential to the development of new or improved treatments. One of the key benefits of integration is that it becomes far easier, quicker and cheaper to recruit patients for clinical trials. Indeed the pharmaceutical industry nowadays needs to work with very large populations – 500m or more – in order to find the right patients in a timely way. That means that countries with smaller populations are overlooked in favour of places like China or regional groupings of countries like the European Union.

This requirement for large populations with standardised electronic healthcare records has emerged because biomedical research has been able to identify new potential medicines that are effective in just a small number of individuals. The new medicines act more precisely than ever in treating those individuals. This new medicine is sometimes called 'precision medicine'. A number of public health researchers also can see benefits to population health from using population-wide datasets and they have coined the term 'precision public health' to describe this. There is therefore an overlap between 'precision public health' and the construction of the Health Society. However, to end the modern plagues, improvement of data management infrastructure alone is, we must emphasise, insufficient.[7]

This summary of the importance of health data to population health improvement may mislead readers into thinking that the issues are relatively straightforward. This is not the case. To get some idea of the difficulties, look below at the list of stakeholders in a current UK-led European project called the European Institute for Innovation through Health Data:

- Patient organisations.
- Healthcare professionals and provider organisations.
- Pharmaceutical and biotechnology companies.
- Healthcare payers and policymakers.
- Health data brokers.

- Health information and communications technology sector.
- Scientific and academic organisations.
- Standards development organisations and industry associations.

The improvement of healthcare data management via this project calls for all these types of stakeholder to work together. Even more stakeholders are required to improve data management for health improvement since that calls for data on vital, social and agency needs.

As we construct the Health Society these ways of collecting information, once organised systematically, will enable the measurement of risk reduction and thereby help improve the ways in which risks are reduced.

Let us imagine, for example, that a football team's fan club has a Health Society Champion. 'Which way can supporters get to normal weight quicker and then keep it that way?' asks the champion. 'Is it with a buddy system with three members or ten members?' If all the data on the members is collected and made accessible to researchers, not only can this question be answered but also other questions – such as how many cases of diabetes, depression, cancer or heart disease have been averted.

In other words we can start to develop evidence-based strategies for risk reduction by measuring reduced risks in the real world. It is impossible to do this in a conventional observational epidemiological study where only 'natural' behaviour is studied. The very idea of interfering in such natural processes by having Health Society Champions and professionals is considered anathema because bias may be introduced. But the Health Society wants to turn that bias to good effect.

Data danger

There is no getting away from the fact that construction of the Health Society requires the use of large quantities of data from different sources on all of us from cradle to grave. And, there is no getting away from the fact that this requirement cannot be satisfied without the strictest control on access to the data. In the UK, the current arrangements for data from healthcare sources involve data storage in 'safe havens' that are overseen by Health Data Research UK. This is jointly funded by ten research funders and the data is stored by twenty-two research institutes across the UK. In a Health Society, this structure provides a good starting point. However, there will be major new challenges. For example, the Health Society will see high levels of involvement by ordinary people in improving their own health and that of their communities. They will need access to some data to see how they are doing. This access will require amending current rules and processes and providing appropriate support to individuals and organisations. This support would help ensure that data is properly interpreted with strict controls to prevent any invasion of privacy.

These controls are very important for the maintenance of public trust and for the continued involvement of individuals who permit personal data to be stored in the first place. For a brief period, the UK government wanted to allow private companies easy access to healthcare data. But the government retreated in the face of protests when it recognised the problems that easy access would cause.

Miscalculations like this will slow down the development of the Health Society and the cost of that is, of course, the persistence of the modern plagues. It is difficult for us to know the value systems of other societies, but recent developments in China would certainly challenge values commonly held in the UK. Alibaba is the Chinese equivalent of Amazon and, as part of a consortium approved by the government, it is building an online credit scoring system called Sesame. By publishing their score, people are able to book a hotel room without a deposit, or to get a loan. The score is calculated from data on individuals' online purchasing history. The government is due imminently to complete construction of a similar national 'social credit' scoring system. This will measure every citizen's 'trustworthiness' using data on everything from financial information to traffic violations. It is clear that data management systems today can put power over citizens in the hands of others. But the systems can also empower the individual. Getting this balance right is critically important for the Health Society to succeed.

Movement in the right direction

Some interesting initiatives are underway, which aim to combine research with action on health improvement. They are overcoming some of the barriers that have constrained classical epidemiological observational research. Here are two examples from the US.

100K Wellness Project

In 2014, the Seattle Institute for Systems Biology initiated the 100K Wellness Project.[8] In the pilot phase, 107 participants gave consent for research and provided blood, urine, saliva and faecal samples every three months for metabolite, proteomic and gut microbiome testing and whole-genome sequencing. They also provided information on lifestyle habits, and data from wearable fitness trackers. 'Health coaches' provided participants individually with feedback from data analysis and advised on risk reduction actions. Overwhelmingly, the participants were white and upper middle class.[9] It turned out that everyone needed to reduce one or other risk factor, everyone was advised of this, and seven out of ten followed that advice. During the nine months of the study, some participants showed a decrease in risk while in others the risks materialised as disease. The main goal of this study is a research goal: the identification of new biomarkers. The goal of increasing the healthspan of the US population as a whole is not addressed.

Kavli HUMAN project

The proposed Kavli HUMAN Project in New York City aims to run for 25 years, recruiting 10,000 individuals from approximately 2,500 family units in the five city boroughs.[10] Their biology and behaviours will be measured from analysis of biological samples combined with a full record of their health, education, environmental and 'lifestyle' profiles. Environmental conditions and events affecting participants will be captured using a new Geographic Information System currently under construction. Linkage to secondary healthcare electronic records is anticipated. Wearable health-related devices will be deployed. The organisers hope that the project will enable evidence-based change for improved health and well-being, particularly in an urban context.

Can Britain lead the way in building the Health Society? We think so. There is widespread and popular appreciation of the value of a universal system to treat illness, which is free when it is needed. A universal system to prevent illness is conceptually little different. While the British enjoy their privacy, they also enjoy socialising through clubs and other community organisations. Putting health maintenance on the agenda of every club will strengthen the club and help it attract more members. Employers have a history of supporting sports clubs for their staff. All major political parties recognise that prevention of the common long-term conditions has to be moved up the agenda of government action, if only to save money. The technological know-how exists. The key obstacle is that prevention is wrongly thought of as the professional responsibility of people who are already very over-stretched trying to deal with consequences of the absence of effective prevention.

17

Your health is my health

We have argued that to save sick Britain, we need to start building the Health Society. This is a society that reduces the risks to us all of the modern plagues, of the common long-term conditions like diabetes, depression, heart disease and cancer. Building that Health Society requires a new way of life achieved through institutional, community and technological change.

The idea of the Health Society challenges what most people today think society is for, it re-thinks what is meant by 'health' and then applies this in a rational and evidence-led manner. The theoretical underpinning for this re-think comes from separate British works of scholarship. Noble's theory of biological relativity is based on observations of the interconnectedness of all living systems including ours. Hamilton's political philosophy of needs argues that 'health' is the state wherein there is optimal satisfaction of human needs. When we bring these two ideas together, we replace older perceptions of the purposes of society – to increase prosperity, to gain power, to assert certain economic, political or moral values – with that of achieving health through optimal satisfaction of our needs. The scale of the modern plagues and the societal risks that they engender make this new purpose for society necessary and timely.

While the idea of a Health Society is challenging, it is not radical in the conventional political sense: it is merely the modern version of an ancient aphorism, of Cicero's flash of insight when he wrote that the health of the population is the over-riding purpose of government. There was little that the Romans could do to turn this idea into reality: they had virtually no tools for the job. Cicero was ahead of his time.

This then is our central message.

We started by looking at the burden on individuals and on society as a whole of the rising incidence of the modern plagues, of what are commonly called chronic non-communicable diseases such as Type 2 diabetes, heart disease, cancer, depression, and so on.

We justified the use of the word 'plagues' by comparing the numbers of people affected by these diseases with those affected by an infectious epidemic like flu or by the bubonic plagues of the past.

We challenged the idea that they are non-communicable by noting that a major risk factor – obesity – spreads through social networks. And we showed how one disease leads to another so that people can have multiple diagnoses at the same time.

We saw how the span of people's lives can be divided in two. Healthy lives often end with a diagnosis with one of the modern plagues. Diagnosis marks the end of healthspan and is followed by years or decades spent living with increasing disabilities until the end of lifespan. This second period of life is marked by, on the one hand, individual isolation that exacerbates social fragmentation and, on the other, results in time off work that affects income and can limit career prospects.

The other side of the problem is the inadequacy over the decades of policy responses that have largely comprised fine words and feeble efforts.

We then looked at the scientific landscape: the birth of epidemiology and the constraints on its ability to experiment; an understanding of the molecular level at which diseases act offering possibilities not only for treatment but also for effective prevention;

an understanding of all the levels of organisation of ourselves and our society that modify disease risks.

We found that only those risk factors that the individual and society can actually reduce are practical targets for action – risk factors such as obesity, physical inactivity and isolation.

We argued that an appreciation of risk is essential to understanding the need for change but that the idea of risk is not, in general, well understood.

Is there a scientific basis for proposing that society is based on health? We delved into this question, looking at the theory of biological relativity, looking at how 'health' can be defined in a positive way that allows preventive action to maintain health – Systems Prevention. This was contrasted with natural prevention – processes in nature that are often indistinguishable from natural selection.

How do we refashion society for health, starting from where we are now? Our answer was to specify change across public policy with the three pillars of institutional, community and technological change. And, we proposed setting an initial target: to reduce the average gap between healthspan and lifespan in the UK to that seen today in the least deprived of the population.

Here is a summary of the initial changes that we say are needed (others say similar things).

Enshrine in UK law the World Health Organization principle of 'health in all policies' with the explicit aim of prevention of the modern plagues.

Deputy Prime Minister to head a 'war cabinet' so that change is coordinated across all aspects of public policy. Initial goal: reduce the gap between healthspan and lifespan to ten years for all neighbourhoods. Perform an audit on how much is really spent on prevention pure and simple. Double this amount immediately. A comprehensive Universal National Health Service Health Check. Every pound saved on treatment to be used for prevention. Establish a publicly visible oversight mechanism for policy implementation and service delivery. Appoint a Royal Commission to reform all public policy.

Data: deliver fully integrated, digitised and standardised records of information that contribute to health risk and its reduction. New locations for data entry (e.g. in the community). Data harmonisation across England, Northern Ireland, Scotland and Wales for data-sharing and reviews of best practice.

Employers' duty of care to extend to prevention of the modern plagues. Help, support and advice via Health Society professionals to both public and private employers.

Help, support and advice from Health Society professionals to community and social organisations and to Health Society Champions recruited via a universal Health Society Check.

Help, support and advice from Health Society professionals to Health Society Champions working more widely to mobilise their communities and workplaces.

Primary and secondary school curriculum to include population health. In higher education, the social responsibility mission of institutions to include improving health of the local population.

Maintain and increase Public Health's public education, promotion of improved legislation and role as an observatory. The four Public Health bodies (in England, Northern Ireland, Scotland and Wales) might report directly to the Deputy Prime Minister and execute coordination across departments.

A couple of diversions

The profound changes required to build the Health Society will provoke opposition. Some will be diversionary – trying to blow us off track – and some will be direct.

One diversion says: 'There are more important health issues to tackle.' This is the line taken by a major UK lobby group, the Institute of Economic Affairs. Its head of 'lifestyle economics',

Chris Snowdon, is critical of the World Health Organization. He said:

> The WHO has become obsessed with western lifestyles at the expense of more serious health matters in the developing world. They worry too much about 'reward-risk' scenarios like sugar and plain packaging on cigarettes. It'd be better off educating the public on infectious disease rather than endless prohibition and pushing poor countries into protocol after protocol.[1]

It is plain wrong to suggest that the obesity epidemic – the principal modifiable risk factor for the chronic diseases that the WHO wants to tackle – is a 'western' phenomenon: it is a global phenomenon. It is plain irresponsible to suggest that the modern plagues are less significant than infectious diseases. Hundreds of millions of people in both rich and poor countries have diabetes, depression, heart disease or cancer. It is surely incomprehensible to them that these diseases and conditions are the WHO's 'obsession'.

A more subtle variant of this type of diversion is to change the subject by sleight of hand. For example, a politician might say: 'Yes, of course, I want to prevent this or that disease. That's why I shall ensure that there is better detection and treatment of the disease.' But, clearly, they have changed the subject because, whereas better detection and treatment require only a national health service, effective prevention additionally requires a Health Society. A problem that requires profound change has, in the unconscious blink of an eye, by a turn of phrase, been turned into a quite different problem.

Here is an example of how it works. Poor mental health affects millions of people and costs the country £99bn a year. So, in January 2017, the then Prime Minister asked two experts 'to undertake an independent review into how employers can better support the mental health of all people currently in employment including those with mental health problems or poor well-being to remain in and thrive through work'.

Notice how the terms of reference refer both to 'all people' and 'those with mental health problems'. Instantly, there is a conflation of prevention and treatment. This is then reinforced by stating that the aim is to help 'those with mental health problems or poor well-being to remain in and thrive through work'. And, naturally, no-one will disagree with the Prime Minister when she wrote: 'More needs to be done so that employers provide the support needed for employees with mental health conditions.'

The experts who performed the review duly obliged and came up with forty recommendations.[2] Most of these are aimed at helping those already found to have poor mental health. To be fair, a small number of recommendations concerned with prevention were sneaked in. For example, the review says employers should be rewarded with tax breaks when they manage mental health better. Two ministers announced jointly that they accepted the review in full.[3] But there was no new funding or legislative back-up. Both ministers then moved on to other jobs. A problem of prevention that requires profound change was turned into a problem of treatment and then kicked into the long grass.

More direct arguments against the national Health Society can be made. The main ones are:

- It's all down to individual choice; the market knows best; things will sort themselves out naturally.
- It is more important to address socio-economic inequality.
- Legal reform is more important so as to establish the right of every individual to prevention measures.

These arguments, discussed more fully below, are all faulty for the same fundamental scientific reason. They give precedence to one level of organisation of our species as the determinant. They ignore the theory of biological relativity whereby no single level takes precedence in determining survival. The arguments are deterministic – and that is a fault.

It's my choice

'How people lead their lives is all down to them. It's an individual choice – and that goes for health, food, physical activity and anything else.' This is a commonly held view. It can take a more robust expression in the form: 'Why should I pay tax to prevent others getting ill?' Or it can be dressed up with a fancy name like 'rational choice theory'. This theory claims that when each human being chooses to act in their own self-interest (i.e. making a 'rational choice' is presumed to be a selfish choice), then, overall, this realises the public good.

But these ideas just do not work in the real world. To appreciate this, consider what happens when a major flu epidemic comes along. Every individual recognises that, if other people catch flu, then their own risk of flu rises dramatically. In other words, we recognise that our own health is dependent on the health of others. Governments may recognise this too and so may act to develop a vaccine as quickly as possible and to make it universally available. When it comes to flu, we all recognise that it is plainly not just down to us as individuals. We recognise that when your health is protected, then my health is protected too. We recognise that 'Your health is my health'.

But it isn't just flu. Chapter 9 described the network transmission of obesity from person to person. This means that 'Your obesity is my obesity'. In *The Spirit Level*, the authors describe how, round the world, the health of different groups in society affects each other for better or for worse.[4] Using data from twenty nation states in Europe, Asia and North America they found that the proportion of the adult population that is obese rises dramatically as income inequality rises. The lowest proportion was in Japan (at about 3%) and the highest in the US (at 30%). Japan has the lowest income inequality of the twenty nation states; the US has the highest. The same trend is evident for overweight teenagers. Even within a nation state like the US, comparing individual states of the union, those with the least income inequality also had the least obesity. Life expectancy follows the same pattern: you live longer in nation states, or within areas of nation states, with lower income inequality. Mental health is no different: Japan had the lowest proportion (8%) of mental illness while the US had the highest (26%).

This suggests health benefits will accrue to all citizens of a nation state that reduces its income inequality. But it is also the case that everyone's health suffers as a consequence of more deprivation, whether or not they are deprived. We have analysed life expectancy data comparing different regions of England. The data shows that life expectancy is shorter for the least deprived in the North West than for the least deprived in the South East. And the same is true for the most deprived. To be direct, this means that the health of the rich is bound up with the health of the poor – and vice versa. Your life expectancy is my life expectancy; your obesity is my obesity; your health is my health.

As a consequence, it just is not enough for each of us individually to make the right health choices. To reduce individual risks and improve individual health, we have to ensure that others also make the right health choices. We are responsible for each other, whether we like it or not, whether we choose to believe it or not.

A further problem with 'rational choice theory' is that, in reality, individual citizens may not be in a position to make a rational choice. Consider our levels of physical activity. At the height of the Industrial Revolution, working men, women and even children had far higher physical activity levels than today. They had no choice: they had to work and that nearly always meant intense physical activity. Today, by contrast, working men and women cannot choose to work in that way because work is increasingly sedentary. In the US, the proportion of workers carrying out 'light activity' (predominantly sitting at a desk) doubled between 1970 and 2000 from two in ten to four in ten. In the same thirty-year period, the number of people carrying out jobs requiring 'high-energy output' (construction, manufacturing, farming) fell from three in ten to two in ten.[5] In those thirty years – and even more so since – the 'high-energy' jobs have become increasingly mechanised. People cannot, in general, make the rational choice to work at a job that ensures the optimal levels of physical activity needed for health. Making rational choices between brands of jeans or T-shirts may be possible. But are such choices possible between the various human needs that define health?

Another way of looking at this change in work is by following the growth of the 'knowledge economy' – work broadly associated with the production, distribution and exchange of knowledge and information. 'Knowledge-based services' include communications, financial services, business services, education and health.[6] In the UK between 1970 and 2006, this knowledge economy more than doubled, while manufacturing more than halved. Figure 17.1 illustrates the broader picture of the relative decline of manufacturing and the rise of the service sector.

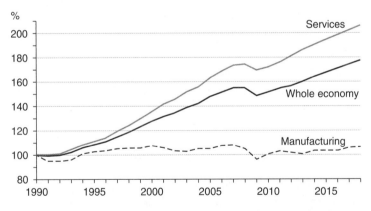

Figure 17.1 Graph from the House of Commons Library showing that the service sector of the economy is growing while manufacturing is not. These big changes are not due to choices by individuals yet they impact on everyone's health. In the UK in 2018, £1.5 trillion of total UK economic output was from the services industry (including retail, accommodation, business administration and finance), £186bn was from manufacturing output and £115bn was from the construction sector.

These far-reaching changes in our way of life have precious little to do with individual choice. Yet they have profound consequences for health, for healthspan and for optimal satisfaction of human needs.

Why people 'believe in' individual choice is explained, in part, surely, by the fact that almost every individual yearns to have control over their own life. This yearning is a fantasy because we are a social species that evolved as such out of necessity, not choice. If individuals want to take back control, then this generally needs to be a collaborative and collective enterprise, not an individualistic one.

If, on the other hand, we know absolutely that we cannot take control, then we have no choice but to grin and bear it. This outlook on life is called stoicism. The classic exponent of this view was a Roman Emperor, Marcus Aurelius Antoninus, who controlled every slave and citizen in his vast empire but could not control a major plague (probably smallpox). This so-called Antonine Plague – named after him – probably took his life too. Stoicism is all that is left if we, as individuals and as a society, have already tried everything and it has all failed. If we haven't tried everything, if, as today, governments are guilty of dithering, then stoicism is merely an excuse for defeatism, cowardice, negligence and hard-heartedness.

Don't worry, we'll find a cure

We referred earlier to the view of the pharmaceutical industry, that its 'Holy Grail' is the discovery of some elixir of youth – a new medicine to prolong life (and implicitly to prolong healthspan). Increasing numbers of publicly funded researchers have turned their attention to this and so this view must carry some weight with funding agencies. It certainly carries weight with some British MPs who have formed an All Party Parliamentary Group for Longevity. At the time of writing, the current issue of the journal of the Gerontological Society of America (gerontology being the study of ageing) includes numerous research papers on drugs and human proteins that seem to offer a route to an elixir. The funders include US and EU research funders, charities and industry.

We are deeply sceptical of this approach. Seeking to extend healthspan using a magic bullet to counter the effects of non-optimal satisfaction of the vital, social and agency needs that we have identified as constituting health seems to us to be, at best, scientifically naive. It is a simplistic extrapolation from the observation that different animals have different lifespans.

However, let us say there were an elixir out there waiting to be discovered. We would be wrong. But we are still right because, here and now, that elixir is unknown to all and so humanity cannot just wait around for the elixir to become known at some unknown time in the future. We need to do what we can with the knowledge and the tools that we already have. We need to construct the Health Society.

More dismally, if we are wrong and an elixir were to be discovered that somehow prevents all the common long-term conditions, then this still leaves plenty of long-term conditions out there. These conditions would still terminate healthspan earlier than needs be. Moreover, the needs that define health would still remain unsatisfied – unless we were to have constructed the Health Society.

Inequality is the problem

Another common argument states that the way to reduce the differences in healthspan in the population and to improve population health is by acting to end socio-economic inequalities across society. Socio-economic deprivation, it is pointed out, is strongly associated with shorter healthspan, reduced life expectancy, poorer access to healthcare and lack of agency. As a socio-economic project, the case for addressing inequalities is attractive to many. It is a matter of justice for all. Unequal prospects for children at birth, for school children, in working life and the plight of stricken communities are matters that damage many lives and prick consciences.

However, the fact is that a swathe of opinion treats these matters as contentious. Many people remain locked into narratives about individual choice. They say: 'Why should I pay tax to benefit the feckless poor?' As a consequence, an unending debate continues on justice and injustice or on individual rights. In the process, the issue of preventing the modern plagues is lost, or at least diluted.

Take the 2010 Marmot Review, 'Fair Society, Healthy Lives', on how to tackle inequalities in health. It set the benchmark in examining solutions to the issues of health inequality. It informed subsequent policy proposals from the World Health Organization. It argued that health inequalities are a matter of social justice and fairness and that tackling them involves tackling social inequalities as well as tackling climate change. It went on to demonstrate the scale of health inequality in England and its human and economic costs. It specified the social determinants of health and then moved on to a critique of UK public policy followed by proposals for change. These proposals fell into six themes:

- Give every child the best start in life.
- Enable all children, young people and adults to maximise their capabilities and have control over their lives.
- Create fair employment and good work for all.
- Ensure healthy standard of living for all.
- Create and develop healthy and sustainable places and communities.
- Strengthen the role and impact of ill-health prevention.

The policy proposals are persuasive and the proposals for implementing them are detailed. The problem is: who has been persuaded? Since the review appeared in 2010, things have got worse, not better. Evidence for this comes from the rising gap in life expectancy between the most and the least deprived: this gap has risen between 2001 and 2016 by 1.8 years for women and by 0.7 years for men.[7]

Clearly, not enough people have been persuaded. But, whose job is it to do the persuading? Ending inequality is a very hot political potato where divisions of opinion boil down to divisions about individual choice theory. What biology and the related sciences can offer is a very strong case that 'Your health is my health'. Putting that idea into practice in the form of the Health Society not only has its own merits, but it also counteracts individual choice theory by establishing the interdependence of all humans, whether for the purposes of extending healthspan or of ensuring prosperity for all. In brief, enabling the construction of the Health Society is the most appropriate, most necessary, and probably the best way for biologists and epidemiologists to contribute to ending social inequalities.

A key advantage of the Health Society concept is that it builds on the principle behind the most treasured of Britain's public institutions – the National Health Service. The service is universal because it is obliged to treat every patient's illness, regardless of them being rich or poor. The same universality applies to the Health Society.

It just won't work

Saying 'It just won't work' is perhaps the easiest fall-back position of those who resist reform. It is also the most desperate position because there is no evidence to support this view, at least until we start to construct the Health Society. This negative thinking brings to mind the web page that lists 'Fifty Reasons Why We Cannot Change'.[8] Here is a selection of those excuses (slightly modified):

- We've never done it before.
- We don't have the money.
- We tried it before.
- It's not my job.

- Nobody else has ever done it.
- We don't have the time.
- We've been doing it the old way for years.
- It will put people out of work.
- It won't work in a small group.
- It's contrary to policy.
- It won't work in a large group.
- It's not our problem.
- It won't work here.
- It's too complicated.
- Why change – it's working OK.
- We're not ready for it.
- It's too much trouble to change.
- It needs more thought.
- Our country is different.
- We can't take the chance.
- Someone won't like it.
- We'd lose money on it.
- It's too visionary.
- It takes too long.
- It's too radical.
- We're doing all right as it is.
- It can't be done.
- It needs sleeping on.

Of these excuses, the one that might seem most compelling is 'We don't have the money – there is no money tree'. While this may be batted away with the principle that you can't put a price on human life, the fact is that some politicians want to do this (as long as it is not their own life) and some economists are happy to do various sums. A better line of reasoning to counter this excuse is based on recognising that the Health Society is a new way of making the wheels of industry and commerce turn. It is a society driven by seeking to satisfy needs, measured by parameters of health and guided by the usual combination of regulation, incentives and disincentives. The changes inherent in the Health Society are not some cost added onto today's expenditures, but are a completely new budget with the same budget items as today (income, expenditure, borrowing and repayment) but with new sources of income and new forms of expenditure.

Transitioning to this Health Society is a process. To help that process, the funding that previously went into treating the modern plagues can, over time, be re-directed toward preventing those conditions. Every case of diabetes prevented is a saving from the £100bn-plus NHS budget. Currently it spends about £10bn a year on treating diabetes which is £2,000–3,000 per patient. In 2010, the costs of cancer diagnosis and treatment in the UK were estimated at £9.4bn. This is equivalent to an average of £30,000 per person with cancer.

Every case of, say, diabetes that is prevented in a year saves not just that sum, but a similar sum each and every year that a patient remains alive. If the patient lives for a further twenty years, the total saved is £40,000–50,000. Preventing about twenty cases in the first year would pay the salary for a full-time Health Society professional for a lifetime. Thus it is prevention that is cheap, while it is treatment that costs so much.

Your Earth is my Earth

The case for the Health Society works at three levels. First, there is the fact of the modern plagues and the failure of current public policy. Second, the theory of biological relativity says humans can do it the easy way (via Systems Prevention) or the hard way (via natural prevention). The third line of argument is one that we have not yet described. Scientists have identified another major source of risk to humanity: global heating due to human activity. This has major implications for health-as-needs because it is reducing our ability to satisfy those needs.

This is illustrated in Table 17.1, in which we use information from 'Countdown on Health and Climate Change', a study by 150 experts from twenty-seven universities and institutions including the World Health Organization and the World Bank.[9] In the table, the first column lists human needs and the second column specifies observations that put those needs at risk. Only the most direct risks are specified, but the indirect risks are just as important. For example, climate change is causing migration, where the immediate motive for moving away is, say, crop failure that

Table 17.1   Human needs and climate change

Human needs	Risks to health from global heating
Nutrition (including air and water)	• 30 countries are experiencing downward trends in crop yields • Sea surface temperatures have risen in 16 of 21 fishing basins, risking marine primary productivity • Air pollution worsened in 70% of cities from 2010 to 2016 • Ambient air pollution resulted in more than 2.9 million premature deaths globally from fine particulates alone in 2015
Shelter	• Vulnerability to heat exposure is rising. 42–43% of over-65s in Europe and the East Mediterranean are vulnerable • Heatwave exposure events rose 11% in one year from 2016–17, affecting 157 million people • South America and Southeast Asia are regions most exposed to flood and drought • Frequency has risen of floods and extreme temperature since 1990
Vital and agency needs	• Migration by thousands of people is caused solely or largely by climate change • Hours of labour lost due to extreme heat rose by 40% between 2000 and 2017
Disease	• Mortality from dengue fever and malignant skin melanoma is rising • Susceptibility to dengue fever has risen 10% since the 1950s • Susceptibility to diarrhoea and sepsis has risen 25% on the Baltic and US northeast coast since the 1980s • Susceptibility to malaria has risen 21% in highland areas of Africa since the 1950s

Source: based on data from 'Countdown on Health and Climate Change'.

puts at risk the vital need for nutrition. However, migration also puts agency needs at risk since loss of population can decimate a community or region and so leave in tatters the social structures within which agency needs are met. The result can be a failed state. Furthermore, individual climate refugees are at high risk of loss of satisfying of their own agency needs because they have left the social structures that had provided it to some degree and because they are likely to end up in a place where they are socially isolated (or worse). Social impacts include risk of war and violent conflict, a risk that is usually thought of separately from 'health'. However, for us, war and conflict put all the needs that comprise health at high risk.

What ending the modern plagues and ending global heating have in common is that both require joined-up public policy with progressive reforms. If we are serious about implementing a comprehensive joined-up approach, then there is no obvious reason to do so for one reason but then not to do so for the other. Indeed, it would be irrational and counter-productive if public policy changes were made to tackle one problem that exacerbated the other problem. Moreover, the task of explaining the need for the change becomes far easier. For example, in the UK, it seems probable that most people will support public policy to stop global heating. Most people recognise that 'Your Earth is my Earth' because the scientific evidence has been explained by scientists, by global institutions and sometimes by government. If people can recognise this, then there is every reason also to accept that your health is my health and that to save sick Britain we should build the Health Society.

18

Postscript:
the COVID-19 pandemic

In this postscript, we want first to comment on the global character of COVID-19. Then we shall follow the four sections of *Saving sick Britain* so as to draw some parallels between this pandemic and what we have been calling the modern plagues.

The COVID-19 pandemic highlights the global character of viral diseases, while this book has largely focussed on the common long-term conditions in an insular, even Anglo-centric, fashion. The reasons for our focus were not only because we felt we had to recognise the reality of rising parochialism in Britain but also because we recognised that we were, ourselves, most familiar with societal structures in the UK: we too suffer from parochialism.

COVID-19 has exposed a weakness in this book: it is not solely about saving sick Britain. The pandemic demonstrates that we are far more intimately connected to each other across our planet than Little Englanders can admit. Had we started on this book post-COVID-19, we might well have entitled it 'Saving our sick societies'. We may well have referred not to the 'modern plagues' but to the 'modern pandemics'. The case we make for the Health Society is actually global because humanity as a whole needs to recognise the fundamental fact that we come together as a species so as to seek to meet the needs that optimally define health.

If we fail to do this on COVID-19, there is a risk that humanity will leave a dangerous reservoir of infection in low income countries (or in susceptible animals) so that the virus can then initiate a second pandemic. For common long-term conditions there is a comparable global aspect. If solely high-income countries – and not medium- and low-income countries – end the modern plagues, then their prosperity will shrink. Diminished prosperity in one country means that the second country suffers diminished trade with that country. Their health is our health.

The same is true within individual countries where there are locations or social groups that endure deprivation. In the case of COVID-19 this has been starkly revealed by the elevated mortality among people of colour in the UK and US. The American Medical Association has identified racism as a risk to public health. In other words, racism risks everyone's health either by allowing a 'pool' of infection to persist or by diminishing the prosperity of society as a whole. If a virus can exacerbate society's tensions and inequalities, so can the modern plagues by causing slow-motion social disintegration.

Racism is a modifiable risk factor, not only for COVID-19 but also for the modern plagues, because racism denies optimal satisfaction of vital, social and agency needs. Like obesity and other modifiable risk factors, it spreads through social networks. Initially it targets the health of a separate social network (people of colour) but goes on to damage the health of the network from which racism has emerged. The social network that produces and reproduces racism suffers a self-inflicted loss of optimal satisfaction of agency needs and, ultimately, of vital needs.

The value of global coordination on COVID-19 is clear from the World Health Organization 'Solidarity mega-trial'. This experiment is running many clinical trials on candidate drugs in many countries simultaneously. The key advantage of this is that all the trials can follow the same standards and so their results become fully comparable. While randomised clinical trials normally take years to design and conduct, the Solidarity Trial will take just a fifth as long, the WHO believes. Similarly, great efficiencies would arise if countries jointly undertook experiments to build the Health Society. Experiments on government, industrial and voluntary sector action could be standardised and the results compared swiftly. Low- and middle-income countries would also participate and benefit.

COVID-19 is not a modern plague like those that we have described here. Rather, it is an old-fashioned infectious disease that has spread around the globe to cause a pandemic. What is new about this infection is that, for the first time ever, we humans have the tools to defeat it, although our societal organisation needs reforms so as to be able to use those tools to their best advantage. For example, the World Health Organization has no powers of enforcement over irresponsible governments despite the risks they create for other nations, let alone their own populations. Much the same is true for the pandemics in diabetes, depression and heart disease, where not only some governments but also some global industries lack responsibility.

With the case of COVID-19, getting accurate information on how many people are affected has been proving to be inefficient. For example, deaths per day were given by government but these excluded COVID-19 deaths outside of hospitals. Similar problems were described in Chapter 2, with data being discussed for the different modern plagues, but actually we never quite know if we are double-counting or underestimating. When data for people of colour is neglected, the risk factor of racism is ignored.

When we quoted Hamlet, writing that 'sorrows come ... in battalions' we did not think of how the COVID-19 virus targets those already enduring one or more of the common long-term conditions. Yet that is what the Intensive Care Units tell us: 91% of COVID-19 deaths arise in people with long-term conditions (the latest observations on COVID-19 indicate that Alzheimer's is one of these conditions – this is a condition we did not include in our short list of common long-term conditions but which we are aware might be so considered, especially since obesity is a risk factor

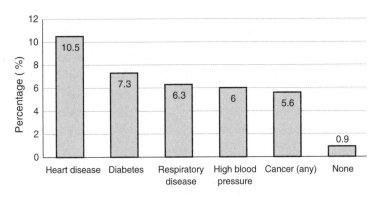

Figure 18.1 Underlying conditions increase the risk of death from COVID-19. Each column represents the proportion of COVID-19 patients in China who have died when they had an underlying condition. The data comes from a research paper examining data on over 70,000 patients in China.

for it). The Centre for Disease Control and Prevention in China found that diabetes, heart disease (including raised blood pressure) or cancer in COVID-19 patients increased the fatality rate by up to twelve-fold[1] (see Figure 18.1). The death rate from COVID-19 would be far lower if we had ended the modern plagues. If society wants to avoid the worst consequences of the next new viral epidemic, it needs to start now by building the Health Society and thereby reducing the risk of the common long-term conditions.

We noted the estimate by Public Health England that the overall annual price we pay for poor population health is £147–185bn. But, of course we failed to include the costs arising from another consequence of this poor health – the total financial cost of pandemics like COVID-19. The SARS-COV-2 virus targets the most serious disease at those already enduring the common long-term conditions. If we had those plagues under control, then the costs due to COVID-19 would be much reduced. Therefore it is reasonable to attribute much of the total financial cost of COVID-19 – trillions of pounds – to our failure to spend the relatively tiny amounts required to improve and maintain good population health. Those trillions include the costs arising from people being absent from work as a consequence of lockdown: COVID-19 has created absenteeism on a scale that the common long-term conditions only achieve after five to ten years.

The dithering and delay of governments confronted with COVID-19 may not surprise us – it has been the decades-long story of societal inaction on disease prevention where moving deckchairs around has been a substitute for action. The UK government has not quite been the worst: Brazil and the US are, at the time of writing, at the bottom of the COVID-19 class. However, the UK has proceeded from failure to stockpile the essentials, to a failed attempt at contact tracing, to a do-nothing policy of awaiting 'herd immunity', to a lockdown that was started without a plan to end it. Where a huge effort is required in public health education involving discussion and debate led by government, UK citizens have simply been told what to do. Politicians have tended to abdicate responsibility for telling us what to do: that responsibility has largely been placed at the door of 'scientists'. They say: 'We follow the science – and so should you'. What is needed for COVID-19 as well as for the Health Society is the active involvement and engagement of the population since that is also what 'following the science' means.

The work of Sir Michael Marmot has illustrated the gap between healthspan and lifespan across the population and shown how the most deprived spend more of their lives with disability. This deprivation is due in some measure to lower income. COVID-19 has cast a new light on those low income groups that hold critical jobs: nurses, hospital cleaners and porters, drivers of ambulances and buses, drivers bringing food to the door and taking rubbish away from the door. Government calls them heroes but they are mainly low-paid heroes and so are at elevated risk of a shortened healthspan and lifespan, of a lengthened period of disability – and of serious COVID-19 disease. Ending health inequality is not only a question of social justice but of need: society needs the work to be done that is carried out by the least rewarded by society.

In Part II we insisted that epidemiology is, in its origins and at its best, an experimental science but that it has been constrained by government to be primarily observational. The experiments involve observation before and after some activity or intervention. Such activity is precisely what has been made absolutely necessary by COVID-19. Preparatory action (stockpiling emergency supplies) was blocked by government, and the first experimental action was on contract tracing. This aims to nip an epidemic in the bud. It failed because the number of tracers had been reduced year after year and so those left could not handle the large number of COVID-19 cases. The second experiment was to advise on hand-washing, but it is difficult to measure its effectiveness directly. The third experiment was a national lockdown. Would it stop transmission or, at least, reduce the number of new cases? It achieved the latter, prompting further experiments on what elements of the lockdown worked best. No experiment is required to test whether masks reduce transmission. On that issue, the problem is how to overcome cultural or ideological opposition to mask wearing. Deploying a safe, effective and long-lasting vaccine will involve experiments for years to come.

All these experiments are needed to end the COVID-19 crisis. All are classic general approaches in experimental infectious epidemiology. All of them except vaccination differ from clinical experiments in posing no direct risk to an individual's health. That means we don't need the classic experiment of clinical research: the blind random clinical trial. We just need to do the experiment with careful observation to identify unintended and undesirable indirect effects, perhaps with pilots to test different experimental strategies for efficacy. Precisely the same goes for the experiments on the Health Society that we suggest will end the modern plagues.

This experimental approach needs to be fully under the control of epidemiologists and other specialists. Politicians are needed to facilitate the experiments, but not to spin the results as they emerge. In brief, scientists should lead the work and politicians should follow. Following is not a role to which conventional politicians aspire. Getting these roles sorted out has proved difficult with COVID-19 – as with the common long-term conditions. In all the briefings by every government, almost invariably the main spotlight has been on a politician. Only the WHO has put a specialist in the spotlight (although he is a former politician). What politicians in general need to know is that experimental science means finding what works. And so that means getting it wrong sometimes. If politicians were wise enough to risk failure, that would be fine but they had better prepare the public for this through better education on the role of politics and science in society. Some politicians may be better communicators than some scientists, but if they do not understand what it is that they are communicating, then they will communicate confusion.

One scientific idea that needs a better appreciation is the idea of risk. For example, infectious pandemics recur and every year without a recurrence is a year closer to the next one. Politicians need to appreciate this rising risk in order that preparation for the next pandemic is as advanced as possible – with the specialists all trained, ready to go and, in the meantime, working on the common long-term conditions. However, the rest of society also needs to appreciate better the risks to individuals and to populations. In the context of the common long-term conditions, a number of apps are now accessible where one enters some personal data and one gets back a risk calculation for this or that condition. While these apps are certainly easy to use, they do not of themselves increase our understanding of the complex issues around health. Yet it is this understanding that we need if we are to change our way of life. Public health education should not underestimate how much people understand and how much they want to understand. The same goes for COVID-19: people want to weigh up the evidence for and against decisions by government and others and do not want to be fobbed off. There is a genuine need for government and Parliament to look at their different roles and how this translates into different modes of communicating. Parliament exists, in part, to hold government to account. To do that effectively, it needs to have a public that is informed on health and science and it needs to help create that better informed public.

The links we have illustrated between COVID-19 and the common long-term conditions demonstrate the important theoretical principle of biological relativity that we outlined in Part III. But the virus itself illustrates the same point: SARS-COV-2 is promiscuous. It is known to infect large and small cats, bats, pangolins and, of course, our own species. All species and all their individual members are inseparable. The indiscriminate character of transmission from person to person – rich or poor, young or old, male or female – combined with the way that the severity of the disease depends on the presence of underlying conditions, requires us to understand that health for all of us is a matter of optimal satisfaction of the needs of each of us. This line of reasoning is supported by the experience of the 'Spanish' flu a century ago. The lethal effects of that virus are widely considered to have been exacerbated by the poor underlying health of populations subjected to years of war.

Let us illustrate this by examining some of the potentially more contentious needs that we have identified as comprising part of what defines the status of being healthy.

One of the vital needs we identified was for 'social conversation'. We mentioned that the state of solitary confinement to which prisoners are sometimes subjected is damaging to their health. This was strong enough to make our case. But look now, in the time of COVID-19, at how difficult distancing is for people – especially for young adults. Think of your own experiences when you have been cooped up at home. Many of us get back in touch with old friends, not so much because we can or we should, but because we just feel we have to. We wave to strangers out of the window, like children used to do from the railway embankments at passengers on passing trains. We are doing whatever it takes to maintain some level of social conversation. We love it. We need it. It is a vital need.

Another vital need is adequate shelter. Its absence increases the risk of contracting COVID-19, just as for the common long-term conditions. Dr Deborah Potts at Kings College London points out that 'hot-bedding' (sleeping in shifts in one bed) is a feature of over-crowded accommodation and a probable cause of viral spread.

Then there is the television or perhaps the smartphone that we specified as a social need. Again, being cooped up has been demonstrating the existence of this need over and over. It may be a surrogate for social conversation at times. But we also need these items to know what to do and when to do it. They are the tools of communication between government and people as well as between people. It is true that the other social need we listed – the car – is far less useful during lockdown. But that serves to empha-sise how necessary it is for us to be able in normal times to get to and from work (in the absence of safe, frequent, cheap, reliable public transport).

As COVID-19 took hold in the UK, three-quarters of a million people volunteered to help the National Health Service. People insist that the NHS belongs to them: it is our most treasured institution. That sense of ownership is one way in which people have agency in society through believing in and acting in support of social institutions. And that social agency is made real when people volunteer to help. At the same time, volunteering to end the crisis gives people something to do when their usual activities have been interrupted. This leads to a reasonable and testable hypothesis: the satisfaction of agency needs in these ways is good for the volunteers' own health and the health of those who live with them. When I have agency in ensuring that your health is my health, the health of both of us is improved. These NHS volun-teers could – we would say 'should' – turn out to be the harbingers of the Health Society Champions that we describe. In addition to these volunteers, there are all those people who are being good neighbours and good members of their communities. They are demonstrating the reality of our proposal for a Health Society and its champions.

Building the Health Society involves prioritising the prevention of disease rather than down-grading it in the name of 'efficiency'. In the COVID-19 pandemic, many countries have appeared to prioritise treatment over prevention. There has been, for example, far more media discussion of shortages of ventilators than of masks. In the UK, government even relinquished direct responsibility for stockpiling of personal protective equipment. An emphasis on people who are already sick is of course understandable. In fact, such behaviour is seen in other primates as well. Our special human attribute is our potential for conscious behaviour that prevents disease.

COVID-19 indicates that this human potential has not yet been fully realised. A stark illustration comes from opponents to the lockdown. They claim and campaign that a lockdown – a method of prevention – infringes human rights (see Figure 18.2). In campaigning, they are unconsciously satisfying, in part, their need for social agency. Yet, at the same time, they favour abstract, legalistic arguments about their rights and oppose optimal conscious satisfaction of their own needs.

Part of the basic infrastructure needed to prevent an infectious pandemic is a national strategic stockpile of protective equipment. But tracing and testing for COVID-19 requires infrastructure to allow population-wide health data management and biological sample management. This infrastructure is what we described in Chapter 16. If we had been investing in building the Health Society we would have saved trillions and we might well have been able to nip COVID-19 in the bud. We would have been able to implement rapidly the mantra of the World Health Organization throughout the pandemic to 'test, test, test' because the biological

Figure 18.2 A protest in Ohio against public health measures aimed at preventing the spread of COVID-19. Patrick Henry (1736–99) was an American slave owner who campaigned for independence from Britain. Policies – even the most anodyne – that promote health for everyone prompt debates about social agency, authoritarianism and mutual dependency.

sample management infrastructure we propose is designed to enable such mass testing. Bill Gates has made constructive proposals on prevention of future pandemics, including on public sector therapeutics development (the market has failed and will fail on this, he notes).

The Health Society is the recognition that 'your health is my health', and the COVID-19 lockdown provides a vivid and dramatic verification of this. At the time of writing, we still lack a full appreciation that the purpose of my wearing a face covering is to protect you. Unlike the Japanese, we tend to think it is only, or largely, to protect ourselves. The idea that your health is my health surely has to be one of the general lessons from the pandemic. Blaming the 'feckless poor' or asserting an individual right that actually harms us all are attitudes that will surely become rarer.

If the UK had undertaken the institutional and community changes that we propose, then the national responsibility for tackling COVID-19 would have fallen to the Deputy Prime Minister. Instead, it seems that, if anyone had responsibility before the virus arrived, then it was, in principle, a junior minister. The brief of the Parliamentary Under-Secretary of State (Minister for Prevention, Public Health and Primary Care), Jo Churchill MP, included 'lead minister for crisis response'. She did not, at the time of writing, appear to be leading on COVID-19. We do not know why. But it is clear that preparing for health crises and preventing them requires a stable and consistent evidence-based approach over decades. This has been singularly lacking.

One route to achieving stability and consistency is through the use of the national and community risk registers. These exist to identify and monitor risks and prepare plans to deal with them. For example, global warming has raised the risk of flooding. The registers recognise this, leading to action on improved flood defences. When it comes to health, the registers recognise the general risk of infectious disease pandemics. But this has not led to a corps of trained contact tracers that could nip a pandemic in the bud. That strategy had to be abandoned within days of COVID-19 arriving in the UK. Tracing work had been financially decimated. In addition, the registers have completely ignored the risks from the modern plagues. And then, the registers ignore the way that a respiratory virus can become a killer when people already have an underlying condition. The risk registers are a useful tool for national and local government, but they are now in urgent need of improvement. Furthermore, there is an urgent need for both government and civil servants to use the register as a tool. For example, senior civil servants told the Commons' Public Accounts Committee that Whitehall had not devised a plan for dealing with the consequences for the economy of an infectious pandemic. Schemes were devised to help businesses 'as they went along', Sir Thomas Scholar told the 'dumbstruck' chair of the committee. Had government followed the guidance for its own risk register, it would not have needed to make things up as it went along.

We dealt in Chapter 17 with arguments based on excessive individualism opposing the Health Society. The COVID-19 pandemic has seen the emergence of new but related arguments:

- More people could die as a consequence of trying to defeat the virus than will die from it.
- Despite the virus, we need to end the lockdown and get back to work (Donald Trump).
- The pandemic will 'cull' some 'elderly dependents' and this may prove 'mildly beneficial' from a 'disinterested economic perspective' (*Daily Telegraph*).
- Efforts to contain the virus should be challenged because they reduce our liberty (former Supreme Court Justice Lord Jonathan Sumption).

It is rather like opposing the Health Society because:

- People will die from too much exercise.
- The economy is a bigger problem than diabetes and the like.
- If, owing to obesity, you are not as productive as you might be, then your life is worth less.
- True liberty means having the right to live in a society where population health is not an issue.

Readers can decide for themselves whether these arguments have any substance logically, scientifically or morally.

Postscript: the COVID-19 pandemic

How will life change after COVID-19? It is hard to imagine that UK citizens will not want to see in place more effective prevention against any new viral pandemic. After the coronavirus epidemics (SARS in 2002 and MERS in 2012), governments in the Far East and Middle East were obliged to improve prevention. For this to become more effective, action moving us in the direction of the Health Society is inevitable. Mere tweaks of the system will seem inadequate when the total cost of COVID-19 is added up. Therefore the argument will be strengthened that we need to continue to 'follow the science' by implementing the institutional, community and technological changes that we have described for ending the modern plagues. One simple example of the need for wide-ranging reform is based on the finding in the UK and elsewhere that COVID-19 is concentrated in the most crowded areas of housing in the country. Bad housing and planning policy denies optimal satisfaction of a vital need for shelter – and it brings bad outcomes both for infectious disease and long-term conditions.

This case for reform is simply a re-phrasing of our concept of Systems Prevention: the uniquely human attribute of having the capacity to go beyond the slow processes of natural prevention – that is, of natural selection. Natural prevention refers either to herd immunity or to the slower processes of change that can be transmitted between generations. Both these mechanisms involve millions of deaths worldwide and confer protection from just one virus. By contrast, Systems Prevention rapidly minimises death and maximises the breadth of protection. It means using all the imagination and ingenuity that we collectively can muster for scientific and social innovation to help our societies meet our needs.

Notes

Preface

1   F. Engels, *The Condition of the Working Class in England* (London: Penguin Classics, 1987).
2   D. Noble, *Dance to the Tune of Life: Biological Relativity* (Cambridge: Cambridge University Press, 2016).
3   R. Dawkins, *The Selfish Gene* (Oxford: Oxford University Press, 2016).

Introduction

1   C. R. Darwin. *On the Origin of Species by Means of Natural Selection, or the Preservation of Favoured Races in the Struggle for Life* (London: John Murray, 1859).
2   L. A. Hamilton, *The Political Philosophy of Needs* (Cambridge: Cambridge University Press, 2008).

Chapter 1

1   HM Chief Inspector of Prisons, *Report on an Announced Inspection of Isle of Man Prison* (2011), www.gov.im/media/55040/prisonreport2011.pdf (accessed 22 May 2020).
2   S. Turton, 'Prisoners switch to e-cigarettes', *IoM Today*, 8 February 2018, www.iomtoday.co.im/article.cfm?id=38525&headline=Prisoners%20switch%20to%20e-cigarettes&sectionIs=news&searchyear=2018 (accessed 22 May 2020).
3   Commission on Chronic Illness, *Chronic Illness in the United States, Vol. 1* (Cambridge, MA: Harvard University Press, 1957).
4   J. Last, *A Dictionary of Epidemiology* (New York: Oxford University Press, 1995), cited in J. Bousquet and N. Khaltaev (eds), *Global Surveillance,*

Notes

Prevention and Control of Chronic Respiratory Diseases: A Comprehensive Approach (New York: World Health Organization, 2007).

5 S. Stinson, *Human Biology: An Evolutionary and Biocultural Perspective* (Hoboken, NJ: John Wiley & Sons, Inc., 2012).

6 World Health Organization, *Preamble to the Constitution of the World Health Organization as Adopted by the International Health Conference* (1946), www.who. int/governance/eb/who_constitution_en.pdf (accessed 22 May 2020).

7 World Health Organization, *Ottawa Charter for Health Promotion First International Conference on Health Promotion, Ottawa* (1986), www.who.int/ healthpromotion/conferences/previous/ottawa/en/ (accessed 22 May 2020).

Chapter 2

1 US Centers for Disease Control and Prevention, *Remembering the 1918 Influenza Pandemic*, www.cdc.gov/features/1918-flu-pandemic/index.html (accessed 22 May 2020).

2 H. Sung, R. L. Siegel, Philip S. Rosenberg and A. Jemal, 'Emerging cancer trends among young adults in the USA: analysis of a population-based cancer registry', *Lancet Public Health* 24, no. 3 (2019): 137–47. doi: 10.1016/S246-2667(18)30267-6.

3 National Health Service, *Clinical Depression: Causes*, www.nhs.uk/condi tions/clinical-depression/causes/ (accessed 22 May 2020).

4 World Health Organization Media Centre, *Diabetes Factsheet* (2016), www. who.int/mediacentre/factsheets/fs312/en/ (accessed 22 May 2020).

5 S. S. Zghebi, D. T. Steinke, M. J. Carr, M. K. Rutter, R. A. Emsley and D. M. Ashcroft, 'Examining trends in type 2 diabetes incidence, preva-lence and mortality in the UK between 2004 and 2014', *Diabetes, Obesity and Metabolism* 19, no. 11 (2017): 1537–45. doi: 10.1111/dom.12964.

6 National Diabetes Audit Report 1, *Care Processes and Treatment Targets 2015–16*, https://digital.nhs.uk/catalogue/PUB23241 (accessed 22 May 2020).

7 W. Hinton, A. McGovern, R. Coyle, T. S. Han, P. Sharma, A. Correa, F. Ferreira and S. de Lusignan, 'Incidence and prevalence of cardiovas-cular disease in English primary care: a cross-sectional and follow-up study of the Royal College of General Practitioners (RCGP) Research and Surveillance Centre (RSC)', *BMJ Open* 8, no. 8: e020282. doi: 10.1136/bmjopen-2017-020282.

8 Public Health England, *Hypertension Prevalence Estimates in England: Estimated from the Health Survey for England* (2016), www.gov.uk/government/publica tions/hypertension-prevalence-estimates-for-local-populations (accessed 22 May 2020).

9   P. Bhatnagar, K. Wickramasinghe, E. Wilkins and N. Townsend, 'Trends in the epidemiology of cardiovascular disease in the UK', *Heart* 102, no. 24 (2016): 1945–52. doi: 10.1136/heartjnl-2016-309573.

10 Office for National Statistics, Cancer Registration Statistics (2014), www. ons.gov.uk/peoplepopulationandcommunity/healthandsocialcare/condi tionsanddiseases/bulletins/cancerregistrationstatisticsengland/previous Releases (accessed 22 May 2020).

11 Adult Psychiatric Morbidity Survey, *Survey of Mental Health and Wellbeing, England* (2014), https://digital.nhs.uk/data-and-information/publications/ statistical/adult-psychiatric-morbidity-survey (accessed 22 May 2020).

12 S. McManus et al., *Mental Health and Wellbeing in England: Adult Psychiatric Morbidity Survey, 2014* (2016), https://digital.nhs.uk/data-and-information/ publications/statistical/adult-psychiatric-morbidity-survey/adult-psychia tric-morbidity-survey-survey-of-mental-health-and-wellbeing-england- 2014 (accessed 22 May 2020).

13 World Health Organization, *Towards a Common Language for Functioning, Disability and Health: The International Classification of Functioning, Disability and Health (ICF)* (Geneva, 2002), www.who.int/classifications/icf/icfbe ginnersguide.pdf?ua=1 (accessed 27 May 2020).

14 The Marmot Review, *Fair Society, Healthy Lives* (2010), www.local.gov.uk/ marmot-review-report-fair-society-healthy-lives (accessed 22 May 2020).

15 F. McGuinness, *Income Inequality in the UK* (2018) (House of Commons Library Briefing Paper Number: 7484), www.parliament.uk/commons- library (accessed 22 May 2020).

16 Institute for Health Metrics and Evaluation, *Global Burden of Disease*, www. healthdata.org/gbd (accessed 22 May 2020).

Chapter 3

1   C. Salisbury, L. Johnson, S. Purdy, Jose M. Valderas and Alan A. Montgomery, 'Epidemiology and impact of multimorbidity in primary care: a retrospective cohort study', *British Journal of General Practice* 61, no. 582 (2011): e12–e21. doi: 10.3399/bjgp11X548929.

2   A. Cassell, D. Edwards, A. Harshfield, K. Rhodes, J. Brimicombe, R. Payne and S. Griffin, 'The epidemiology of multimorbidity in pri- mary care: a retrospective cohort study', *British Journal of General Practice* 68, no. 669 (2018): e245–e251. doi: 10.3399/bjgp18X695465.

3   Department of Health, *Long-Term Conditions: Compendium of information* (2012), www.gov.uk/government/uploads/system/uploads/attachment_ data/file/216528/dh_134486.pdf (accessed 22 May 2020).

4   American Heart Association, *Cardiovascular Disease and Diabetes*, www.heart. org/en/health-topics/diabetes/why-diabetes-matters/cardiovascular-

Notes

disease-diabetes (accessed 22 May 2020). World Health Organization, *Cardiovascular Diseases (CVDs) Key Facts* (2017), www.who.int/news-room/fact-sheets/detail/cardiovascular-diseases-(cvds) (accessed 22 May 2020).

5 Mayo Clinic, *Diabetic Nephropathy*, www.mayoclinic.org/diseases-condi tions/diabetic-neuropathy/symptoms-causes/syc-20371580 (accessed 22 May 2020).

6 E. Bullmore, 'From depression to dementia, inflammation is medicine's new frontier', *The Guardian*, 19 January 2020, www.theguardian.com/com mentisfree/2020/jan/19/inflammation-depression-mind-body (accessed 22 May 2020).

7 T. Kraynak, A. L. Marsland, T. D. Wager and P. J. Gianaros, 'Functional neuroanatomy of peripheral inflammatory physiology: a meta-analysis of human neuroimaging studies', *Neuroscience & Biobehavioral Reviews* 94 (2018): 76–92. doi: 10.1016/j.neubiorev.2018.07.013.

8 Wellcome Trust Consortium for the Neuroimmunology of Mood Disorders and Alzheimer's Disease, www.neuroimmunology.org.uk/ (accessed 22 May 2020).

9 P. Anderson, *The Impact of Alcohol on Health* (2011), www.euro.who. int/__data/assets/pdf_file/0003/160680/e96457.pdf (accessed 22 May 2020).

10 Health Effects Institute, *State of Global Air 2019: A Special Report on Global Exposure to Air Pollution and its Disease Burden* (2019), www.stateofglobalair. org/sites/default/files/soga_2019_report.pdf (accessed 22 May 2020).

11 R. Peto, S. Darby, H. Deo, P. Silcocks, E. Whitley and R. Doll, 'Smoking, smoking cessation, and lung cancer in the UK since 1950: combination of national statistics with two case-control studies', *British Medical Journal* 321, no. 7257 (2000): 323–9. doi: 10.1136/bmj.321.7257.323.

12 NHS Digital, *Statistics on Smoking – England* (2018), https://digital.nhs.uk/data-and-information/publications/statistical/statistics-on-smoking/stat istics-on-smoking-england-2018 (accessed 22 May 2020).

13 Health and Social Care Information Centre, *Statistics on Smoking: England* (2014), https://digital.nhs.uk/data-and-information/publications/statis tical/statistics-on-smoking/statistics-on-smoking-england-2014 (accessed 22 May 2020).

14 Public Health England, *Smoking Prevalence for Local and Unitary Authorities in England 2012–13* (2013), www.gov.uk/government/uploads/system/uploads/attachment_data/file/341228/Smoking_prevalence_and_tobac co_sales_-_modelling_of_net_savings.xlsx (accessed 22 May 2020).

15 NHS Information Centre for Health and Social Care, *Smoking, Drinking and Drug Use among Young People in England in 2014* (2014), https://digital. nhs.uk/data-and-information/publications/statistical/smoking-drinking -and-drug-use-among-young-people-in-england/2014 (accessed 22 May 2020).

16 NHS Digital, *Smoking, Drinking and Drug Use among Young People in England 2018*, https://digital.nhs.uk/data-and-information/publications/statistical/smoking-drinking-and-drug-use-among-young-people-in-england/ 2018 (accessed 22 May 2020).

Chapter 4

1 Thucydides, *The History of the Peloponnesian War*, trans. David Grene (Chicago, IL: University of Chicago Press, 1989), pp. 115–18.

2 International Panel on Social Progress, *Rethinking Society for the 21st Century* (Cambridge: Cambridge University Press, 2018), www.ipsp.org (accessed 22 May 2020).

3 Department of Health, *The Long-Term Conditions Year of Care Commissioning Programme Implementation Handbook* (2017), https://assets.publishing.service. gov.uk/government/uploads/system/uploads/attachment_data/file/216 528/dh_134486.pdf (accessed 22 May 2020).

4 OECD, *Health at a Glance 2017: OECD Indicators* (Paris, OECD Publishing: 2017) https://dx.doi.org/10.1787/health_glance-2017-en (accessed 22 May 2020).

5 House of Commons Health Select Committee, *Obesity: Third Report of Session 2003/04* (London: The Stationery Office, 2004).

6 B. McCormick, I. Stone and the Corporate Analytical Team, 'Economic costs of obesity and the case for government intervention', *Obesity Reviews* 8, no. 1 (2007): 161–4. doi: 10.1111/j.1467-789X.2007.00337.x.

7 Frontier Economics, *Submission to the Marmot Review: Overall Costs of Health Inequalities*, www.ucl.ac.uk/gheg/marmotreview/Documents (accessed 22 May 2020).

8 C. Black, *Working for a Healthier Tomorrow* (Department for Work and Pensions, 2008), www.gov.uk/government/publications/working-for-a-healthier-tomorrow-work-and-health-in-britain (accessed 22 May 2020).

9 S. Morris, 'Body mass index and occupational attainment', *Journal of Health Economics* 25, no. 2 (2006): 347–64. J. Erikkson, T. Forsén, C. Osmond and D. Barker, 'Obesity from cradle to grave', *International Journal of Obesity* 27, no. 6 (2003): 722–7. doi: 10.1038/sj.ijo.0802278.

10 D. M. Gates, P. Succop, B. J. Brehm, G. L. Gillespie and B. D. Sommers, 'Obesity and presenteeism: the impact of body mass index on workplace productivity', *Journal of Occupational and Environmental Medicine* 50, no. 1 (2008): 39–45. doi: 10.1097/JOM.0b013e31815d8db2.

11 E. A. Finkelstein, M. DaCosta DiBonaventura, S. M. Burgess and B. C. Hale, 'The costs of obesity in the workplace', *Journal of Occupational and Environmental Medicine* 52, no. 10 (2010): 971–6. doi: 10.1097/ JOM.0b013e3181f274d2.

Notes

12   K. McPherson, T. Marsh and M. Brown, *Modelling Future Trends in Obesity and the Impact on Health. Foresight Tackling Obesities: Future Choices* (2007), www.foresight.gov.uk (accessed 22 May 2020). B. McCormack, I. Stone and the Corporate Analytical Team, 'Economic costs of obesity and the case for government intervention', *Obesity Reviews* 8, no. 1: 161–4. doi: 10.1111/j.1467-789X.2007.00337.x.

13   UK Health Forum and Cancer Research UK, *Tipping the Scales: Why Preventing Obesity Makes Economic Sense* (2016), www.cancerresearchuk.org/sites/default/files/tipping_the_scales_-_cruk_full_report11.pdf (accessed 22 May 2020).

14   N. Hex, C. Bartlett, D. Wright, M. Taylor and D. Varley, 'Estimating the current and future costs of Type 1 and Type 2 diabetes in the UK, including direct health costs and indirect societal and productivity costs', *Diabetes Medicine* 29, no. 7 (2012): 855–62. doi: 10.1111/j.1464-5491.2012.03698.x.

15   British Heart Foundation, *Coronary Heart Disease Statistics* (2010), www.bhf.org.uk/~/media/files/research/heart-statistics/hs2010_coronary_heart_disease_statistics.pdf (accessed 22 May 2020).

16   Centre for Economics and Business Research, *The Economic Cost of Cardiovascular Disease from 2014–2020 in Six European Economies* (2014), www.cebr.com/wp-content/uploads/2015/08/Short-Report-18.08.14.pdf (accessed 22 May 2020).

17   Department of Health, *Cancer Reform Strategy*, webarchive.nationalarchives.gov.uk/20130107105354/; www.dh.gov.uk/prod_consum_dh/groups/dh_digitalassets/documents/digitalasset/dh_081007.pdf (accessed 22 May 2020).

18   H. Featherstone and L. Whitham, *Policy Exchange Research Note: The Cost of Cancer* (2010), www.policyexchange.org.uk/images/publications/the%20cost%20of%20cancer%20-%20feb%2010.pdf (accessed 22 May 2020).

19   Public Health England, *NHS Health Check Implementation Review and Action Plan* (2013), https://assets.publishing.service.gov.uk/government/uploads/system/uploads/attachment_data/file/224538/NHS_Health_Check_implementation_review_and_action_plan.pdf (accessed 22 May 2020).

20   E. Whitley, D. Gunnell, D. Dorling and G. D. Smith, 'Ecological study of social fragmentation, poverty, and suicide', *British Medical Journal* 319, no. 7216 (1999): 1034–7. doi: 10.1136/bmj.319.7216.1034.

21   C. Hsu, S. Chang, E. S. T. Lee and P. S. F. Yip, 'Geography of suicide in Hong Kong: spatial patterning, and socioeconomic correlates and inequalities', *Social Science & Medicine* 130 (2015): 190–203. doi: 10.1016/j.socscimed.2015.02.019.

22   M. K. Stjärne, A. P. de Leon and J. Hallqvist, 'Contextual effects of social fragmentation and material deprivation on risk of myocardial infarction – results from the Stockholm Heart Epidemiology Program (SHEEP)', *International Journal of Epidemiology* 33, no. 4 (2004): 732–41.

23 R. Pabayo, B. E. Molnar, A. Cradock and I. Kawachi, 'The relationship between neighborhood socioeconomic characteristics and physical inactivity among adolescents living in Boston, Massachusetts', *American Journal of Public Health* 104, no. 11 (2014): e142–9. doi: 10.2105/AJPH.2014.302109.

24 D. Russell, L. A. Peplau and C. E. Cutrona, 'The revised UCLA Loneliness Scale: concurrent and discriminant validity evidence', *Journal of Personality and Social Psychology* 39, no. 3 (1980): 472–80. doi: 10.1037//0022-3514.39.3.472. See: https://artemciy.gitlab.io/loneliness-scale/#/ (accessed 22 May 2020).

25 D. Kusaslan Avci, 'Evaluation of the relationship between loneliness and medication adherence in patients with diabetes mellitus: a cross-sectional study', *Journal of International Medical Research* 46, no. 8 (2018): 3149–61. doi: 10.1177/0300060518773223.

26 M. A. Whisman, 'Loneliness and the metabolic syndrome in a population-based sample of middle-aged and older adults', *Journal of Health Psychology* 29, no. 5 (2010): 550–4. doi: 10.1037/a0020760.

27 A. Richard, S. Rohrmann, C. L. Vandeleur, M. Schmid, J. Barth and M. Eichholzer, 'Loneliness is adversely associated with physical and mental health and lifestyle factors: results from a Swiss national survey', *PLoS One* 12, no. 7 (2017): e0181442. doi: 10.1371/journal.pone.0181442.

28 M. Gonçalves, R. Amici, R. Lucas, T. Åkerstedt, F. Cirignotta, J. Horne, D. Léger, W. T. McNicholas, M. Partinen, J. Téran-Santos, P. Peigneux, L. Grote and the National Representatives as Study Collaborators, 'Sleepiness at the wheel across Europe: a survey of 19 countries', *Journal of Sleep Research* 24, no. 3 (2015): 242–53. doi: 10.1111/jsr.12267.

29 H. W. Bakos, R. C. Henshaw, M. Mitchell and M. Lane, 'Paternal body mass index is associated with decreased blastocyst development and reduced live birth rates following assisted reproductive technology', *Fertility and Sterility* 95, no. 5 (2011): 1700–4. doi: 10.1016/j.fertnstert.2010.11.044.

30 H. Levine, N. Jørgensen, A. Martino-Andrade, J. Mendiola, D. Weksler-Derri, I. Mindlis, R. Pinotti and S. H. Swan, 'Temporal trends in sperm count: a systematic review and meta-regression analysis', *Human Reproduction Update* 23, no. 6 (2017): 646–59. doi: 10.1093/humupd/dmx022.

Chapter 5

1 A. Thomas, 'I was the first baby delivered by the NHS. It has saved my life eight times', *The Observer*, 17 September 2017, www.theguardian.com/society/2017/sep/16/first-baby-born-under-nhs-national-health-service-aneurin-bevan (accessed 22 May 2020).

2 NHS, 'NHS Vaccinations and When to Have Them', www.nhs.uk/conditions/vaccinations/childhood-vaccines-timeline/ (accessed 22 May 2020).

3 Confederation of Meningitis Organisations, 'Life Course Immunisation Initiative', www.comomeningitis.org/projects/life-course-immunisation-initiative/ (accessed 22 May 2020). Also, European Commission, *Proposal for a Council Recommendation on Strengthened Cooperation against Vaccine Preventable Diseases* (2018), https://eur-lex.europa.eu/legal-content/EN/TXT/HTML/?uri=CELEX:52018DC0244&from=EN (accessed 22 May 2020).

4 Office for National Statistics, *Causes of Death Over 100 Years*, www.ons.gov.uk/peoplepopulationandcommunity/birthsdeathsandmarriages/deaths/articles/causesofdeathover100years/2017-09-18 (accessed 22 May 2020).

5 F. Dobson and T. Jowell, *Our Healthier Nation: A Contract for Health*. Department of Health and Social Care. 9 February 1998. www.gov.uk/government/publications/our-healthier-nation-a-contract-for-health.

6 Department of Health, *Putting Prevention First – NHS Health Check* (2008), www.healthcheck.nhs.uk/document.php?o=227 (accessed 22 May 2020).

7 Department of Health, *Living Well for Longer: A Call to Action to Reduce Avoidable Premature Mortality*, www.gov.uk/government/uploads/system/uploads/attachment_data/file/181103/Living_well_for_longer.pdf (accessed 22 May 2020).

8 Local Government Association, *Local Authority Public Health Allocations 2015/16 In-Year Savings*, www.gov.uk/government/consultations/local-authority-public-health-allocations-2015-to-2016 (accessed 22 May 2020).

9 S. Lafond, *Funding Overview: Current NHS Spending in England* (2015), www.health.org.uk/sites/default/files/FundingOverview_CurrentNHSSpendingInEngland.pdf (accessed 22 May 2020).

10 HM Government, *Childhood Obesity: A Plan for Action* (2016), www.gov.uk/government/publications/childhood-obesity-a-plan-for-action (accessed 22 May 2020).

11 Department of Health and Social Care, *Advancing Our Health: Prevention in the 2020s* (2019), https://assets.publishing.service.gov.uk/government/uploads/system/uploads/attachment_data/file/819766/advancing-our-health-prevention-in-the-2020s-accessible.pdf (accessed 22 May 2020).

Chapter 6

1 J. Snow, *On the Mode of Communication of Cholera* (London: John Churchill, 1855), www.ph.ucla.edu/epi/snow/snowbook.html (accessed 22 May 2020).

2 R. Bloch, *Healers and Achievers: Physicians who Excelled in Other Fields and the Times in Which They Lived* (Bloomington, IN: Xlibris, 2012).
3 F. Hoffman, 'Cancer and smoking habits', *Annals of Surgery* 93, no. 1 (1931): 50–67. See also: A. Morabia, 'Quality, originality, and significance of the 1939 "Tobacco consumption and lung carcinoma" article by Mueller', *Preventative Medicine* 53, no. 3 (2012): 171–7. doi: 10.1016/j.ypmed.2012.05.008.
4 R. Doll and A. B. Hill, 'Smoking and carcinoma of the lung', *British Medical Journal* 2, no. 4682 (1950): 739–48.
5 R. Peto, S. Darby, H. Deo, P. Silcocks, E. Whitley and R. Doll, 'Smoking, smoking cessation, and lung cancer in the UK since 1950: combination of national statistics with two case-control studies', *British Medical Journal* 321, no. 7257 (2000): 323–9. doi: 10.1136/bmj.321.7257.323.
6 Health and Social Care Information Centre, 'Statistics on Smoking. England', (2014), https://digital.nhs.uk/data-and-information/publications/statistical/statistics-on-smoking/statistics-on-smoking-england-2014 (accessed 22 May 2020).
7 Public Health England, *Smoking Prevalence for Local and Unitary Authorities in England 2012–13* (2013), www.gov.uk/government/uploads/system/uploads/attachment_data/file/341228/Smoking_prevalence_and_tobacco_sales_-_modelling_of_net_savings.xlsx (accessed 22 May 2020).

Chapter 7

1 C. Wild, 'Complementing the genome with an "exposome": the outstanding challenge of environmental exposure measurement in molecular epidemiology', *Cancer Epidemiology, Biomarkers & Prevention* 14, no. 8 (2005):1847–50. doi: 10.1158/1055-9965.EPI-05-0456.
2 C. Bernard, *Leçons sur les phénomènes de la vie communs aux animaux et aux végétaux* (Paris: J.-B. Baillière et fils, 1885).
3 E. Smith, 'HPV: the whole story, warts and all', Science blog, 16 September 2014, https://scienceblog.cancerresearchuk.org/2014/09/16/hpv-the-whole-story-warts-and-all/ (accessed 22 May 2020).

Chapter 8

1 Motorcycleminds, *The Motorcycle Helmet Law* (2017), http://motorcycleminds.org/2017/02/15/the-motorcycle-helmet-law (accessed 22 May 2020).
2 L. Trevena, H. M. Davey, A. Barratt, P. Butow and P. Caldwell, 'A systematic review on communicating with patients about evidence',

Journal of Evaluation in Clinical Practice 12, no. 1 (2006):13–23. doi: 10.1111/
j.1365-2753.2005.00596.x.
3   R. Feng and J. Garrido, 'Actuarial applications of epidemiological
    models', *North American Actuarial Journal* 5, no. 1 (2012): 112–36.
4   A. Kawthar, A. Lophatananon, M. Yuille, W. Ollier and K. R. Muir,
    'Review of non-clinical risk models to aid prevention of breast
    cancer', *Cancer Causes & Control* 29, no. 10 (2018): 967–86. doi: 10.1007/
    s10552-018-1072-6.
5   Joint British Societies for the prevention of Cardiovascular Disease,
    'JBSR Risk Calculator', www.jbs3risk.com (accessed 22 May 2020).

Chapter 9

1   World Health Organization, 'Growth Reference 5–19 Year's'
    (2007), https://who.int/growthref/who2007_bmi_for_age/en/index.html
    (accessed 22 May 2020).
2   P. S. Shetty and W. P. James, 'Body mass index – A measure of chronic
    energy deficiency in adults', *FAO Food and Nutrition Paper* 56 (1994):
    1–57, www.fao.org/docrep/t1970e/t1970e08.htm (accessed 22 May
    2020).
3   M. Franco, U. Bilal, P. Ordúñez, M. Benet, A. Morejón, B. Caballero,
    J. F. Kennelly and R. S. Cooper, 'Population-wide weight loss and regain
    in relation to diabetes burden and cardiovascular mortality in Cuba
    1980–2010: repeated cross sectional surveys and ecological comparison of
    secular trends', *British Medical Journal* 346 (2013): f1515. doi: 10.1136/bmj.
    f1515.
4   T. A. Henken, *Cuba: A Global Studies Handbook* (Santa Barbara, CA: ABC-
    CLIO, 2008), p. 438.
5   National Obesity Observatory, 'UK Obesity Data for the Adult
    Population' (2012), www.slideshare.net/deheij/vid-17667-slides-for-web
    siteadultdec2013 (accessed 22 May 2020).
6   B. Butland, S. Jebb, P. Kopelman, K. McPherson, S. Thomas, J. Mardell
    and V. Parry, *Tackling Obesities: Future Choices – Project report* (2007), www.
    gov.uk/government/uploads/system/uploads/attachment_data/file/28
    7937/07-1184x-tackling-obesities-future-choices-report.pdf (accessed 22
    May 2020).
7   NCD Risk Factor Collaboration, 'Worldwide trends in body-mass index,
    underweight, overweight, and obesity from 1975 to 2016: a pooled analy-
    sis of 2416 population-based measurement studies in 128.9 million chil-
    dren, adolescents, and adults', *The Lancet* 390, no. 10113 (2017): 2627–42.
    doi: 10.1016/S0140-6736(17)32129-3.

Notes

8   Annual Report of the Chief Medical Officer, *The Health of the 51%: Women* (2015), www.gov.uk/government/uploads/system/uploads/attachment_data/file/484383/cmo-report-2014.pdf (accessed 22 May 2020).

9   L. Donaldson and R. J. Donaldson, *Essential Public Health, Second Edition* (Oxford: Petroc Press, 2003).

10 World Health Organization. *Controlling the Global Obesity Epidemic.* Press release, 3 March 2003. www.who.int/nutrition/topics/obesity/en/.

11 A. Astrup, C. Lundsgaard and M. J. Stock, 'Is obesity contagious?', *International Journal of Obesity and Related Metabolic Disorders* 22, no. 4 (1998): 375–6.

12 N. Christakis and J. H. Fowler, 'The spread of obesity in a large social network over 32 years', *The New England Journal of Medicine* 357, no. 4 (2007): 370–9. doi: 10.1056/NEJMsa066082.

13 R. Hunter, K. de la Haye, J. Murray, J. Badham, T. Valente, M. Clarke and F. Kee, 'Social network interventions for health behaviours and outcomes: a systematic review and meta-analysis', *PLoS Medicine* 16, no. 9 (2019): e1002890. doi: 10.1371/journal.pmed.1002890. G. Spencer-Bonilla, O. J. Ponce, R. Rodriguez-Gutierrez, N. Alvarez-Villalobos, P. J. Erwin, L. Larrea-Mantilla, A. Rogers and V. M. Montori, 'A systematic review and meta-analysis of trials of social network interventions in type 2 diabetes', *BMJ Open* 7, no. 8 (2017): e016506. doi: 10.1136/bmjopen-2017-016506.

14 K. Powell, J. Wilcox, A. Clonan, P. Bissell, L. Preston, M. Peacock and M. Holdsworth, 'The role of social networks in the development of overweight and obesity among adults: a scoping review, *BMC Public Health* 15, no. 996 (2015): 1–13. doi: 10.1186/s12889-015-2314-0.

15 D. Holtgrave and R. Crosby, 'Is Social Capital a Protective Factor Against Obesity and Diabetes? Findings From an Exploratory Study', *Annals of Epidemiology* 16, no. 5 (2006): 406–408. doi: 10.1016/j.annepidem.2005.04.017.

16 World Health Organization, *Environment and Health Risks: A Review of the Influence And effects of Social Inequalities* (2010), www.euro.who.int/__data/assets/pdf_file/0003/78069/E93670.pdf (accessed 22 May 2020).

17 C. Wen, J. Wai, M. Tsai, Y. Yang, T. Cheng, M. Lee, H. Chan, C. Tasao, S. Tasi and X. Wu, 'Minimum amount of physical activity for reduced mortality and extended life expectancy: a prospective cohort study', *The Lancet* 378, no. 9798 (2011): 1244–53.

18 UK Chief Medical Officer, *Physical Activity Guidelines* (2019) www.gov.uk/government/publications/physical-activity-guidelines-uk-chief-medical-officers-report (accessed 22 May 2020).

19 R. Chatterjee, T. Chapman, M. Brannan and J. Varney, 'GPs' knowledge, use, and confidence in national physical activity and health

guidelines and tools: a questionnaire-based survey of general practice in England', *British Journal of General Practice* 67, no. 663 (2017): e668-e675. doi: 10.3399/bjgp17X692513.

20 Centers for Disease Control and Prevention, 'Adult participation in aerobic and muscle-strengthening physical activities United States, 2011', *Morbidity and Mortality Weekly Report* 62, no. 17 (2013): 326–330.

21 L. Farrell, B. Hollingsworth, C. Propper and M. A. Shields, 'The socioeconomic gradient in physical inactivity: evidence from one million adults in England', *Social Science & Medicine* 123 (2014): 55–63. doi: 10.1016/j. socscimed.2014.10.039.

22 E. B. Kahn, L. T. Ramsey, R. C. Brownson, G. W. Heath, E. H. Howze, K. E. Powell, E. J. Stone, M. W. Rajab and P. Corso, 'The effectiveness of interventions to increase physical activity. A systematic review', *American Journal of Preventative Medicine* 22, no. 4 (2002): 73–107. N. Artinian, G. F. Fletcher, D. Mozaffarian et al., 'Interventions to promote physical activity and dietary lifestyle changes for cardiovascular risk factor reduction in adults: a scientific statement from the American Heart Association', *Circulation* 122, no. 4 (2010): 406–41. doi: 10.1161/ CIR.0b013e3181e8edf1.

23 J. Zhang, D. Brackbill, S. Yang, J. Becker, N. Herbert and D. Centola, 'Support or competition? How online social networks increase physical activity: a randomized controlled trial', *Preventative Medicine Reports* 4 (2016): 453–8. doi: 10.1016/j.pmedr.2016.08.008.

24 R. West, M. Edwards and P. Hajek, 'A randomized controlled trial of a "buddy" system to improve success at giving up smoking in general practice', *Addiction* 93, no. 7 (1998):1007–11. doi: 10.1046/j.1360-0443.1998.93710075.x. S. May, R. West, P. Hajek, A. McEwen and H. McRobbie, 'Randomized controlled trial of a social support ("buddy") intervention for smoking cessation', *Patient Education and Counseling* 64, nos. 1–3 (2006): 235–41. doi: 10.1016/j.pec.2006.02.008.

Chapter 10

1 C. P. Snow, *The Two Cultures* (Cambridge: Cambridge University Press, 1961).

2 DNA songtext: www.songtexte.com/songtext/little-mix/dna-5ba5a7b4. html (accessed 22 May 2020).

3 C. Murray, 'Where Are the Female Einsteins?', American Enterprise Institute, 22 November 2005, www.aei.org/articles/where-are-the-female-einsteins/ (accessed 22 May 2020). A. Jensen, *The g Factor: The Science of Mental Ability* (Santa Barbara, CA: Praeger, 1998). Jensen invents a 'general intelligence measure' that he calls 'g' and claims that

'white-black difference in *g*' has 'a biological component' that is a 'result of natural selection'.

4 R. Dawkins, 'It's all in the genes', *The Sunday Times*, 12 March 2006, www. thetimes.co.uk/article/its-all-in-the-genes-p655hlx2j2n (accessed 22 May 2020).

5 D. Gibson, J. I. Glass, C. Lartigue et al., 'Creation of a bacterial cell controlled by a chemically synthesized genome', *Science* 329, no. 5987 (2010): 52–6. doi: 10.1126/science.1190719.

6 F. Griffith, 'The significance of pneumococcal types', *Journal of Hygiene* 27, no. 2 (1928):113–59. doi: 10.1017/s0022172400031879.

7 W. Hayes, *The Genetics of Bacteria and their Viruses* (Oxford: Blackwell Scientific Publications, 1965).

8 D. Noble, *Dance to the Tune of Life: Biological Relativity* (Cambridge: Cambridge University Press, 2016).

9 A. Barabási, 'Network medicine – from obesity to the "diseasome"', *The New England Journal of Medicine* 357 (2007): 404–7. doi: 10.1056/NEJMe078114.

10 J. Sturmberg and C. M. Martin, 'Diagnosis – the limiting focus of taxonomy', *Journal of Evaluation in Clinical Practice* 22, no.1 (2016):103–111. doi: 10.1111/jep. 12113.

11 G. Schwalfenberg, 'The alkaline diet: is there evidence that an alkaline pH diet benefits health?', *Journal of Environmental and Public Health* (2012). doi: 10.1155/2012/727630.

12 S. Cheuvront, 'The zone diet and athletic performance', *Sports Medicine* 27, no. 4 (1999): 213–28. doi: 10.2165/00007256-199927040-00002.

13 NHS Choices, 'Caveman fad diet' (2008), www.nhs.uk/news/food-and-diet/caveman-fad-diet (accessed 22 May 2020).

Chapter 11

1 C. R. Darwin. *On the Origin of Species by Means of Natural Selection, or the Preservation of Favoured Races in the Struggle for Life* (London: John Murray, 1859), Chapter IV, p. 81.

2 E. Andersen, S. Ali, E. Byamukama, Y. Ken and M. P. Nepal, 'Disease resistance mechanisms in plants', *Genes* 9, no. 7 (2018): E339. doi: 10.3390/genes9070339.

3 J. de Roode, T. Lefèvre and M. D. Hunter, 'Ecology: self-medication in animals', *Science* 340, no. 6129 (2013):150–1. doi: 10.1126/science.1235 824.

4 J. Weiner, *The Beak of the Finch: Story of Evolution in our Time* (London: Jonathan Cape, 1994).

5 V. Labrie, O. J. Buske, E. Ohet al., 'Lactase nonpersistence is directed by

DNA-variation-dependent epigenetic aging', *Nature Structural & Molecular Biology* 23, no. 6 (2016): 566–73. doi: 10.1038/nsmb.3227.

6 G. H. Perry, N. J. Dominy, K. G. Claw et al., 'Diet and the evolution of human amylase gene copy number variation', *Nature Genetics* 39 (2007): 1256–60. doi: 10.1038/ng2123.

7 Hippocrates, *The Law, Oath of Hippocrates, on the Surgery, and on the Sacred Disease*, trans. Francis Adams (Moscow: Dodo Press, 2009).

8 Hippocrates, *On Airs, Waters and Places*, trans. Francis Adams (Moscow: Dodo Press, 2009).

Chapter 12

1 M. Huber, J. A. Knottnerus, L. Green et al., 'How should we define health?', *British Medical Journal* 343 (2011): d4163. doi: 10.1136/bmj.d4163.

2 L. Hamilton, *The Political Philosophy of Needs* (Cambridge: Cambridge University Press, 2008).

3 S. Hasstedt, H. Coon, Y. Xin, T. D. Adams and S. C. Hunt, 'APOH interacts with FTO to predispose to healthy thinness', *Human Genetics* 135, no. 2 (2016): 201–7. doi: 10.1007/s00439-015-1629-3.

4 A. Pearce, E. Rougeaux and C. Law, 'Disadvantaged children at greater relative risk of thinness (as well as obesity): a secondary data analysis of the England National Child Measurement Programme and the UK Millennium Cohort Study', *International Journal for Equity in Health* 14, no. 61 (2015): 1–12. doi: 10.1186/s12939-015-0187-6. T. J. Cole, K. M. Flegal, D. Nicholls and A. A. Jackson, 'Body mass index cut offs to define thinness in children and adolescents: international survey', *British Medical Journal* 335, no. 7612: 194. doi: 10.1136/bmj.39238.399444.55.

5 NHS, 'Homeless die 30 years younger than average' (2011), www.nhs.uk/news/lifestyle-and-exercise/homeless-die-30-years-younger-than-average/ (accessed 22 May 2020).

6 M. Baker, A. McNicholas, N. Garrett, N. Jones, J. Stewart, V. Koberstein and D. Lennon, 'Household crowding a major risk factor for epidemic meningococcal disease in Auckland children', *The Pediatric Infectious Disease Journal* 19, no. 10 (2000): 983–90. doi: 10.1097/00006454-200010000-00009.

7 P. Wilkinson et al., 'The health problems associated with poor housing and home conditions, inadequate water supplies, flooding, poor sanitation and water pollution' (2016), *HealthKnowledge*, www.healthknowledge.org.uk/public-health-textbook/disease-causation-diagnostic/2f-environment/health-problems-poor-housing (accessed 22 May 2020).

8 Z. Shan, H. Ma, M. Xie et al., 'Sleep duration and risk of type 2 diabetes: a meta-analysis of prospective studies', *Diabetes Care* 38, no. 3 (2015): 529–37. doi: 10.2337/dc14-2073. F. Cappuccio, D. Cooper, L. E'Elia,

P. Strazzullo and M. A. Miller, 'Sleep duration predicts cardiovascular outcomes: a systematic review and meta-analysis of prospective studies', *European Heart Journal* 32, no. 12 (2011): 1484–92. doi: 10.1093/eurheartj/ehr007.

9   M. Gilbert-Ouimet, H. Ma, R. Galzier et al., 'Adverse effect of long work hours on incident diabetes in 7065 Ontario workers followed for 12 years', *BMJ Open Diabetes Research & Care* 6, no. 1 (2018): e000496. doi: 10.1136/bmjdrc-2017-000496.

10 NHS Digital, *National Diabetes Audit – 2012–2013: Report 1, Care Processes and Treatment Targets* (2013), https://digital.nhs.uk/data-and-information/publications/statistical/national-diabetes-audit/national-diabetes-audit-2012-2013-report-1-care-processes-and-treatment-targets (accessed 22 May 2020). See also: Scottish Diabetes Survey (2012), www.diabetesin scotland.org.uk/publications/#survey-docs (accessed 22 May 2020).

11 T. Kupers, *Prison Madness: The Mental Health Crisis Behind Bars and What We Must Do About It* (San Francisco, CA: Jossey-Bass, 1999). See Foreword by H. Toch.

12 V. Van Rode, M. Rotsaert and M. Delhaye, 'Loneliness and adolescence: clinical implications and outlook', *Revue Médicale de Bruxelles* 36, no. 5 (2015): 415–20. J. Yanguas, S. Pinazo-Henandis and F. J. Tarazona-Santabalbina, 'The complexity of loneliness', *Acta Biomedica* 89, no. 2 (2018): 302–314. doi: 10.23750/abm.v89i2.7404.

13 IARC Working Group on the Evaluation of Carcinogenic Risks to Humans, 'Diesel and gasoline engine exhausts and some nitroarenes', *IARC Monographs on the Evaluation of Carcinogenic Risks to Humans* 105 (2014): 9–699.

14 Office of the Mayor: City of New York, *Executive Order No. 359. Incorporating Active Design Principles in City Construction* (2013), www.nyc.gov/html/records/pdf/executive_orders/2013EO359.pdf (accessed 22 May 2020).

15 S. A. Kinner and E. A. Wang, 'The case for improving the health of ex-prisoners', *American Journal of Public Health* 104, no. 8 (2014): 1352–1355. doi: 10.2105/AJPH.2014.301883.

16 K. Clark, 'A soil soldier: Ron Finley on cultivating coronavirus life skills and erasing food prisons', *Complex*, 1 May 2020, www.complex.com/life/2020/05/ron-finley-gangster-gardener-masterclass-interview (accessed 22 May 2020).

Chapter 13

1   P. Cairney, *Understanding Public Policy: Theories and Issues* (London: Red Globe Press, 2011), p. 26.

Notes

2 J. Locke, *Second Treatise of Government* (Oxford: Oxford University Press, 2016 [1689]), chapter XIII, paragraph 158.

3 I. Kickbusch et al., *Governance for Health in the 21st Century* (2012), www.euro. who.int/__data/assets/pdf_file/0019/171334/RC62BD01-Governance-for-Health-Web.pdf?ua=1 (accessed 22 May 2020).

4 Local Government Association, *Health in All Policies: A Manual for Local Government* (2016), www.local.gov.uk/health-all-policies-manual-local-government (accessed 22 May 2020).

5 A. M. Connolly and R. Jaipaul, 'A guide to our new health equity collections page', 16 January 2018, https://publichealthmatters.blog.gov.uk/2018/01/16/a-guide-to-our-new-health-equity-collections-page (accessed 22 May 2020).

6 J. Dudman, 'Dispelling the myths around health and safety', *The Guardian*, 30 June 2010, www.theguardian.com/society/2010/jun/30/judith-hackitt-health-safety-work (accessed 22 May 2020).

7 P. Gøtzsche, K. J. Jørgensen and L. T. Krogsbøll, 'Authors' reply to Lauritzen and colleagues, Newton and colleagues, and Mangin', *British Medical Journal* 349 (2014): g4790. doi: 10.1136/bmj.g4790. J. Newton, A. Davis, J. Waterall and K. Fenton, 'NHS Health Check programme: too early to conclude', *British Medical Journal* 349 (2014): g4785. doi: 10.1136/bmj.g4785. P. Gøtzsche, K. J. Jørgensen and L. T. Krogsbøll, 'General health checks don't work', *British Medical Journal* 348 (2014): g3680. doi: 10.1136/bmj.g3680. T. Lauritzen and A. Sandbaek, 'General health checks may work', *British Medical Journal* 349 (2014): g4697. doi: 10.1136/bmj.g4697.

8 A. Forster, H. Dodhia, H. Booth et al., 'Estimating the yield of NHS Health Checks in England: a population-based cohort study', *Journal of Public Health* 37, no. 2 (2015): 234–40. doi: 10.1093/pubmed/fdu079. T. Cochrane, R. Davey, Z. Iqbal, C. Gidlow, J. Kumar, R. Chambers and Y. Mawby, 'NHS health checks through general practice: randomised trial of population cardiovascular risk reduction', *BMC Public Health* 12, no. 944 (2012):1–11. M. Artac, A. R. H. Dalton, A. Majeed, J. Car and C. Millett, 'Effectiveness of a national cardiovascular disease risk assessment program (NHS Health Check): results after one year', *Preventative Medicine* 57 (2013): 129–34. doi: 10.1016/j.ypmed.2013.05.002. P. Barton, L. Andronis, A. Briggs, K. McPherson and S. Capewell, 'Effectiveness and cost effectiveness of cardiovascular disease prevention in whole populations: modelling study', *British Medical Journal* 343 (2011): d4044. doi: 10.1136/bmj.d4044.

9 K. Chang, J. Lee, E. Vamos, M. Soljack, D. Johnston, K. Khunti, A. Majeed and C. Millett, 'Impact of the National Health Service Health Check on cardiovascular disease risk: a difference-in-differences

matching analysis', *Canadian Medical Association Journal* 188, no. 10 (2016): E228-E238. doi: 10.1503/cmaj.151201.

10 O. Mytton, C. Jackson, A. Steinacher, A. Goodman, C. Langenberg, S. Griffin, N. Wareham and J. Woodcock, 'The current and potential health benefits of the National Health Service Health Check cardiovascular disease prevention programme in England: a microsimulation study', *PLoS Medicine* 15, no. 3 (2018): e1002517.

11 G. Baynam, A. Bauskis, N. Pachter et al., '3-Dimensional facial analysisfacing precision public health', *Frontiers in Public Health* 5, no. 31 (2017). doi: 10.3389/fpubh.2017.00031.

12 M. J. Khoury and S. Galea, 'Will precision medicine improve population health?', *JAMA* 316, no. 13 (2016): 1357–1358. doi: 10.1001/jama.2016.12260.

13 M. Yuille, K. Dixon, A. Platt et al., 'The UK DNA Banking Network: a "fair access" biobank', *Cell Tissue Bank* 11, no. 3 (2010): 241–51. doi: 10.1007/s10561-009-9150-3.

14 L. Hood and N. D. Price, 'Demystifying disease, democratizing health care', *Science Translational Medicine* 6, no. 225 (2014): 225ed5. doi: 10.1126/scitranslmed.3008665.

Chapter 14

1 Public Health England, 'Modern life responsible for "worrying" health in middle aged', 28 December 2016, www.gov.uk/government/news/modern-life-responsible-for-worrying-health-in-middle-aged (accessed 22 May 2020).

2 National Cancer Intelligence Network Data Briefing, *Recent Trends in Lung Cancer Incidence, Mortality and Survival* (2013), www.ncin.org.uk/publications/data_briefings/recent_trends_in_lung_cancer_incidence_mortality_and_survival (accessed 22 May 2020).

3 Cabinet Office, *National Risk Register* (2008), www.gov.uk/government/uploads/system/uploads/attachment_data/file/61934/national_risk_register.pdf (accessed 22 May 2020).

4 All Policies for a Healthy Europe, https://healthyeurope.eu/ (accessed 22 May 2020).

5 Annual Report of the Chief Medical Officer, *The Health of the 51%: Women* (2015), www.gov.uk/government/uploads/system/uploads/attachment_data/file/484383/cmo-report-2014.pdf (accessed 22 May 2020).

6 World Economic Forum, *The Global Risks Report 13th Edition* (2018), http://wef.ch/risks2018 (accessed 22 May 2020).

7 Greater Manchester Resilience Forum, *Greater Manchester Community Risk*

Notes

Register (2014), www.preventionweb.net/applications/hfa/lgsat/en/image/href/5770 (accessed 22 May 2020).

8 R. Lawson, *Bills of Health* (Oxford: Radcliffe Medical Press, 1997).

9 Audit Commission, *Building Better Lives: Getting the Best from Strategic Housing* (2009), www.bl.uk/collection-items/building-better-lives-getting-the-best-from-strategic-housing-local-government (accessed 22 May 2020).

10 National Housing Federation, *Housing for Health* (1997).

11 D. Ahrendt, H. Dubois, J. Jungblut et al., *Inadequate Housing in Europe: Costs and Consequences* (2016), www.eurofound.europa.eu/publications/report/2016/quality-of-life-social-policies/inadequate-housing-in-europe-costs-and-consequences (accessed 22 May 2020).

12 Centre for Ageing Better and Care & Repair England, *Home and Dry: The Need for Decent Homes in Later Life* (2020), www.ageing-better.org.uk/publications/home-and-dry-need-decent-homes-later-life (accessed 22 May 2020).

13 M. Marmot and E. Brunner, 'Cohort Profile: The Whitehall II study', *International Journal of Epidemiology* 34, no. 2 (2005): 251–6. doi: 10.1093/ije/dyh372.

14 D. Stevenson and P. Farmer, *Thriving at Work: Independent Review of Mental Health and Employers* (2017), www.gov.uk/government/publications/thriving-at-work-a-review-of-mental-health-and-employers (accessed 22 May 2020).

15 https://gameofthepeople.com/.

16 M. Mazzucato, *The Value of Everything: Making and Taking in the Global Economy* (London: Penguin Books, 2018).

17 R. Costanza, 'How to retool our concept of value', *Nature* 556 (2018): 300–301, www.nature.com/articles/d41586-018-04534-1 (accessed 22 May 2020).

18 J. Stiglitz, J. Fitoussi and M. Durand, *Measuring What Counts: The Global Movement for Well-Being* (New York: The New Press, 2019).

19 Office of National Statistics, *Personal and Economic Well-Being in the UK* (2019), www.ons.gov.uk/peoplepopulationandcommunity/wellbeing/bulletins/personalandeconomicwellbeingintheuk/november2019 (accessed 22 May 2020).

20 J. Breysse, D. E. Jacobs, W. Weber et al., 'Health outcomes and green renovation of affordable housing', *Public Health Reports* 126, no. 1 (2011): 64–75. doi: 10.1177/00333549111260S110.

21 Health & Environment Alliance, *Healthy Buildings, Healthier People* (2018), www.env-health.org/wp-content/uploads/2018/05/Healthy-Buildings-Briefing.pdf (accessed 22 May 2020).

22 Intergovernmental Panel on Climate Change, 'Global Warming of 1.5°C', www.ipcc.ch/sr15 (accessed 22 May 2020).

23 Ministry of Defence, *Obesity in the Armed Forces from 2007 to 31 March 2018*,

Notes

https://assets.publishing.service.gov.uk/government/uploads/system/uploads/attachment_data/file/764869/11002.pdf (accessed 22 May 2020).

Chapter 15

1 H. Clinton, *It Takes a Village: And, Other Lessons Children Teach Us* (New York: Simon & Schuster, 1996).
2 World Health Organization, *Healthy Cities* (2016), www.euro.who.int/en/health-topics/environment-and-health/urban-health/activities/healthy-cities (accessed 22 May 2020).
3 Centers for Disease Control and Prevention, *Healthy Communities Program (2008–2012)* (2016), www.cdc.gov/nccdphp/dch/programs/healthycommunitiesprogram/ (accessed 22 May 2020).
4 A. J. McMichael, 'Standardized mortality ratios and the "healthy worker effect": scratching beneath the surface', *Journal of Occupational Medicine* 18, no. 3 (1976):165–8. doi: 10.1097/00043764-197603000-00009. J. McCambridge, J. Witton and D. R. Elbourne, 'Systematic review of the Hawthorne effect: new concepts are needed to study research participation effects', *Journal of Clinical Epidemiology* 67, no. 3 2014: 267–77. doi: 10.1016/j.jclinepi.2013.08.015.
5 Football Trade Directory, www.footballtradedirectory.com/ (accessed 22 May 2020).
6 R. West, M. Edwards and P. Hajek, 'A randomized controlled trial of a "buddy" system to improve success at giving up smoking in general practice', *Addiction* 93, no. 7 (1998):1007–11. doi: 10.1046/j.1360-0443.1998.93710075.x. S. May, R. West, P. Hajek et al., 'Randomized controlled trial of a social support ("buddy") intervention for smoking cessation', *Patient Education and Counseling* 64, no. 1–3 (2006): 235–41. doi: 10.1016/j.pec.2006.02.008.
7 S. Yoon, D. Go, H. Park and M. Jo, 'The Korean national burden of disease study: from evidence to policy', *Journal of Korean Medical Science* 33, no. 53 (2018): e307. doi: 10.3346/jkms.2018.33.e307.

Chapter 16

1 The Foundational Economy Collective, *Foundational Economy: The Infrastructure of Everyday Life* (Manchester: Manchester University Press, 2018).
2 K. Strimbu and J. A. Tavel, 'What are biomarkers?', *Current Opinions in HIV and AIDS* 5, no. 6 (2010): 463–6. doi: 10.1097/COH.0b013e32833ed177.

3   D. McCartney, R. F. Hillary, A. J. Stevenson et al., 'Epigenetic predic-
    tion of complex traits and death', *Genome Biology* 19, no. 1 (2018): 136. doi:
    10.1186/s13059-018-1514-1.

4   NHS, 'NHS Genomic Medicine Service', www.england.nhs.uk/genom
    ics/nhs-genomic-med-service/ (accessed 22 May 2020).

5   A. Valdes, J. Walter, E. Segal et al., 'Role of the gut microbiota in nutri-
    tion and health', *British Medical Journal* 361 (2018): k2179. doi: 10.1136/
    bmj.k2179.

6   S. Gee, R. Oliver, J. Corfield et al., 'Biobank finances: a socio-economic
    analysis and review', *Biopreservation and Biobanking* 13, no. 6 (2015): 435–51.
    doi: 10.1089/bio.2015.0030.

7   S. Dolley, 'Big Data's role in Precision Public Health', *Frontiers in
    Public Health* 6, no. 68 (2018). doi: 10.3389/fpubh.2018.00068. Prosperi,
    J. S. Ming, Jiang Bian et al., 'Big data hurdles in precision medicine and
    precision public health', *BMC Medical Informatics and Decision Making* 18,
    no. 1 (2018): 139. doi: 10.1186/s12911-018-0719-2.

8   L. Hood and N. D. Price, 'Demystifying disease, democratizing health
    care', *Science Translational Medicine* 6, no. 225 (2014): 225ed5. doi: 10.1126/
    scitranslmed.3008665. See also: www.systemsbiology.org/research/100k-
    wellness-project/ (accessed 22 May 2020).

9   A. Anderson, 'Leroy Hood describes promising results from pilot stage
    of ISB's 100K Wellness Project' (2015), www.genomeweb.com/molec
    ular-diagnostics/leroy-hood-describes-promising-results-pilot-stage-isbs-
    100k-wellness-project (accessed 22 May 2020).

10 O. Azmak, H. Bayer, A. Caplin et al., 'Using Big Data to understand the
    human condition: the Kavli HUMAN Project', *Big Data* 3, no. 3 (2015):
    172–88. doi: 10.1089/big.2015.0012. See also: Kavli Human Project,
    https://kavlihumanproject.org/ (accessed 22 May 2020).

Chapter 17

1   O. Bennett, 'The end is nigh for the World Health Organization', *The
    Independent*, 5 April 2017, www.independent.co.uk/news/world/politics/
    obamacare-trump-health-ebola-flu-pandemic-who-reforms-cancer-tb-a76
    22416.html (accessed 22 May 2020).

2   D. Stevenson and P. Farmer, *Thriving at Work: Independent Review of Mental
    Health and Employers* (2017), www.gov.uk/government/publications/thriv
    ing-at-work-a-review-of-mental-health-and-employers (accessed 22 May
    2020).

3   Department for Work and Pensions and Department of Health and
    Social Care, *Improving Lives: The Future of Work, Health and Disability* (2017),

www.gov.uk/government/publications/improving-lives-the-future-of-work-health-and-disability (accessed 22 May 2020).

4 R. Wilkinson and K. Pickett, *The Spirit Level: Why Equality is Better for Everyone* (London: Penguin, 2010).

5 N. Owen, P. B. Sparling, G. N. Healy et al., 'Sedentary behaviour: emerging evidence for a new health risk', *Mayo Clin Proceedings* 85, no. 12 (2010): 1138–41. doi: 10.4065/mcp. 2010.0444.

6 C. Levy et al., *A Plan for Growth in the Knowledge Economy* (2011), http://creative-blueprint.co.uk/library/item/a-plan-for-growth-in-the-knowledge-economy (accessed 22 May 2020).

7 J. Bennett, J. Pearson-Stuttard, V. Kontis et al., 'Contributions of diseases and injuries to widening life expectancy inequalities in England from 2001 to 2016: a population-based analysis of vital registration data', *The Lancet Public Health* 3, no. 12 (2018): e586–e597.

8 Fast Company, *Fifty Reasons Why We Cannot Change*, www.fastcompany.com/55009/50-reasons-why-we-cannot-change (accessed 22 May 2020).

9 N. Watts, M. Amann, N. Arnell et al., 'The 2018 report of the Lancet Countdown on health and climate change: shaping the health of nations for centuries to come', *The Lancet* 392, no. 10163 (2018): 2479–514. doi: 10.1016/S0140-6736(18)32594-7.

Chapter 18

1 The Novel Coronavirus Pneumonia Emergency Response Epidemiology Team, 'The epidemiological characteristics of an outbreak of 2019 novel coronavirus diseases (COVID-19) – China, 2020', *China CDC Weekly* 2, no. 8 (2020): 113–22. doi: 10.46234/ccdcw2020.032.

Suggested reading

Donaldson, L. and R. J. Donaldson, *Essential Public Health, Second Edition*. Oxford: Petroc Press, 2003.

Hamilton, L., *The Political Philosophy of Needs*. Cambridge: Cambridge University Press, 2008.

Hempel, S., *The Medical Detective: John Snow, Cholera and the Mystery of the Broad Street Pump*. London: Granta Books, 2014.

Jekel, J. F., D. L. Katz, J. G. Elmore and D. Wild, *Epidemiology, Biostatistics and Preventive Medicine*. Philadelphia: Saunders, 2007.

Johnson, S., *The Ghost Map: A Street, an Epidemic and the Hidden Power of Urban Networks*. London: Penguin Books, 2008.

The Marmot Review, *Fair Society, Healthy Lives* (2010), www.instituteofheal thequity.org/resources-reports/fair-society-healthy-lives-the-marmot-review (accessed 22 May 2020).

Noble, D., *Dance to the Tune of Life: Biological Relativity*. Cambridge: Cambridge University Press, 2016.

Noble, D., *The Dance Sourcebook* (2019). https://denisnoble.com/wp-content/uploads/2019/11/The-Dance-Sourcebook-1.pdf (accessed 22 May 2020).

Porter, D., *Health, Civilization and the State: A History of Public Health from Ancient to Modern Times*. London: Routledge, 1998.

Snowden, F., *Epidemics and Society: From the Black Death to the Present*. New Haven, CT: Yale University Press, 2020.

Stinson, S., B. Bogin, and D. H. O'Rourke (eds), *Human Biology: An Evolutionary and Biocultural Perspective*. Hoboken, NJ: John Wiley & Sons, Inc., 2012.

Rosen, G., *A History of Public Health*. New York: MD publications, 1958.

Wilkinson, R. and K. Pickett, *The Spirit Level: Why Equality is Better for Everyone*. London: Penguin, 2010.

Index

Index